ALBERT'S VICTORIA

Tyler Whittle was born in 1927. He began his writing career in 1955 after having served for two years in the Royal Marines. Since then he has broadcast many radio talks and features and television programmes, written children's books, novels, books of essays on botany and gardening, a history of plant hunting, and biographical novels on Richard III and Queen Victoria. His work has been widely translated – into German, French, Polish and Japanese. He lives in Norfolk, his favourite part of England, and also has a home in the South of Italy. His greatest pleasures are collecting and cultivating plants, reading and bathing. *Albert's Victoria* is the second of three novels on the life of Britain's longest reigning sovereign. The first was *The Young Victoria*, and the third is called *The Widow of Windsor*.

By the same author in Pan Books

THE YOUNG VICTORIA

Albert's Victoria

Tyler Whittle

UNABRIDGED

PAN BOOKS LTD : LONDON

First published 1972 by William Heinemann Ltd
This edition published 1973 by Pan Books Ltd,
33 Tothill Street, London SW1

ISBN 0 330 23792 6

Made and printed in Great Britain by
Cox & Wyman Ltd, London, Reading and Fakenham

To Sibyl Harton

AUTHOR'S NOTE

Though a fictional treatment, *Albert's Victoria* is entirely faithful to the known facts. No character has been invented and nothing has been deliberately distorted or omitted simply to make the writing easier or to suit a preconceived idea. The few small liberties taken to bridge gaps in the documentary evidence lie always within the seemliness of historical probability.

T.W.

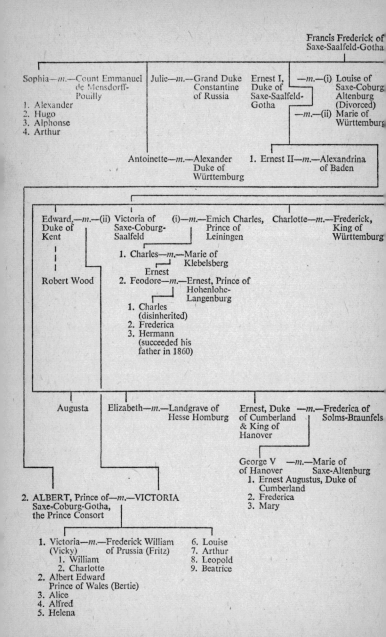

Francis Frederick of
Saxe-Saalfeld-Gotha

Sophia—m.—Count Emmanuel
de Mensdorff-
Pouilly

1. Alexander
2. Hugo
3. Alphonse
4. Arthur

Julie—m.—Grand Duke
Constantine
of Russia

Ernest I,
Duke of
Saxe-Saalfeld-
Gotha

—m.—(i) Louise of
Saxe-Coburg-
Altenburg
(Divorced)

—m.—(ii) Marie of
Württemburg

Antoinette—m.—Alexander
Duke of
Württemburg

1. Ernest II—m.—Alexandrina
of Baden

Edward,—m.—(ii) Victoria of
Duke of   Saxe-Coburg-
Kent   Saalfeld

(i)—m.—Emich Charles,
Prince of
Leiningen

Charlotte—m.—Frederick,
King of
Württemburg

Robert Wood

1. Charles—m.—Marie of
Klebelsberg

Ernest

2. Feodore—m.—Ernest, Prince of
Hohenlohe-
Langenburg

1. Charles
(disinherited)
2. Frederica
3. Hermann
(succeeded his
father in 1860)

Augusta

Elizabeth—m.—Landgrave of
Hesse Homburg

Ernest, Duke —m.—Frederica of
of Cumberland   Solms-Braunfels
& King of
Hanover

George V —m.—Marie of
of Hanover   Saxe-Altenburg

1. Ernest Augustus, Duke of
Cumberland
2. Frederica
3. Mary

2. ALBERT, Prince of—m.—VICTORIA
Saxe-Coburg-Gotha,
the Prince Consort

1. Victoria—m.—Frederick William
(Vicky)   of Prussia (Fritz)
1. William
2. Charlotte
2. Albert Edward
Prince of Wales (Bertie)
3. Alice
4. Alfred
5. Helena

6. Louise
7. Arthur
8. Leopold
9. Beatrice

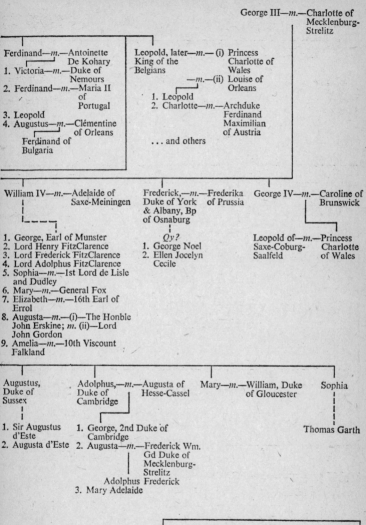

A SIMPLIFIED FAMILY TREE OF
VICTORIA, QUEEN OF GREAT BRITAIN
in the year of the Prince Consort's death
1861
(a dotted line indicates illegitimate descent)

Part One

I

Mr Greville, Clerk to the Privy Council, was nervous and irritable at dawn on February 14th, 1840.

His digestion was imperfect and celebrating the Queen's marriage the day before had upset him. So had the continuous excitement of meeting old friends from the country who were up to see the illuminations and the royal processions. In fact, by the time he reached Windsor, arriving at a discreet interval after the bridal couple, he was quite feverish. Sleep had been denied him, and reading was particularly difficult at the Castle because the ration of two candles a room gave too dim a light, and halved and made into four, as the ladies sometimes did to get sufficient light for their toilette, they burnt for too short a time. By half past seven, when a grey light began to steal in through the uncurtained windows, he was glad to get up, dress, and take himself off for a walk.

He made for the east terrace which, except on Sundays,

the Queen reserved for herself. But Greville liked this garden and at such an early hour he was confident he could walk there without being seen. Therefore he gasped when he rounded a shaped yew hedge and found himself face to face with Lady Palmerston and her maid.

They were no less surprised. Lady Palmerston put her fingers to her mouth. The maid gave a little shriek.

Then, as they recovered from the shock, Greville and Lady Palmerston began to smile simultaneously.

'Mr Greville,' she said. 'I shall have to depend upon your discretion. And you on mine.'

He bowed.

'Excellent. Now give me your arm and we shall trespass this forbidden garden in each other's company.'

Her maid fell in behind and the two walked slowly down the centre path, round the lily pond and back again.

They found they shared the same sleeplessness, and the same inability to manage on the meagre ration of candles.

'Each time Lord Palmerston threatens to bring his own student's reading-lamp,' she told him. 'And each time it is forgotten.'

Greville quickly turned the conversation to the wedding. Though wife to the Foreign Secretary and sister to Lord Melbourne, the First Minister, Lady Palmerston had not been at the ceremony nor at the breakfast. But she knew all about them, and Greville, who loved small gossip, was determined to worm out as many details as he could. She did not mind in the least. She could keep a close mouth over things that mattered but she was happy to quench a little of the Clerk's thirst for tittle-tattle. She told him what the principal guests had worn – by far the oddest, the Duke of Sussex who wore a skullcap and was popinjayed out as Captain General of the HAC, with the Garter, the Bath and the St Andrew all jumbled up about his neck like mayday favours. She told him what they had eaten at the breakfast, a heavy, Hanoverian meal, boiled and roast meats and stodge-wodge food, and all tepid because of the distance between the kitchens and the Banqueting Hall. And the cake, she said, had been topped with Britannia in sugar robed as a Roman matron. But the best titbit she offered him was the news that though the Queen had kissed the Princess Sophia and her aunts of Gloucester and Cambridge, she had not kissed her own mother, the Duchess of Kent.

'Not?' repeated Mr Greville, very gratified.

'Not,' said Lady Palmerston again, and, to his pleasure, continued: 'They remain the best of enemies, though how long Prince Albert will permit it to continue remains to be seen.'

Mr Greville raised his eyebrows. 'You consider, Ma'am, that the Prince will have great influence upon the Queen?'

This was too straight a question to deserve anything but an oblique answer. Lady Palmerston half changed the subject. 'Did you not think, Mr Greville, that they make a beautiful couple?'

'Indeed, yes, Ma'am. The Prince is exceedingly handsome and the Queen has a prettiness which is almost porcelain. So different from the saggy features of her father's family, don't you know.'

'Not being as perspicacious as you, dear Mr Greville, I really can't and won't say,' teased Lady Palmerston. Again she changed the subject. 'How were the celebrations here? We arrived so late last night the lights were gone.'

Greville began to tell her of the confusion in the streets – the bell-ringing, and singing and cheering, the beer-drinking and pie-eating, and the dramatic effect of flights of rockets fired over the town from Eton – when he was interrupted by Lady Palmerston's maid.

'Your ladyship,' she said breathlessly and in great agitation. 'There is her majesty.'

Ahead, walking the gravel which stretched across the length of the Castle, were the Queen and Prince Albert.

Without a moment's hesitation Lady Palmerston stepped behind a hedge and was quickly followed by Mr Greville and the maid. They walked rapidly and unobserved out of the garden.

'I don't believe we were seen,' said Lady Palmerston. 'But how mortifying to feel like a small boy caught apple-stealing.'

3

'There seemed to be no reason to suppose the Queen would be in the garden at this hour of the morning,' murmured Greville. He, too, was vexed by the necessity of making an undignified exit. 'It seems odd,' he continued. 'Particularly on the first day of a honeymoon.'

Lady Palmerston permitted herself to be indiscreet. 'The whole honeymoon is odd,' she said. 'And I'm not at all sure that it isn't indelicate. Instead of being largely alone the bridal pair plan to entertain a host of people. The Castle is already half full, and tomorrow the Duchess of Kent and Prince Albert's father and brother arrive with a score or more other guests. Then, instead of taking three weeks or a month from affairs, the Queen insists that her honeymoon shall only be for three days. It is altogether extraordinary, almost improper.'

Greville looked back towards the garden. The Queen and the Prince were smiling and talking to one another. 'Taking pre-breakfast walks is a peculiar way of honeymooning,' he said. 'You'll agree, Lady Palmerston, that it's hardly the way to get us a Prince of Wales.'

II

Mr Greville's tart remark was repeated throughout the Castle; that is, by those who had the broad view characteristic of cultivated English patricians for the past one hundred and fifty years. Nowadays there were also those whose views were narrower, mostly young Maids of Honour and Women of the Bedchamber who were earnestly Evangelical. When the Queen was under the influence of these ladies she became solemn and introspective and piety was the proper thing at Court; but when, as she put it, she was the niece of George the Fourth, frank, unsqueamish and unshockable, talk was freer and much saltier.

Many at Court enjoyed Greville's *mot*. Some considered

it unbecoming or indelicate. The Queen's young ladies thought it downright improper. They were not innocent in the sense that custom was to make their daughters and granddaughters innocent. They knew what physical love was, but the strictness of their brand of religion made them regard it as an affront to a woman's modesty. It pained them that their dear royal mistress, their Queen, was subjected to this shadowy part of marriage and then made a joke of by the Clerk of her own Privy Council. They went as a body to say so to the Baroness.

Baroness Lehzen, though an elderly maiden lady, smiled at them and she told them they were gooses, a peculiar plural word which betrayed her foreign origin even though she had been in England for eighteen years. She pooh-poohed their gloomy views. Was it likely, she asked, that a gentleman so young and so handsome and so accomplished as Prince Albert would subjugate his bride with what they liked to call bestial passions? She rang for her page who poured tiny glasses of ratafia and handed slices of shortcake round the room.

As calmly and as quietly as she could she endeavoured to persuade the young ladies to be more tolerant of the older generation. She soothed their indignation and though she could not alter their prudish views, at least, when they left her, they were mollified. Without exception they were devoted to the Baroness and highly respected her unique position at Court. She had no official title, being known simply as the Lady Attendant, but she had control of the Queen's Privy Purse and of the royal household. Once nursery governess to Victoria it was she who now trained the Maids of Honour in their duties. It was she who acted as the Queen's Private Secretary and wrote copies of her most confidential papers. It was she who had combined with Lord Melbourne to arrange all details of the royal wedding, and it was she who had made everything ready for the royal honeymoon at Windsor. There was always much to do. A great deal too much, she sometimes thought. But she could always find time to mother the young ladies at Court, and they knew this and appreciated it.

When they had gone, Lehzen sat at her desk and thought about their anxieties. What gooses they were. And how unobservant not to have noticed the Queen's radiance since her marriage. She helped herself to a caraway seed from a small lacquered box and chewed it reflectively as she thought about the change in Victoria.

Because she herself loved the Queen with such single-minded devotion, she could sense that Albert did not yet love his bride. He did not even have the tenderness of old Lord Melbourne who had adored the Queen since her accession. Clearly he had simply been obedient to his family's ambitions, and, being a younger son from a small German duchy, had been told he could consider himself fortunate to marry his cousin Victoria. But he had accepted his duty with little stoicism and had gone to the altar with resigned acceptance and no enthusiasm. Yet Lehzen noticed there was already a difference in his manner. He was less uneasy, far more sure of himself than before the wedding. Victoria's love was giving him confidence. No doubt he was now prepared to enjoy her as a delicate and delicious toy, and one day, maybe, some sort of love for her would germinate and mature. Until then Lehzen decided it was her duty to serve Victoria as before. And it was also her duty, she decided, to accustom herself to the idea that one day she would be no longer needed. When that day came she hoped she would learn the truth painlessly and have the strength to retire without showing a trace of resentment or even of grief. She felt she owed this to Victoria, the product of her own upbringing.

At that very moment the Queen was saying in German to her bridegroom: 'Poor Lehzen, it is the second night we shall not dine together.'

Prince Albert spread his hands. 'Customs vary from place to place but it is universal that on a honeymoon the bridal couple dine alone.'

'We have hardly been separated since I was two,' explained Victoria. 'And though in your company I do not miss Lehzen, she might well be missing me.'

He cupped her oval face in his hands. 'Not even for dear Lehzen can we break the custom.' To prevent her continuing.

he gently pressed her lips together with two fingers. Then he changed the subject. 'Your Opium War, my love,' he said. 'It would please me to know details of your Opium War.'

She looked at him, round-eyed with astonishment.

He smiled. 'I am serious. The subject interests me.' He made himself comfortable on the sofa beside his bride and told her what he already knew of the war then being fought between England and the Celestial Empire. It was considerable.

Victoria was easily bored by business, even when Lord Melbourne compelled her to discuss affairs. She let her mind wander and began to daydream until Albert noticed it, stopped what he was saying, and threw her into confusion by begging her to be attentive. She apologized, blinked into the firelight, and tried hard to concentrate. About twenty-eight hours before she had promised to love, honour and obey him. Very likely this meant she ought to listen carefully and respectfully to what he was saying. But how complicated it all was. Why he had asked her for information she could not imagine. He appeared to know the facts already, and though a little of what he said was familiar to her, the name of Lin, for instance, the imperial commissioner who had started the troubles, most of it was not. Then, to her amazement Albert appeared to be doubting Palmerston's wisdom in declaring war. If she was correct in understanding him, he even appeared to think her country was in the wrong and the war was unjustifiable.

She sat upright. 'My love,' she said, interrupting him. 'We English have treaty privileges in the Far East.'

'To use an enervating drug as an article of trade?' he asked. 'And introduce it in such quantity that in exchange the Chinese empire was being drained of its best silver, tea, and silk, and porcelain?' He smiled at her. 'It is scarcely any wonder that Emperor Tao-Kuang condemned such irresponsibility.'

Her cheeks flushed. 'Albert, you ought not to say such things. Not yet. It is not fitting for you to condemn my merchants or my government.'

Again he cupped her oval face in his hands. Then he put

7

his mouth to her ear and whispered as a lover might: 'Nor is it fitting for you to remind me that I am a stranger.' He held her at arm's length, and repeated mockingly: 'We English have rights!'

'Truly, I beg your pardon.'

'And do the Chinese not have rights, and the poor Germans?'

'My love, dearest Albert.' Victoria's face was puckered. Soon she would cry. 'Forgive my clumsiness.'

'Of course.' Swiftly he kissed her on the tip of her nose.

Afterwards they sat silently side by side looking into the fire.

How forceful he is, she was thinking; how very intelligent. And how difficult it will be both to obey him as his wife and command him as his Queen.

He was facing the same sort of dilemma. Reminded already that his opinions as a German were of small importance, and put in his place for mildly criticizing the *status quo*, he foresaw storms ahead. They were inevitable. It would be his duty, he realized, to make them as small and inconsequential as possible.

Because both were young – neither more than twenty – they soon forgot their differences in the pleasure of being together before the fire.

After dinner they would play chess and sing together at the piano.

Then they would lie in each other's arms.

III

The Queen's marriage made a considerable difference at Court.

Victoria and her mother had been at odds for years. Everyone said it was because the Duchess had had an affair with her good-looking Comptroller, Sir John Conroy, and that Victoria had discovered their guilty passion. This was the talk. More probably the reason was the Duchess had been too familiar with Sir John and had allowed him to be overbearing and cruel to her daughter. Certainly they had both schemed to rule through Victoria when she came to the throne and had been shocked by her determination to be independent. Now Conroy had gone – dismissed by the Queen on the first day of her reign, and later persuaded to leave the Duchess' household – and, by marrying, Victoria was free of her mother's chaperonage.

It now was planned that the Duchess should be given a grace-and-favour house and move from her apartments in Buckingham Palace and at Windsor. But the Prince made it plain by his attitude that she was not to be treated as an exile from Court. She would be in a separate establishment, but Albert wished that his aunt and his wife should be on friendly terms again.

At the same time it was clear that there were to be other changes in influence.

Lord Melbourne, of course, would continue to be the focus of all political power, and the Queen Dowager, Adelaide, would always enjoy the special place she had won at Court and in the hearts of the people by the sweetness of her disposition. But the other Hanoverian aunts, who had enjoyed some influence over the Queen, would no longer do so unless she particularly asked for their advice. This was to rid herself of tiresome Aunt Sophia who nowadays thought and talked of little but her raffish bastard son from Melton Mowbray, and Aunt Cambridge who, though only a princess of tiny Hesse-Cassel was very haughty, and, resentful of the Coburg intrusion into so high a place, was determined to maintain the honour of the '*old* royal family'. Keeping them at arm's length would be a relief and still allow her to enjoy the society of bird-like Aunt Augusta, and the counsel of Aunt Gloucester, who as well as being eccentric and given to bawling, was a sage old lady.

There were also changes in the size of the royal household. The Prince's gentlemen – a Groom of the Stole, two Lords-in-Waiting, two equerries, two grooms, and a Private Secretary – were joined by an extra twenty-three servants.

Most were German and were a source of criticism to those in the Court who did not trust foreign servants. To demonstrate the unreliability of foreigners, they would retell the grisly and true story of a Frenchwoman employed in the Queen's dressmaking department who, after her discharge, took a post as governess in Paris and there systematically tortured five English children, two of them to death. The jägers, valets, and other servants of Prince Albert, with their outlandish tongue and equally outlandish livery, were objects of much mistrust.

Court protocol was tightened. Baroness Lehzen was responsible. She talked with the Queen and the Prince, and afterwards consulted the Lord Chamberlain, Lord Uxbridge. This old soldier – he had had a leg blown off and formally buried at Waterloo – agreed that what had been good enough for a single young lady loosely chaperoned by her mother was not good enough for a married queen. The formalities were made inflexible. Before the Queen's wedding, by her special invitation, gentlemen at Court had occasionally been seated. Now they were forbidden to sit at any time in her presence except at dinner. Prince Albert, denied by Parliament the title of King-Consort, a peerage and a proper annuity, had his dignity maintained at home where his wife's Maids of Honour were not allowed to sit in his presence. Nor could they speak unless he first spoke to them. The protocol for presentation, of ladies at drawing-rooms and of gentlemen at levées, was severely formal, as were the rules governing the dress of courtiers. Ladies at a presentation were obliged to wear lappets if they were married or veils if they were not, and a headdress of three white feathers. Gentlemen not in uniform had to wear a court dress of knee breeches, white stockings, buckled shoes, a sword and a wine-coloured coat. American diplomats were an exception and had special permission to appear in humdrum pantaloons.

Only Baron Stockmar could do as he liked and wear what he wished. He dined in trousers and took the unheard of liberty of avoiding the drawing-room and going straight to his rooms after dinner.

The Baron's return was, in fact, the most considerable change at Court after the Queen's marriage. He had left some time before, assuring the young Victoria it was wiser for her to be without foreign advisers. Her subjects were notorious for their mistrust of foreigners. Even the Latin poet Horace had described them in an apt epigram, as 'the British, cruel to strangers'. He had persuaded the Queen, but she had not liked to let him go. He had always been a power in her life: deciding on the nursery and schoolroom regimen by which she had been brought up; advising her both before her accession and afterwards; showing a realistic understanding of her antipathy to her mother; keeping her in close contact with her uncle, the King of the Belgians. Nevertheless, if he thought it prudent to go he must be allowed to do so, and he had gone, first to stay in Belgium, and afterwards to take an important part in 'furbishing up' Prince Albert. This he had done gently because he did not want the young man to feel too keenly his position as a sacrifice on the dynastic altar. Now that the sought-for marriage had taken place he considered it his duty to be at hand should either of his pupils need him. It meant denying himself the needs of most men of his age – the ease of a comfortable home in his native land and the company of his wife and children. But, then, the Baron had always been prepared to mortify the Stockmar family for the benefit of the Coburgs. Here was no *volte face*, he told the Queen. His opinions had not altered. The British, cruel to strangers, would never alter either, so, for her sake, he would make himself as unobtrusive as possible. He asked only for apartments, use of the royal libraries, and access to the royal ear. Nothing else. Both the Queen and the Prince were delighted. He would be their strength and stay as he had been to the Coburg family since the year of Waterloo. But, though wisely he refused any sort of official appointment and kept himself in the background, and though he was tiny in stature, wore subfusc, and spoke very quietly, his presence in the royal household was as obtrusive as a London sparrow in an exotic aviary. The Baron was back again.

Lord Melbourne had mixed feelings about Stockmar. He commanded attention as Victoria's Merlin, but no English nobleman could relax in his company. The Baron was too severe, and his appearance and manner were against him. His pug-bulgy eyes, the colour of prunes, were so intense, and his soft voice had a timbre which made audible each vowel and consonant. Then there was his snuff-taking. Melbourne thought it an unobjectionable habit. Old gentlemen, even ladies such as the Duchess of Kent and the Duchess of Gloucester, consumed ounces of the stuff a day and appeared to come to no harm. But Stockmar's regular habit was disconcerting. While appearing to use a box of scented rappee and an Indian bandana, no particle of snuff ever reached his nose. It was all show. Finally – and Melbourne admitted to himself that this criticism was carping – in the apparently endless memoranda which were issued from the Baron's apartments like Bulls from Rome, he had a curious method of using capital letters. For example, the page of the backstairs was honoured with capital letters, whereas the office of First or Prime Minister had to do without and the word 'view' (if it happened to be the view of the Prince or the Queen or of Stockmar) merited the same attention, which no one else's did.

These little vexations aside, there was no doubting the Baron's excellence as a political adviser, though some might doubt the wisdom of having such a functionary at Court; and there was no doubting his shrewdness, though seriousness sometimes made him ponderous. Therefore when Stockmar wrote to ask for a private appointment with the Prime Minister he was at once given one.

He arrived armed with a small leather pocket book.

'I am obliged to you for your time, Lord Melbourne,' he said. 'And I should not have troubled you but for some

untruthful and malevolent press attacks on the Prince.'
Stockmar took a cutting from his pocket book. 'First and
worst of all is this.'

'From a provincial newspaper,' said Melbourne when he
had adjusted his spectacles.

'Provincial, yes, my lord; but, dear me, with a wide and
influential circulation.'

Melbourne read the paragraph.

*Prince Albert is a prince respected and to be respected
for all his conduct. But, besides and beyond him, we see
Coburgs in France! Coburgs in Belgium! Coburgs in
Portugal! And we verily believe that if the billionaires
among the children of Israel should buy Jerusalem and all
the land about Jordan, we should doubtless see all the
machinery of diplomacy instantly at work with a Coburg
King of the Jews.*

The Prime Minister was not very good at being serious.
The sort of newspaper irreverence which made other people
so indignant generally served to make him chuckle, but he
managed to keep the proper sort of face when he handed the
cutting back to Stockmar. It was regrettable, he said, but he
felt bound to point out that within certain limits the English
Press had freedom to say what it wished, and in law he
doubted if those limits had been passed.

'But, my lord,' insisted Stockmar, tapping the paper with
an overlong thumbnail. 'Here is a wicked hint of the old
scandal that the Prince is not his father's son, that he is
illegitimate and half-Jewish.'

'Eh?' Melbourne was genuinely astonished. Nor, even
when Stockmar persisted in trying to see an inference, would
be begin to agree that one existed. To turn the point he said:
'Worse things have been said about the Queen herself in
recent years. In England, Baron, the Press is free.'

Stockmar indicated that he was well aware of it, thought it
regrettable. 'Upon my word, such iniquitous attacks deserve
answering,' he said. 'And there have been others.' He re-
opened the small leather pocket book and looked at a

13

memorandum. 'Already the Queen's husband has been abused in the public prints as "The Pauper Prince", "The German Professor", and – Stockmar hesitated – 'and ... "Lovely Albert".'

He was astonished to see the corners of Melbourne's mouth begin to twitch.

'You think it amusing, Prime Minister?' he asked severely.

By gripping the arms of his chair Melbourne just managed to control himself. It would have been unpardonable to burst out laughing at something which the Baron took so seriously. He remained silent, and listened to Stockmar's view that an attack on her husband was an attack on the Queen herself. Reformers, anarchists, republicans, existed everywhere. Before they could manipulate public opinion the government should take the initiative.

'I am anxious,' the Baron finished, 'that a body of opinion should be formed which is as strongly for the Prince as the body of opinion is against him. And this can only be done by influential people talking amongst all classes and making plain the Prince's claim to some regard. If you and your ministers, if the Duke of Wellington and Sir Robert Peel, could form this body of opinion in society, a great deal of potential harm might be avoided.'

Again there was a twitch at the corners of Melbourne's mouth. The Tories, led by the Duke and Peel, had been so against the Prince that he had had great difficulty in persuading the Queen to invite a single one of them to her wedding. The thought of asking them, or almost anyone in Parliament, to speak kindly of their friends about Prince Albert was ludicrous – although, yes, it would avoid all sorts of trouble, and the boy was undoubtedly worthy.

He promised to do all he could to move public opinion in Albert's favour though he knew it was a hopeless task. At the same time he looked carefully at the Baron. Poor man. Was he losing touch with reality?

Apparently not. Sensing Melbourne's rejection of what he thought was a capital plan, Stockmar went on to talk of precedence. Here he was on surer ground. The Prime Minister personally cared not a fig for precedence, but he appreciated how much it mattered at Court.

It was astounding, said the Baron, that while a Queen Consort had precedence over everyone, the consort of a Queen Regent had no sort of position at all. 'It makes the Prince,' he objected, 'of no more account than a hive drone.'

'The English,' said Melbourne patiently, 'have always managed things that way. Though, as you remark, it can lead to difficulties.'

They discussed the situation as it was, examining all aspects to see if any improvement could be made.

The Queen's uncles were not being cooperative.

Because Hanover had Salic law, which barred any woman from inheriting the crown, Ernest, Duke of Cumberland had become King of Hanover on the death of William IV. At the same time, because England did not have Salic law, Victoria had succeeded to the English crown. And King Ernest − hated in his native land where at various times he was accused of political corruption, murder, sodomy, incest, and plotting against the life of his own niece, but loved in Hanover where, despising consitutional government, he ruled as a benevolent despot – was asserting his rights. As the oldest surviving son of George the Third and therefore head of the Brunswick dynasty, he would not yield his precedence to what he termed contemptuously 'a paper Royal Highness'. Nor would he give up his claim to certain of the crown jewels which he believed were his as head of the family. Nor would he give up his grace-and-favour apartments in St James's. Nor would he give up a single right, possession, privilege or claim in Britain simply to please his niece and her Coburg consort who, for all that he was German, wore clothes of such a Latin cut and colour that, as King Ernest snapped out in public, he resembled 'a damned, sneaking Italian tenor'.

Stockmar agreed that not much could be done to get round the problem of King Ernest. He was better left alone, and as long as he stayed in Hanover, all would be well. Melbourne made a note to ask the Duke's help. Wellington

15

had great influence in the old royal family. He might be able to persuade King Ernest to keep away. Later, when blind Prince George inherited his father's throne, they could go into the question of precedence again.

Next in succession was Augustus, Duke of Sussex. Victoria had a high regard for her Uncle Sussex, a genial scientific old gentleman with a passion for clocks. He had given way at once. Albert should have his precedence. And in return Victoria had asked him to give her away in marriage and had partially recognized his morganatic wife by creating her Duchess of Inverness. But there were signs, warned Melbourne, that Sussex's geniality might be souring. Stockmar made a note to see him. He must be kept sweet.

George the Third's seventh son, Adolphus of Cambridge, had also given Albert precedence. But no sooner was it done, and the fact announced to his Duchess, than he regretted it. They were a loving couple and had been through the many years of his Vice-royalty in Hanover, and he was shattered by the manner in which she scolded him. To give way to a tuppence-ha'penny Coburg! she had shouted; to humble the *old* royal family before a brat of doubtful parentage! *Doubtful*, she yelled again, and at twice the volume because the Duke's hearing had almost gone. Finally she had told him a way out; he could pretend not to have heard. This would invalidate his consent, and Albert would be back where he belonged – behind the Hanoverian uncles in strict precedence. Cunningly the Duke had pretended not to hear her suggestion that he pretend not to have heard; and she became so red in the face and frustrated and confused and angry, that her maid had to cut her stays and restore her with sal volatile and feather burning. She realized afterwards it was no use; her Duke could not be made to change his promise. But she had made no promise, and already she was causing trouble by refusing to stand at dinner when Albert's health was drunk with honours.

'She needs,' said Stockmar, 'a sharp lesson.' He made a note in his pocket book.

Melbourne said he hoped it would not be too sharp.

Family quarrels, and that is what this was, were more easily exacerbated than mollified.

'I think,' said the Baron continuing to write, 'that if she were not invited to the Palace ball this month, the Duchess would dislike it.'

Melbourne nodded. The Baron was correct. She would dislike it very much indeed. The idea struck him as equal to poking a stick into a wasps' nest.

The Baron snapped shut his pocket book, and said the next matter of particular concern was the Prince's lack of employment.

Melbourne found himself agreeing. It was important that a man of such capabilities should be given something to do. All he did at present was to shoot a little, wearing long red leather boots which the ladies thought fetching and the gentlemen considered repellent, skate from time to time, play innumerable duets with the Queen, and blot her signature when she signed state papers.

'I have recommended that he study English constitutional history,' said the Baron.

'Very wise.'

'And that he learn from the leaders of all political parties.'

Melbourne cocked an eye at him.

The Baron placed the tips of his fingers together.

'You would not, I am certain, object to him seeing a good deal of Sir Robert Peel.'

'Not in the least. That is, just so long as he does not give the appearance of being a Tory sympathizer.'

'No more, I assure you, than he will appear to be a supporter of the Whigs. And, in case your ministry should fall, it is important that the Prince knows something of your successor.'

'I agree,' said Melbourne wryly. Damn the fellow, he thought, for being a Jeremiah. He made a cordial gesture himself. Or rather, he wished it to appear a gesture. In fact he had already made up his mind to draw the Prince as much as possible into the Queen's work. 'It would be fair, I think,' he said, 'for the Prince to see memoranda and dispatches.'

'Excellent,' said Stockmar in some excitement.

'Which should not be difficult to arrange with the Cabinet,' continued Melbourne. 'But,' he warned, 'the Queen herself might not care to go so far just yet.'

Stockmar frowned. 'Dear me, you think so?'

Melbourne shrugged his shoulders. 'Baron, you know the Queen. For my part I am happy for the Prince to see state papers. But, finally, it must rest with the Queen.'

That ended the interview.

After Stockmar had gone Melbourne sat gazing out of his library window. He had never moved to the official residence of the First Lord of the Treasury and had stayed at home in South Street. At his time of life he saw no point in moving or making himself in any way uncomfortable. Besides, as the Baron had pointed out, he could not stay in office for ever, and then there would have been the business of moving all over again.

He blinked for tears had started to his eyes. Political power mattered to him less than nothing, but the right to go each day to Court to see the Queen was more estimable than anything in the world. When his ministry fell, that privilege would cease, and he could not bear to think of it.

Tears came easily to elderly eyes. He wiped them away, wishing he did not feel her marriage quite so deeply.

As so often happened when he felt low he decided that after the day's business was done he would sup with Mrs Norton. Neither of them ever made it clear whether or not they were lovers. But the world supposed it was so. All Melbourne told his closest friends was that Caroline Norton had the safest mouth, the wisest brain, the wittiest conversation, the most infectious sense of humour, the deftest hands at preparing special dishes, the neatest manner of encouraging the disconsolate, strengthening the weak, and cautioning the rash, of any woman under the sky. She knew him better than anyone alive; knew exactly how tender he was at the present when the young love of his old age was committed irrevocably to another.

V

Victoria was deeply in love.

She showed a glimpse of it in a letter to her Uncle Leopold, describing Albert as an angel and herself as 'the happiest, happiest Being that ever existed'. After a short time of marriage her love was so intense that Albert was a little frightened. He was vain in some respects but less of a coxcomb than most men of his age, and that he should be the subject of so great a passion was as mystifying as it was touching. He tried to please her, made every effort to improve his English and be tolerant of English customs and, to some extent, he began to enjoy himself.

Their daily life together was orderly and plain. After breakfast at nine o'clock they took a longish walk. Then the Queen attended to state papers while the Prince read English history. Before luncheon at two they sketched, occasionally etching and having the plates 'bit' in a special room in the Palace. Lord Melbourne was with the Queen during the afternoon until the Prince drove her out in a pony phaeton. Only infrequently did she ride. She was a matron now, very different from the girl who had led her First Minister and the Court at a gallop through the parks. After tea the Prince read aloud. After dinner he played at double chess while the Queen *cercled* and talked to Lord Melbourne and her other guests at a large round table. Or on occasions which she much enjoyed and he abominated, there was dancing after dinner, and they waltzed together.

Because Albert liked the country, Victoria changed her own opinion and said she now preferred Windsor to London. She, who had been regularly at the opera and the theatre, was content to be there very seldom. Albert was never lively after dinner. He had been brought up to sleep earlier than the English. Late performances were a real trial to him. And so only occasionally did they go to German and

Italian opera or a French play. English drama lost its royal patronage and, as a result, a number of theatres were closed down.

When the Queen's attention was drawn to this unhappy fact she expressed sympathy, but she was not prepared to do anything else. Prince Albert mattered more than English players.

He mattered so much. She loved his voice when he read to her aloud. She loved to hear him play and sing. She loved to see his firm control of horses and dogs. She loved his elegant clothes; the wired stock and the frock-coat which he introduced to England. She thought him the most beautiful man at her Court and, when they had overcome their first shyness, she accepted his embraces with all the frank ardour of a Hanoverian.

She believed that marriage had matured her, and she looked back on the former life with some disgust. Any gaiety she had enjoyed during her three unmarried years as Queen she now condemned as having been irresponsibly frivolous. At the back of her mind she rather blamed Lord Melbourne for leading her astray. Not that she said anything. He was still too dear a friend to expose him to any hurt. And she considered it might have been more fitting if dear Lehzen had warned her against too much levity. But nothing could be said to her either. Lehzen would not defend herself, but one reproachful look from her almond-shaped eyes would melt away any sort of criticism. It was a long time since Lehzen had scolded her with words. Most effectively it was done with her eyes.

Utterly content in her love, Victoria kept it to herself. At the present she was confiding in no one. Its ecstasies were as private as its pains, and she was too level-headed to pretend that the former could exist without the latter. Albert had brought her the most intense joys; but, secretly, she acknowledged the hurts as well.

She accepted that he did not love her as she loved him; but something told her that maybe this might be altered. If she was loving and patient through anything and everything, he might come to love her.

20

It was not easy.

By disposition she was stubborn. Had she not been Queen of England but a simple country girl, she would still have liked her own way. Getting it, in the teeth of Albert's wishes, was sure to make him cold and withdrawn. So, though she longed to forbid him to have anything to do with the Tories – a despicable lot who had done nothing but vex her ever since she came to the throne – she tried to smile on his plan to be friendly to Peel. And though, in herself, she resented his wish to see state papers and help her in the business of ruling, she steeled herself to accept the idea.

She had less control over other pricks.

There was the day when the Duke of Saxe-Coburg went home, and Albert took it badly. He cried at the separation, and, when Victoria tried to comfort him he told her that not having had a father of her own, she could not begin to conceive the extent of his wretchedness. His brother, Prince Ernest, was staying on at the English Court for another month or two, but after that he would be entirely alone and desolate. That evening Victoria wrote in her journal:

Oh, how I did feel for my dearest, precious husband at this moment! Father, brother, friends, country – all he has left, and all for me. God grant that I may be the happy person, the most happy person, to make this dearest, blessed being happy and contented!

This is what she wrote. Privately she felt that her dearest, blessed being had made too much of it. It was not exactly tactful to have reminded her of all he had sacrificed at the hymeneal altar.

Then there was the occasion when he scolded her for being harsh to her ladies. Exasperated by their slowness in bringing her a shawl, she had drawn attention to the fact. Afterwards Albert rebuked her, telling her it was unbecoming to speak harshly to someone who could not answer back. All she had said, and she remembered the exact words, was: 'Duchess of Bedford, I have been waiting for some

21

time.' It was unjust of Albert to say she had behaved unbecomingly and unfairly. She said so – and she regretted it.

After that, she had discovered accidentally that he was reorganizing her private band, changing it from brass to strings. Both appreciated music, both knew the capabilities of strings were larger than those of brass, but Victoria had left the royal band alone because old William the Fourth had loved it so. There was nothing jollier, he'd say, than eating brown soup to the sound of a brass band. She did not like the change. Somehow it seemed disloyal. Nor did she like Albert acting independently and giving orders without her knowledge. She said so – and she swiftly regretted it.

None of this was as bad as when the Prince was rude to Uncle Sussex. The Duke seldom came to Court. When he did, he came in some state; always accompanied by equerries and his Negro page, Mr Blackman. He came one day to give formal thanks to his niece for creating his morganatic wife Duchess of Inverness and afterwards he stayed to luncheon. It was a cold meal, as was the English way, and the Prince, accustomed to hot food at that time, was slightly on edge. The old Duke carried a selection of repeaters in his deep pockets and at the hours and quarters they struck and chimed and tinkled and, far from amusing the Prince, the cacophony of unexpected noise jarred on his nerves. Moreover, though this uncle of Victoria's had given him precedence, he recalled Stockmar's advice that he still be kept sweet for he might go back on his word. The necessity of doing this and being agreeable when he felt the opposite was almost too much. Between the striking of his repeaters the Duke reminisced.

It was as if he spoke of another world when he told them how, as a young prince in Rome, he had fallen in love with and married a Lady Augusta Murray. George the Third was enraged. The marriage had been performed by the English Chaplain in Rome but it was without royal permission and therefore invalid. Neither Gussy nor Goosie, as they called themselves, cared a pin and in course of time produced two children, a boy and a girl. Feeling it was polite if not his duty the Prince had called on the Pope. This enraged his father further. He hated disobedient sons, but hated papists more.

To her alarm Victoria saw that Albert was nodding in agreement with King George's sentiments.

Fortunately the old man did not notice. He went on happily telling the next *faux pas* which threatened to give George the Third a surprise. He had called on the Cardinal of York, the last legitimate descendant of James the Second. It was a kindly and cousinly act, but the Cardinal was known in Jacobite circles as Henry the Ninth, King of England, Scotland, France and Ireland.

'I was young,' chuckled the Duke, 'and I was a romantic. And so I studiously addressed him as "your royal highness", and he was so delighted that he repaid my call. We became good friends . . .' He was interrupted by his repeaters striking the quarter. As soon as the noise had died away he continued: 'My royal father was pleased to disapprove. He was spectacularly angry. Beside himself.'

'Your royal highness will agree it was to be expected?' Albert's voice was thin and disapproving.

The Duke's beam died away. He took snuff. 'Well, yes,' he said at length. 'I suppose you might be right.'

Albert saw at once that he had shown too much of the vexation he was feeling. 'I have seen his tomb,' he said in an attempt to be mollifying, though it merely sounded macabre.

'York's? The Cardinal's?' The Duke was interested. 'Have you now! A grandiose piece of work I expect.'

'Very ornate,' said Albert shortly. Again he seemed disapproving.

Things went from bad to worse. Victoria felt more and more uncomfortable. Thoroughly put out, the Duke relapsed into a gloomy silence while Albert spoke of his own visit to Rome. He said he'd found the Catholic religion irrational, and the superstitions intolerable to a man of intellect and taste. Nor had he cared for the way the Italians managed their antiquities. The Duke had lived in the city for years and had learnt to like the Romans. He had studied the antiquities, had known Gibbon, and was recognized

23

everywhere as a scholar of some distinction. He did not like being patronized.

He made his feelings clear by switching his attention to Victoria. Then, as tall men can, he took advantage of his great height and deliberately towered over Albert when he said goodbye. Though not far from seventy he was still fifteen inches taller than the Prince, who felt very small indeed at that moment.

The young man knew that he had behaved badly, and yet he was unprepared for Victoria's anger. She told him she would not have her uncle treated so. As for his rudeness to the Catholic religion, she hoped it did not represent his real opinion for a more irreligious view she had seldom heard.

Realizing he was in the wrong Albert said so; but his apology was barely out before the Queen suddenly relented of her anger. Tears burst from her eyes and streamed down her face as she begged his pardon. Not for worlds, she said, would she hurt him. She had not wished to be so peremptory. She never wanted to be so outspoken. Would he forgive her?

He took her in his arms and kissed her. 'Little one,' he murmured. 'My sweetheart! Of course; of course!' There was salt from her tears on his tongue.

'Oh, thank you!' she said. 'Thank you!'

... She loved him so deeply and all manner of unlikely things about him; his shadow thrown by candlelight on a wall; the soft rhythm of his breathing as he lay beside her; the way he cupped her head in his hands; those rare occasions when he looked straight at her and his formal smile changed into something else which grew out of his beautiful face like a flower.

From that date there was always hot luncheon at the Palace; even on shooting days.

VI

The Duke of Wellington had many distinguished titles and appointments – a principality, several dukedoms, marquisates and marshal's batons – and a number of offices in England ranging from Chancellor of Oxford to leader of the Tory party. He was known in society simply as the Duke, by his closest friends as the Beau, and affectionately by his men as 'that long-nosed bugger what licked the French'. To everyone in England he was a living hero, and to a privileged few he was a valued adviser and friend.

It seemed natural, therefore, to Mr George Anson, Private Secretary to Prince Albert, that, when he was in great perplexity about a difficult matter of some importance, he should go to the Duke's room at the House of Lords and ask for his advice and help.

Because of his position in the royal household he was admitted at once to the Duke's presence. He came to the point immediately.

'I ought to make it plain, your grace, that I have not come as a plenipotentiary of Prince Albert. In fact, he does not know that I am here, and I was reduced to a small deception in order to make it possible.'

The Duke nodded.

'I justify the deception by the fact that I am here in his interest,' continued Anson.

'Then sit down, man, you'll talk better off your feet.'

For a moment Anson did so, but he was too unused to sitting at Court, and felt more at his ease standing. 'In such a grave case I would, ordinarily, have gone to Lord Melbourne, but since I left his service I have thought it prudent for both of us to keep apart. Besides, as we may say in the secrecy of these four walls, in matters which closely concern the Queen he is too involved emotionally to be objective. All this, and because for many years you have heard and kept a

25

number of royal secrets, is why I have come to you, your grace.'

'One moment, young man.' The Duke rang a bell, and instructed the steward that he was engaged and must not be disturbed on any account. When the steward had gone, the Duke himself sported the oak. 'I take it,' he said, moving to sit at his desk, 'that the matter is very confidential?'

'It is, your grace.' For a moment Anson hesitated. Then he said: 'May I be entirely frank?'

'We shall never get anywhere unless you are,' said the Duke with some asperity. 'Come, Anson. Speak out.'

Anson hesitated no longer. He said it was evident, and the Duke nodded his agreement, that the Queen was devoted to her husband but, unfortunately, it was making her very possessive. She wished to keep him so entirely to herself that she would not share him with anything or anyone. Even the sight of him close to one of her ladies had made her so sick with jealousy that she had taken her troubles to Stockmar. He had done much to calm her; telling her there was no danger of the Prince's eye lighting on anyone else. He had never, said Stockmar, shown much desire or regard for the ladies. So possessive was her love that the Queen barely noticed the outstanding tactlessness of the Baron's remark, and had merely found it comforting. Stockmar had then warned Anson to make sure his master did not unintentionally aggravate the situation, expressing the opinion that in time the Queen's extravagant expressions of affection would be rationalized.

'With which view,' said Anson, 'I am bound to agree. But now, your grace, the very worst has happened. A lady has been writing to the Prince in an exaggerated and bold manner—' Anson broke off. He was no puritan, though in two months a little of the Prince's prudery had brushed off on to his Private Secretary. He simply wondered if the old Duke had really murmured: 'Lucky dog!'

'You spoke, your grace?'

Wellington looked him straight in the eye. 'Of course not, young man. Pray continue. Tell me more of these bold and exaggerated letters. Do they please the Prince?'

Anson permitted himself to smile. 'He has not seen them. I saw no reason to trouble him.' He took a packet from his pocket. 'The last, which arrived yesterday, is the only one which causes me concern.' He passed the top letter to the Duke. 'The lady announces her intention of coming to England, and I really do not know what to do.'

The letter had been sealed by a wafer and did not carry the sender's name. Nor did the signature mean very much to the Duke.

Anson told him her name. 'Countess Resterlitz, your grace. She is from Carlsbad but is of no importance socially.'

Wellington read the letter with a glint in his eye. His unsatisfactory duchess, Kitty, had been dead for some nine years, and most of his life he had had the reputation of a philanderer. He wished very much that a countess who wrote such saucy letters was coming all the way from Carlsbad to see him.

Anson brought him back to reality. 'You will understand my concern,' he said quietly. 'If she comes to England she will cause trouble.'

'Yes, by God,' exclaimed the Duke. 'As the Queen's so touchy and jealous there'd be the devil of an explosion. But tell me, has this lady any claims on him?'

'I should think not,' said Anson slowly. 'It is reasonable to suppose that at some time the Prince has been tempted to be indiscreet in Carlsbad, but I do not believe he ever fell to the temptation. He is too rigorous, too strict with himself, and far too severe on unchastity. That is why I did not pass on the letters. Countess Resterlitz is probably an adventuress. She hopes to profit by implying an affair which never took place. The Prince would have been angry. He would have made a fuss, and then undoubtedly it would have come to the Queen's ear.'

The Duke nodded slowly. 'You were right,' he agreed. 'And for the same reason we must scotch this adventuress before he learns of her imminent arrival.' He put the tips of his fingers together, a sign amongst those in the know that he was about to plan a campaign. 'And how do you propose we scotch her, eh?'

'It would be a safe wager,' said Anson, 'that the Countess will travel by packet steamer to Dover.'

'Agreed.' Wellington smiled. 'And Dover is one of the Cinque Ports, of which I am Lord Warden. Young man, you're a conspirator, damn it!'

Anson returned the smile. 'I confess I had not forgotten that it is one of your grace's many offices.'

The Duke glanced again at the letter on his desk. 'We do not know what she looks like. But I take it she is pretty?'

'Attractive undoubtedly. From her letters I judge her to be attractive in a *demi-monde* sort of way.'

'More like a spray of lilac, eh,' suggested the Duke, 'than a woodland violet, eh?'

'Exactly, your grace. And we do have her name.'

'Very well.' The Duke stopped pressing his fingertips together. He reached for the standish and paper, and began to write.

It was four days later. The March skies were dark. Grey clouds chased each other over the Channel. The sea was as grey and was patterned with a feather stitch of white foam.

A French packet had rolled her way over from Calais, not sufficiently ballasted to keep her paddles in the water. Waddling from side to side and surging up and down she had taken four times as long to make the crossing as on a normal run. And it had been frightful for the passengers – a long and regular torture to the bad sailors amongst them.

One of the very worst sufferers was carried ashore prostrate on a stretcher. She longed to die. Her clothes – and she was dressed expensively in the highest mode – were ruined. She called for her maid, but the girl was busy seeing to the boxes and did not hear. As if to sharpen her misery, the rain which had held off all afternoon suddenly began to fall. The clouds opened, and her stretcher was on the quayside. Weakly she scrambled to her feet but before she could reach shelter she was soaked to the skin.

It was then, as she stood drenched and wretched, that two men came up to her. They were hatted and dressed in drab and looked official. One politely raised his hat and in good German he asked her name. She told him, adding that she was travelling from Carlsbad to London and, as she was personally known to Prince Albert of Saxe-Coburg, she felt sure she could rely on their help out of her present difficulties.

When she mentioned the name the two officials exchanged glances. Then the first once more raised his hat and said he regretted she was not permitted to land. They had an authorization signed by the Lord Warden of the Cinque Ports. Dover, he added, was one of the five ports under his special governance.

Countess Resterlitz was a woman of spirit. Under ordinary circumstances she would have resisted, and physically if necessary, the order to return aboard the hated packet which had only just brought her from Calais. But she was wet and cold and exhausted, and her head was spinning with the after effects of a prolonged sea-sickness, and she was daunted when she saw that the two officials were supported by several constables. She would not stoop, she told them, to stay in England after so preposterous an insult. But they and their Lord Warden had not heard the last of it. Like everyone in Europe she knew the name of one Englishman of untarnished honour and great power. She would write to him about her unbelievable predicament.

As she was being helped aboard by a seaman and her maid, she turned to her persecutors. 'I shall complain,' she told them haughtily, 'to the Duke of Wellington.'

VII

Unaware of having been saved from serious embarrassment, Prince Albert concentrated his frustrated energies on settling his aunt and mother-in-law into a hired house.

Belgrave Square was a newly-built area. Fourteen years

earlier it had been a dismal, boggy tract of land. Now one of its stuccoed houses was considered worthy of the Queen's mother.

The Duchess did not agree. She had spent holidays in humble houses, even cottages, but all her life she had lived in a palace or a castle or a country seat. Ingestre House in Belgrave Square was a comedown. Moreover, though Sir George Couper, a kind but delicate gentleman, had taken Conroy's place as her Comptroller, and she had her household of ladies and equerries, she felt she was living alone for the first time in her life.

But she found that being away from Court had its compensations. Victoria was being pleasanter to her than for years past. With a reasonable distance between them, and regularly persuaded by Albert, the Queen had warmer feelings for her mother. For her sake she had tried to persuade the King of Hanover to vacate his apartments in St James's, but he stubbornly refused to cooperate. She apologized to her mother for the inconveniences of Ingestre House and assured her it would only be a temporary arrangement. As soon as a grace-and-favour house was available, she should have it. The Duchess pouted a little, and she mewed, because she was that sort of woman; but she was invited to lunch or dine at the Palace on most days of the week and, in fact, she saw more of her daughter and son-in-law than she had as a resident there. Victoria was kind and considerate. Her mother thanked God for it and was content. After what had passed between them she did not expect more. Nor did she really want it. If Victoria had unexpectedly made protestations of filial love, she would have believed her insincere. Her own maternal love was quickly given to Albert. She adored him.

It was the Prince who arranged the furniture in her public rooms. It was he who chose her books, though she was forced to pretend an interest in the selection. And it was he who heard and sometimes admired the military airs which she composed so easily. They often made music together in the afternoons while across the park Victoria tussled with state affairs under the guidance of Lord Melbourne; she

30

playing and he singing arias from opera, and on the rare occasions when she could persuade him to be frivolous – they played selections from light operas *à quatre mains.*

As often as not his brother was with him. This did not please the Duchess who considered Ernest as boorish as his father. He was also as ugly, she thought, looking with distaste at his pale, spotty complexion. It was incredible that Albert, with all his grace and striking good looks, should be his brother ... She was reminded of the old scandal, and because she half believed it and knew she ought not to, she pushed it to the back of her mind again.

Ernest was quite aware of her dislike. She made it plain she far preferred Albert; but he took it good-naturedly and was prepared to sit against the wall and daydream while Albert and their aunt supervised the arrangement of bijouterie, or looked at folios, or while they played and sang from *Don Giovanni*, or, daringly, from *Le Pré aux Clercs.*

One day he was less good-natured. He fidgeted. The Duchess was showing Albert her collection of political cartoons and she was irritated when Ernest began to stride up and down before the fireplace. She begged him to sit still.

Ernest glanced at her. 'Madam, my aunt,' he said. 'Your daughter is the Queen of this country, but you ought not to treat the Hereditary Prince of Saxe-Coburg as a footman.'

'Hoity-toity!' she said.

His sallow face was suddenly suffused with blood. Albert who knew this presaged a hurricane of temper managed to keep him in restraint until they were out of the house. The Duchess, piqued by their abrupt departure, sulked. Fortunately she did not hear what Ernest said at her own front door.

Albert walked his brother up and down Belgrave Square until he had calmed down. Then he nodded to the grooms to bring up their horses. They rode silently into the Park, two equerries behind.

'You may scold me now,' said Ernest quietly. His temper had given way to dejection.

'I had no intention of doing so,' said his brother. He

31

tipped his hat to a lady in a carriage who bowed graciously as they passed. 'But since you mention it, I can remark that it's unlike you to take offence at anything Aunt Kent might say or do.'

'I know. She's damned cantankerous, but I can usually put up with it. That is, until my patience snaps . . .' His voice trailed off.

Albert looked at him. 'Well?' he said sharply. 'What is it?'

'You've not guessed?'

For a moment Albert looked baffled, then incredulous. He frowned. 'You mean to say you have it again?'

His brother nodded, suddenly jabbed in his spurs and went ahead.

It gave Albert time to think. He gave a signal to the equerries to remain out of earshot. His face grey and lined with anxiety he caught up with Ernest.

'Who was it?' he demanded.

Ernest grinned. 'If you knew her, I should be surprised.'

'Probably you do not know yourself.'

Ernest was surprised by the bitterness in his brother's voice. His grin vanished.

'It is not enough for you to foul our name by getting the pox in Carlsbad, but you have to get it here in England where you are a guest and where your brother is husband to the Queen.'

'My young brother,' snapped Ernest, emphasizing the word 'young', 'who owes me some duty and who should remember that I, too, was an equal candidate for Victoria's hand . . .'

'Be silent!' Albert interrupted him in fury. It was true. Both of them had been groomed by their grandmother and by King Leopold and Stockmar as potential husbands for the Queen. The choice had been hers. Albert could not bear to hear his brother hint that but for fate their places would be reversed. Hardly able to contain his rage, he hissed out: 'You have dishonoured our hospitality and consorted with whores. It makes you despicable, unworthy . . .'

This time it was Ernest who interrupted. 'Virtuous

32

Albert!' he mocked. 'The purest of all Coburgs. How you hate it all; the ordinary itches and pleasures of ordinary men, the coupling, the rutting, the mating. How you'll beget an heir for England is a mystery. And it's your job. You're England's stallion. Poor Victoria!'

Albert wanted to crack his crop across the sneering face. Only by the strictest self-control did he prevent it. As it was, his face was crimson with rage. 'I will arrange for your departure immediately,' he said. 'You will take your insults with you back to Coburg, and I vow I shall never see your face again.'

Ernest suddenly panicked. He realized he had gone too far. He could not face his father nor anyone in the family if he was sent in disgrace from England. And he wanted help in his present trouble.

He tried to apologize. Fright made him gabble. If Albert wanted vengeance for the hurt he had suffered, he was getting it. Ernest was a weak character. He showed it then, to the full. Begging for pardon, he became so hysterical that Albert had to seize his rein and quietly lead him to a clump of trees where his behaviour would not be so conspicuous. Quietly but urgently he demanded that he control himself and hold his tongue. Simply to quieten him he promised that he could remain in England until the proper time. He promised medical help. He promised to forgive him for all his insults, though he knew perfectly well he could not forget them.

Eventually Ernest was calmed. 'It is this clap,' he said miserably. 'It makes me see things in a twisted way. I hardly meant what I said. Believe me.' And then, as if giving his brother a compliment, he added, 'And I've no call to taunt you with being virtuous. Until today I'd no idea you were such a dog.' Albert looked completely foxed. 'Don't pretend you don't know,' smiled Ernest – and told him he had had a letter only that morning from Carlsbad describing Countess Resterlitz's fury at being sent home from England just when she had tried to land. 'She threatened to make a scene: but she can't. You've all the cards in your hand, you lucky dog.'

The Prince sent for his Private Secretary.

'I am having difficulties with my brother and require your help.'

Anson spread his hands and bowed. It signified he was prepared to serve the Prince in any way. He meant it.

'On occasions he behaves outrageously. Today he has confessed to contracting the Neapolitan disease. You will know what I mean. How may he be treated while he is still in England?'

Anson had served the Prince long enough to know a little of the anxieties which pressed upon him. All the household and visitors to Court consulted the Queen's physician, Sir James Clark, when they needed a doctor, but if he suggested this the Prince would be shocked. That anyone so close to the Queen should be aware of his brother's disgrace was unthinkable.

'Would his serene highness object to seeing my brother's doctor in Kensington?'

'He is reliable?'

Anson bit back the warm retort he wanted to make. The very insecurity of his position in England caused the Prince to make such gauche remarks. It was not his fault.

'Absolutely, Sir,' he replied. 'He is a skilled practitioner and of course the case would be treated in the strictest professional confidence. For example, the doctor would not even discuss it with me or with you, Sir.' The Prince opened his mouth as if to object, but Anson hurried on: 'Once Prince Ernest is in his hands that is the end of the matter so far as we are concerned.'

The Prince nodded. 'Perhaps it is better so. Let your brother's doctor treat him until he leaves. I am obliged to you, Anson.'

The Private Secretary bowed.

'And there is one other matter.' The Prince drummed his fingers on the desk. 'My brother, as I have said, is not at all well. Maybe he imagines things. But he remarked today on a certain lady being refused admission to this country. It seems she was coming to see me.'

'A lady, Sir?'

'A Countess Resterlitz from Carlsbad.' He looked his secretary in the eyes. 'I can hardly believe that such a thing would happen without our knowledge. Have you heard of it, by any chance?'

'No, Sir,' replied Anson. 'Otherwise, of course, I should have informed you.'

'Of course.' The Prince nodded. 'Thank you, Anson. That will be all for the present.'

When the door had closed behind him, Albert stared out of the window. He had bitterly resented it when, before their marriage, Victoria had written to say he was to have Lord Melbourne's secretary as his own. It would look partisan, he had written back, and the Tories would be justified in believing he was being made to see England for the first time through Whig spectacles; and he had pleaded the liberty of every man to choose his most intimate associates. But she had been firm, and he had been disgruntled; that is, until he met George Anson. Now already they were fast friends. Anson helped him over many, many difficulties which the English at Victoria's Court could barely guess at. He was patient with his master's faults, and, at a pace he could digest, he corrected them. In some ways, too, he was far wiser than Stockmar. The Baron had taught Albert to counter the English hostility to foreigners with princely hauteur and indifference. Anson had a better solution. Laugh, he advised; laugh with them. Join in their games. Even trying to do this had made life more bearable. Most important of all he was utterly loyal to Albert first, and to the Queen, to England, to Lord Melbourne afterwards. His master's interests mattered most.

Anson made all the difference. Albert felt confident that Ernest would be well looked after, and with the utmost discretion. And he could be sure Anson would keep Resterlitz at bay. How well he tried to lie, and solely for his master's benefit.

He smiled and went over to the piano. There with great solemnity he played the National Anthem, but the words he sang were from a hostile street ballad:

35

God save sweet Vic, my Queen,
Long live my little Queen,
God save the Queen.
Albert's victorious;
The Coburgs are glorious,
All so notorious;
God save the Queen.

At his desk in the small room next door George Anson laid down his pen and listened to the hearty singing. He smiled. 'Well done,' he said softly. 'You are learning.'

VIII

When Sir James Clark confirmed it, the Queen was silent.

He thought for a moment that she was overcome with fright. It would have been reasonable. Childbirth carried off so many. It was always a hazard, and some women were quite naturally afraid of the pain. But neither of the ladies in attendance made any move to comfort her and Sir James realized he was mistaken. The Queen was deliberately savouring the news. When she began to smile with contentment it was a small smile at first which broadened and grew like an opening flower until her whole face was full of joy.

She took Sir James' hand and clasped it. Carefully he extracted his hand, kissed hers, bowed and left the room. His work was done.

Lady Lyttelton spoke first. A mother herself and from a huge family, she could guess at most of the Queen's feelings. 'He will be exactly like his father,' she murmured.

The Queen took her hand. 'Oh, Lady Lyttelton. Do you think so? It is my dearest wish.'

Mrs Brand, a Woman of the Bedchamber, said nothing

was more certain. A big-boned, good-natured woman, she sometimes shocked the ladies by mothering the Queen and by absent-mindedly addressing her as 'dear'. It was a liberty no one, not even Lehzen, would have taken before other people, and Mrs Brand only kept her place because Victoria loved her managing ways and pretended not to hear the offending endearment. Clapping her hands with excitement, Mrs Brand suggested they inform the other ladies at once. The Queen nodded her consent.

In the next room there was a collection of Ladies-in-Waiting, Maids of Honour, and Women of the Bedchamber. Lehzen was there as well, and Miss Skerrett, the Queen's First Dresser. As maiden ladies delicacy had forbidden their attendance during Sir James' examination; otherwise, being so close to the Queen, they would certainly have been there. Mrs Brand gave out the news and, as they exclaimed and cried in delight, she reminded them to keep the matter to themselves. Then she ushered the Baroness and the Dresser into the Queen's presence.

Victoria ran into Lehzen's arms and kissed her. Then she kissed Miss Skerrett. Had she been their own child they could not have been more thoroughly pleased to see her happiness.

Miss Skerrett was the daughter of a West Indian nabob and was a blue-stocking. Her title as First Dresser was misleading. It merely gave her a place close to the Queen's person. In fact it was she who 'bit' the plates of etchings made by the Queen and the Prince, and it was she who communicated with artists, writers, musicians and players acting as a royal ambassador to art. Now, though she had a restricted knowledge of the subject, she took it upon herself to be admonitory. Using the plural pronoun universally beloved by those who have the care of invalids and infants she said exactly what we could and should do and what we should not. Amongst the prohibitions was that we should not only give up riding but even deny ourselves the pleasure of visiting stables, and high in the list of recommendations was that we should eat quantities of milk puddings flavoured, if possible, with bay.

On this occasion no one took Skerrett's preaching very

seriously though the Queen was polite and pretended to. She kissed the Dresser once more and thanked her for her advice. Then she took Lehzen's hand and together they went out to the window balcony.

It was an April day and the Windsor countryside was unexpectedly warm. 'Oh, Lehzen,' said Victoria. 'Dear Lehzen.'

The Baroness pressed her hand. She guessed why she was so exceedingly happy, beyond the happiness of most women when told they are carrying their first child. Victoria's childhood had been grey and part of the greyness had been caused by her solitude. Without any brothers or sisters, her father dead and her mother generally indifferent to her and even sometimes hostile, she had felt desolately lonely. That was why she had given so much devotion to her governess, why Lehzen herself had been the first repository of her love. That was why she had loved Lord Melbourne, and why now she so passionately adored Prince Albert. They gave her a sense of family – but none of them, not even the Prince, was bonded to her as the child now growing in her womb.

Lehzen said nothing for a long time. Victoria looked out over the Great Park, her face alive with joy. In repose it was less beautiful than when alert, but there was an animal liveliness and grace about her which made Lehzen catch her breath. Here was a fulfilment of her own dream. She felt a lump in her throat as she realized her good fortune. She was seeing Victoria as she had hoped and prayed she would be one day. Then, ironically, slow tears blurred the picture.

Victoria turned. 'Why, Lehzen dear; what is it?'

Lehzen could not manage a reply. Instead she hugged her, and in half a minute both were in tears.

Afterwards Lehzen wiped her eyes and admonished Victoria for blowing her nose in so unladylike a fashion.

The Queen smiled. It was quite like the old days. But then she remembered what temporarily she had forgotten, and the excitement of carrying a child came back to her. She talked about it to her old governess, and Lehzen was frank and admitted she knew next to nothing about the matter – though probably more than Miss Skerrett, she added with a smile. She advised Victoria to rely in all things on Lady Lyttelton. Being a dowager she had no reason to be away from Court, and could be permanently at the Queen's right hand. It would be tactful, too, to consult her mother. Victoria pulled a face.

'Now that,' said Lehzen with mock seriousness, 'is hardly becoming in the Queen of England, wife to Prince Albert of Saxe-Coburg, and mother of a prince or princess.'

'Must I?' pleaded Victoria.

Lehzen nodded. 'Your mother will expect it. Under the circumstances you ought to.'

Victoria's oval jaw began to set in the obstinate line so familiar to Lehzen. Clearly she was thinking that her mother had abnegated all claims to have her feelings considered. But it softened again. Life had certainly been more comfortable since February. The Palace and Ingestre House were on good if not loving terms, and the Duchess had come to Windsor for Easter. Victoria decided to tell her mother the news personally. Later, as occasion permitted, she would seek her advice.

Lehzen had a motto or a proverb to suit most occasions. 'Cactus prickles are only drawn by oil,' she said approvingly.

They discussed who else should be given formal notice that towards the end of November the Queen hoped to bear a child. Victoria would write herself to the family – that is, to her grandmother in Coburg, Uncle Leopold's queen, Louise, and to the Hanoverian aunts. Lehzen as the Queen's confidential adviser would tell the Prime Minister, and he would know who else ought to be informed.

As for the rest, it was easily done, said Lehzen with a smile. 'Leave it, my dear, to your ladies. Mrs Brand told them to hold their tongues, but what lady, with such a delicious secret, ever did?' Mischievously she added: 'Baron Stockmar need not be told. He will divine it all in his crystal ball.'

Victoria laughed. She, of course, was to tell Albert.

Breathlessly she told Albert the good news.

His reaction was surprising. He accepted it with massive calmness. Had she already given him ten children and the process become a regular event, he could not have been less moved. That is, so far as his appearance showed. Beneath it he was anxious.

To her relief he took Victoria in his arms and murmured an endearment.

'You are not pleased, Albert?' she asked, puzzled.

'But of course. It is the best possible news, and she will be exactly like you.'

'He,' she corrected.

'Exactly like you,' he continued with a smile. 'Contradictory and obstinate.'

'England,' she insisted, 'expects a Prince of Wales.'

He would not argue. Instead he kissed her. She relaxed in his arms. It would have been pleasanter if he had showed some of the boundless joy she felt herself but then, she supposed, gentlemen had different feelings about such things.

'Albert, you really do want to have a son?' she said anxiously.

There was a barely perceptible pause before he answered: 'I shall refuse to say "of course" any more.'

She pushed herself away from him. What was it? She insisted on knowing why he was being restrained, why he was being so odd.

'We were almost strangers in February when we married, but now I feel I am part of you. I know you are uneasy.'

He smiled wanly. 'I confess,' he said, and he put his arms right round her, 'I confess that I am a little worried. But it is only a little. Not enough to distress you.'

'For me?' she said. 'You need not. Sir James is confident, and so am I. I have always been healthy.'

'Most of us appear to be healthy,' he said. 'And, truly, I am not frightened for you, though I wish you had not so much pain to go through. It is the child I fear for.'

She looked at him round-eyed. 'The bleeding?' she said.

He nodded. On the day after the wedding he had told her that some of the Coburgs had haemophilia. He was free from it himself but Ernest and their father had to be careful

40

not to cut themselves while shaving because their blood was difficult to staunch. A deep wound could cause them to bleed to death.

Victoria had inquired privately of Lehzen why no one had troubled to mention the Coburgs' haemophilia before, and Lehzen had been astonished, claiming complete ignorance of the matter. As no one had said anything, they concluded Victoria's mother had either forgotten all about it or, like everyone concerned with the marriage negotiations, had not thought it important. It had been reassuring at the time, but Albert's anxiety for their child renewed some secret doubts and fears. They had to be faced rationally.

'But you don't have it,' she objected. 'You said yourself only your brother and father have the disease.'

He held her very close to him. 'There are those who say . . .' he began, and he broke off. He swallowed. 'There are those who say I am not my father's son. That my father is Alexander von Haustein, my mother's lover before she was divorced and remarried . . .'

The small face so close to his own smiled and said: 'There is no need to continue, my dearest. I know the story.'

He regarded her in amazement.

She answered his unspoken question. 'From Lord Melbourne,' she said. 'Who else? It was his duty to tell me, and it made not the slightest difference to my intention to marry you.'

'You cannot know it all,' he protested hotly.

She laid a finger across his lips.

'I know enough,' she said softly.

'If it is true,' he said bitterly, 'and we shall never know whether it is or not, at least we need not fear the bleeding will pass to our children through me.'

'Then why are you such a Jeremiah?' she said, playfully slapping the back of his head.

'I fear,' he murmured, 'that it may pass to them through you.'

She frowned.

'You are half Coburg,' Albert reminded her. 'We are first cousins.'

'Women,' she said quickly, 'never have the disease.'

He nodded. 'That is why I hope all our children are daughters. With women like you in the royal family England has no need of kings.'

She liked the compliment.

'But there is something else,' he continued. 'Some of the observers who have tried to trace the course of bleeding in certain families are sure it is passed through the females. The men suffer the disease. The women carry it.'

Victoria felt cold. She shuddered. He felt her trembling and hugged her closer.

'We must pray that they are wrong,' he said.

Victoria shook off her fears and by an act of will she pulled herself together. On occasions she rather enjoyed being deliberately solemn, and candidly she relished the rituals of illness and death; but she had too much commonsense to be overwhelmed by Albert's morbid anxieties.

'Nothing has yet been proved one way or the other,' she said firmly. 'And until it is, I intend to enjoy carrying this child as much as I can.'

His long face seemed to grow longer.

She kissed him to comfort him.

Privately she was rather vexed to have to bolster him up. Really on this occasion it should have been the other way round.

IX

Easter Day passed happily. The Duchess of Kent was delighted with the news and was sincerely concerned for her daughter's health. Victoria was touched. She was affected too by Lord Melbourne's reception of the news. He simply clasped her hands and shook them up and down. No, he said, he was not crying; his eyes were rheumy. She did not believe her old friend, and shed some tears of joy with him.

After she and Albert had received the Sacrament together they spent most of the day in each other's company. Only on such days did they dine alone, apart from company, and they treasured them all the more.

But from Easter Monday Victoria's happiness was threatened in several ways.

On that day there was a meet of the Stag Hounds at Ascot. The Prince said he would hunt. His brother, noticeably more cheerful and less sallow, decided to drive to the Heath with the Queen.

Miss Skerrett made profound objections. It would not do, she said, for her royal mistress to drive so far even in a well-sprung pony carriage. She was unprepared for the Queen's vigorous reaction.

'Nonsense, Skerrett; it will do us good.'

Not five minutes passed before Miss Skerrett had the gloomy satisfaction of receiving the fainting Queen in her arms.

She had been standing at the window to see the Prince ride off from the Castle. Accompanied by two equerries and a groom, he saluted her with his whip, and then turned to go. His mount, a vicious kicker called Tom Bowling, stood stock still. Albert was an excellent horseman. He tried to soothe the beast into obedience but it was too spirited, too bad tempered. With rolling eyes it suddenly seized its bit, reared back, and bolted.

The Queen gripped Skerrett's hand. 'Oh, come quickly, Ernest,' she called over her shoulder.

The Hereditary Prince was at her side at once. They watched Albert turn the horse right about and thunder past below the window. He turned him again. Victoria knew well how to handle horses. She gasped. Four times the Prince turned and then he lost a stirrup. The bolter felt the difference. He tore for some trees growing out from a wall and threw his rider against one of them.

Foliage prevented the Queen from seeing what had happened, but when Tom Bowling appeared alone and thundered past, she gave a little shriek and fainted into the arms of Skerrett. The Hereditary Prince ran for the door.

By the time he returned, the room seemed to be full of white-faced ladies, and the air was thick with sal volatile and burning feathers. He was not welcomed by Miss Skerrett or Mrs Brand or any of the other ladies. They thought a Queen suffering from the vapours should not be seen by gentlemen, even her royal brother-in-law. Prince Ernest paid no attention. It was important that Victoria hear from his own lips what had happened.

He knelt beside her. As soon as she saw him, she sat bolt upright, and this put him at a disadvantage as she was so high above him.

'He is not hurt,' he said looking up at her. 'Not seriously. He has bruised his hip and knee and scraped the skin off his arm.'

'Nothing else?'

'Yes,' he said. 'His coat is torn.'

Victoria's relief was such that Skerrett tried to give her more sal volatile. The Queen pushed it away. 'But where is he?' she demanded.

'He has a new coat, a fresh horse, and has gone on.'

Victoria did not know whether to be glad or angry at this sure sign from Albert that he was unhurt.

Sensing her feelings Prince Ernest said: 'You would have been needlessly alarmed if you had seen him torn and dirty and pale.'

'We shall follow,' she decided.

'Ma'am,' said Skerrett severely. 'It won't do.'

The Queen insisted, and with great vigour. Very soon she and Prince Ernest were being driven out to the Heath.

Victoria was more upset than she would admit to anyone. The accident could have been very serious. For a few brief minutes she had stared widowhood in the face. It had been quite unbearable.

Then, early in May, there came shocking news from London. The brother of Lord John Russell, one of the Queen's ministers, was brutally murdered by his valet. Victoria was horrified by this evidence of anarchy, and revolted to hear that the poor man had been three-quarters beheaded by one blow in his own bed. No one, not even the highest in the land, could consider himself absolutely safe any longer.

Victoria's nerves had only just recovered from this jarring when her favourite dog fell ill. Dash had been her constant companion for ten years and she had petted and loved him at those bleak times when it seemed as if no one in all the world cared for her save Lehzen. Now he was suffering from having been spoilt. His teeth had rotted and he had bad breath. Something inside him was making him very ill. Cavalier spaniels generally remained fit for much longer than ten years. Victoria now had the misery of seeing her beloved Dash suffering, knowing that she herself might have been the cause of it.

Albert could not be expected to know quite why Dash was so precious to her and, thinking her affection sentimental, he was not very sympathetic. Victoria tried to make the point that he himself was devoted to his greyhound Eos and it was no comfort to be told that working dogs were one thing and lap dogs another, and that if Eos had such unpleasant symptoms he would be shot directly.

Victoria found herself angry out of all proportion. She supposed it was because of her condition. Lady Lyttelton assured her that many things could be exaggerated and thrown out of true when one was carrying a child. Whatever the reason, she was pleased to be revenged on Albert when the day of Ernest's departure drew near. He was not to go directly home and planned to visit their Coburg cousin Ferdinand, the King-Consort of Portugal. Sometime before he left Albert confessed that the thought made him miserable. 'Why?' asked the Queen. He tried to explain, but she who had been so outwardly sympathetic when his father left England, was less than consoling when he complained that soon, soon he would be alone and bereft of all his family. In fact, she was painfully forthright. She had noticed, she said, a certain coolness between the brothers for a month past; therefore she wondered why Albert should feel the loss so keenly. This as she hoped vexed him. She rubbed in salt, saying it was hardly complimentary to her, to their expected child, to her family and friends and to her nation for him to claim that henceforth he would be alone.

Once again Albert tried to explain himself, and failed miserably; but when Ernest did go, it was obvious how much he felt the parting, and Victoria relented and was sympathetic. She wrote in her journal on May 9th:

The two brothers sang a very pretty song together called Abschied, *which students generally sing before they part. Albert was much affected, and when I ran upstairs he looked as pale as a sheet and his eyes full of tears ... After a little while he said, 'Such things are hard to bear (Solche Sachen sind hart)', which indeed they are.*

Victoria then needlessly upset herself by feeling remorse for neglecting Lord M. and dear Lehzen. They had been so important to her happiness in the past and she charged herself with ingratitude for overlooking their claims upon her. She surprised both by a sudden burst of affection.

Albert was amused until he felt the Queen might be making an exhibition of herself. Stockmar warned him that it did not do for sovereigns to mix too intimately with their subjects, and the Baron made another shrewd observation which Albert passed on to Victoria.

'How often, my love, has Viscount Melbourne urged you to be kind to Lehzen, and not forget old friends?'

'Very often,' replied Victoria. 'He has such a good and thoughtful nature. It rebukes my own thoughtlessness.'

'And how often, my love, has the Baroness urged you to be kind to Lord Melbourne, and not forget old friends?'

'Quite often,' she said. 'Because she, too ...' Her voice trailed away. She looked at her husband, sincerely shocked. 'Do you infer they are in collusion?' she asked hotly. 'That they keep themselves before my notice by helping each other?'

He said nothing, but he smiled.

'How could you find it amusing?' she cried, in a voice he had never heard before. 'It is shocking to make such a base inference, to cast doubt on the integrity of two noble disinterested friends, and then make fun of it.'

He apologized for offending her. He had thought it his duty to speak; that was all.

She forgave him, though for a long time she resented his interference. She knew it was ignoble to suspect either Lehzen or Lord M. of trying to keep in her notice for their own reasons. Therefore whenever she thought of the matter she set her mouth in an obstinate line and tried to think of something else. She was the same, or liked to think she was the same to both her friends; but Albert's questions had subdued her. Somehow or other they had altered things.

Lady Lyttelton was very understanding. For the moment she had become everything to the Queen: confidante, adviser, friend and mother. She assured her that there was nothing very dreadful in her repeated tiffs with the Prince. He was her only equal, or near equal at Court; the only man who could spark from her and make life real. After three years in exalted loneliness it might be that the Queen, lowered by her condition, was resentful of any competition.

It was good advice. Victoria thought about it a great deal. For the first time she recognized and faced up to the real reason why she did not care to have Albert help her with state affairs. Lehzen and her tutors had done their best, and as women at the Court went, she was a well-educated woman; but try as she might, she remained an ignoramus in political science. Albert's opportunities for getting information were restricted to a daily reading of the highly prejudiced newspaper *The Times*, but he was always several leaps ahead of her. In Far Eastern affairs, for instance, her head ached with details of the Opium War, and she thought the Chinese tiresome and wicked. Albert, on the other hand, seemed to understand it all, and he actually appeared to consider the British were in the wrong. When an impudent young member called Gladstone had stood in her own House of Commons and said the Chinese had every right to poison their wells in order to keep away the British, Albert had actually agreed with his insolence. Privately, of course. Only to her. Albert was always discreet. She could count on him absolutely. But deep down inside her she was jealous of his undoubted ability to rule, and it was this, she saw now, which had prevented her from letting him help her. Lord Melbourne, the Baron, Lehzen, the Duke, all sorts of good people had tried to persuade her to let Albert see state papers, but she had never agreed. Now that Lady Lyttelton's talk had made her see the reason why, she thought, perhaps, she ought to change her mind.

By an uncomfortable coincidence, on the very day she sent for Albert to tell him what she had decided, he had also decided to seize the nettle on his own account and complain.

His brother Ernest had written from the Court in Portugal with a glowing account of the liberties and powers enjoyed by their cousin the King-Consort. In comparison, Albert's own position was pathetic. His frustrations smarted. The inefficiency, as he saw it, of Baroness Lehzen smarted still more.

He went to the Queen and, seeing she was smiling and in high spirits, was encouraged to be very frank.

'May I mention three matters to you, my dear?' he said. Their importance as he rated them, affected his manner. He sounded as ponderous as Stockmar.

The Queen's heart sank a little but she kept her smile until he told her one of her ladies was a scurrilous gossip.

'Come,' she said, trying to keep her tone light. 'Surely not, Albert. After all, they are my chosen ladies.'

He did not take the hint and blundered on. The Duchess of Bedford, he told her, had spread it about that he did not love the Queen.

Victoria flushed scarlet. This touched her on an extremely sensitive nerve.

'My heart is not on my sleeve as you English say, and therefore the English think I have no heart. My deep devotion for you is unseen, and so one of your own chosen Ladies-in-Waiting insists that it does not exist.'

He walked to the window and looked out. She followed him and slipped her arms round his waist. She murmured endearments.

'She must be disciplined, Victoria,' he insisted. 'My love,

my honour, even my manhood, have been impugned by your duchess.'

'I will speak to her,' she promised.

'She must be disciplined.'

'I will speak to her,' repeated Victoria. 'She will not gossip again.'

Albert was not really satisfied, but Victoria's tone was unmistakable. With her ladies she was like a cat with kittens. He went on to the next point. He hoped, he said, that he had now sufficiently mastered the English language and customs to be of some help to her with affairs of state.

Victoria's smile returned. She remarked on the co-incidence. She had taken advice and had planned to suggest it herself that very day. Stupidly for the moment she had forgotten Albert's extraordinary sensitivity.

'Whose advice, my dear?' he asked coldly.

She realized her mistake and was flustered. Instead of making light of it she answered his question. 'Why, Lord Melbourne, of course,' she began.

'Of course,' he repeated.

'And the Duke . . . and Baron Stockmar . . .'

'Not the Baroness?' he asked.

'Well, yes, as you know she is one of your great admirers and she said at once you ought to be given a sight of state papers.'

Albert was so enraged at being beholden to Lehzen of all people that he then made a mistake. He took Ernest's letter from his pocket.

'I should prefer to think that my claim to be considered as your adviser in state affairs depended less upon the warm-heartedness of your friends than on my inalienable right as a husband.'

Victoria stiffened. Words like 'claim' and 'right' fell hard on her ears. She said nothing until she had taken the letter and had read it.

'What Cousin Ferdinand does in Portugal bears no re-lation to what you do here,' she said at length.

'You are right,' he said, trying to keep the bitterness out of his voice.

'Ferdinand is King-Consort. You are the Queen's consort without a title. Portugal is Portugal. England is England.' If she hoped, by hammering home these hated facts, to mollify him, she was mistaken.

'Then for the time being,' he said stonily, 'we may leave aside the matter of whether or not I shall be your adviser in state affairs. For the moment I should prefer not to.'

She showed neither vexation nor dismay. Nor did she cry nor throw herself into his arms and beg him to reconsider, as he half expected. She merely arranged the folds of her dress and asked: 'And what was the third matter you wished to mention?'

He had intended to ask politely for larger influence in her private affairs. In other words, like any husband, he wished to order his own home, and he wanted to take over some of the tasks which Lehzen had managed ever since the Queen's accession. He had intended to reason quietly, and point out the injustice and the embarrassment of having to play second fiddle in his own home to the Lord Chamberlain, Uxbridge, who was official head of the Royal Household, and to Baroness Lehzen, the unofficial head. But a reasoned argument in his present mood was out of the question. He began where he might have ended if the necessity had arisen, by attacking Uxbridge and Lehzen.

Victoria listened coldly. He said little that she had not heard before, though never indeed from him; how the Paget family, with Lord Uxbridge at their head, at Court were overpowerful, how some hostile critics went so far as to call the Court the Paget Club House, and how Lord Alfred Paget was said to be so much in love with Victoria that in addition to carrying her portrait about his neck, he had another hung round the neck of his dog.

This last fact did surprise the Queen, but she hastened to defend her courtiers. 'How extraordinary!' she said. 'But how typical. Lord Alfred is always doing and saying the oddest things. Did you know he made a pilgrimage to the field of Waterloo simply to see where his father's leg lies buried? No, I suspect not. But then, my dear, I do not think you quite understand the exuberance of the Pagets.'

Albert was dismayed by the light-hearted way she accepted such disrespect to her dignity.

'It is not proper for gentlemen to declare a passion for you at your own Court,' he protested. 'And certainly not now that you are a married lady.' He faced her squarely. 'Nor is it proper for such declarations to be kept from me your husband. I understand that one of the officers attached to the household has already drawn considerable attention to himself by fancying himself madly in love with you, but I heard nothing of it until recently.'

Victoria, who had heard about it a long time before and had not paid the slightest attention, remained silent.

'Either Uxbridge or the Baroness should have informed me. It is I, your husband who has to protect your honour, as Anson has made plain to the Baroness.'

Victoria started. 'What has Mr Anson done?'

'Under my instructions he has told the Baroness that in future all such threats to your reputation are to be mentioned to me immediately.'

Smiling, she tried to calm his fears. 'You take their idiocy too seriously,' she insisted. She told him about the man who had paid regular visits to Kensington Palace to blow kisses at her when she was a girl; a harmless little man with a pair of Sir Robert Peel's policemen to keep an eye on him whom they had nicknamed Mr Tunbridge Wells. Since then there had been other lunatics who imagined themselves deeply in love with her; a Scotsman who travelled south at regular intervals simply to catch a sight of her on the terraces at Windsor, and a haberdasher who was found in the private gardens looking, as he explained, for a wife. These men meant no real harm. Lehzen had had experience of them for years. Either she humoured them or she ignored them; but she never took them seriously.

'Which illustrates,' broke in the Prince, 'her startling incompetence. Now that you are married she should have realized her duty in keeping me informed.'

Victoria, feeling pushed and pulled about by her exacting husband, and exhausted by the stupid progress of their argument, suddenly flared. 'You have no right, no right at all, to

51

say such things of Lehzen. Nor, without my permission, should Mr Anson have said anything to her.'

'It is my province as your husband to guard your honour and save you if possible from the inefficiency of your confidential secretary.'

She gave a little shriek. As if by magic Mrs Brand and Miss Skerrett appeared through the door. She did not seem to see them.

'It is my province as your Queen to forbid you to meddle,' she cried.

White-faced, Albert turned to go.

'Stay!' she commanded.

Very bravely Miss Skerrett tried to calm her. She knew their dear sweet Queen had not meant what she said.

Victoria made it clear she had meant every word of it.

Mrs Brand tried, and, for the first time in her life, was cauterized for addressing the Queen as 'dear'.

It took a great deal of time and all Albert's patience to restore the situation to where it had been before. Victoria wept over him and asked that all should be forgotten and forgiven. Dejected because he had made no progress at all Albert had to leave her to Lady Lyttelton's understanding care. Lady Lyttelton could soothe Victoria's nerves. But who could cure his problems? He could not guess that within four days an event would take place which brought him and Victoria together and a greater degree of understanding between them than ever before.

X

Mr Millais had a passion for trees and appreciated them in a variety of ways; examining species from a distance, in different lights and weathers, and close at hand; sketching them; collecting their flowers and fruits, peels of bark and foliage, pressing the leaves and encouraging his son John to do the same. In June most trees were at their best – beyond the apple-green stage of spring, not yet heavy with sap and overlaid with dust. The Green Park was a daily pilgrimage for father and son; the former carrying a stick and a pocket vasculum; the latter, already determined to be a painter, invariably with a sketch book.

On the tenth of June at half past five in the afternoon John drew his father's attention to a low carriage coming up Constitution Hill. They recognized it as the Queen's for she often drove out at this time and behind the carriage rode two or three gentlemen.

Mr Millais was interested to see if she was accompanied by the Prince. He had only seen him at a distance, never close at hand, and he wanted to see what he really looked like. They said he was handsome, yes, but dour and un-smiling, a thorough son of Germany. But as the carriage bowled nearer he saw the Prince appeared to be rather the opposite – smiling and talking contentedly with the Queen. Their faces were quite close together.

Father and son removed their hats, and Mr Millais was in the act of bowing to his sovereign when he heard a cry.

He looked up and saw the Prince had flung his arms round the Queen. It was he who had shouted. Now one of the attending gentlemen was shouting and pointing with his whip, at a young man who had stepped from the pavement beside Millais and was presenting two pistols at the royal carriage. Before he could move, before he could think of doing anything, the young man had fired one of the pistols. He fired the second a split second before Millais seized him by the shoulders and threw him to the ground.

Neither the Queen nor the Prince was hurt, said John Millais, telling the story afterwards to a police inspector, and the young man had made no resistance when his father picked him up and seized the two pistols. An equerry had thanked them, assured the Queen there was no more danger, and they had driven on as though nothing extraordinary had

53

happened at all. His father agreed. He was full of admiration for the Queen's pluck and her coolness.

'Shot at and shaken up,' he told the inspector, 'and yet she made no more fuss than if the villain had offered her a sandwich instead of bullets.'

They went directly to Ingestre House in case news of the attempt should reach her mother and alarm her. Producing herself, alive and smiling, was irrefutable proof against any rumour. As it was, the Duchess of Kent fainted when Albert told her the news, and she had to lie down.

Victoria was also glad to lie down, and when Albert returned from a hurried consultation with the equerries and grooms as to how such a thing could possibly have happened, she asked him to stay with her.

'It is not that I am frightened,' she told him. 'Why should I be now that the man has been arrested? But I would like you to stay.'

She pressed his hand and he returned the pressure.

'I shall be here for as long as you wish,' he told her.

There he sat silently beside the chaise-longue, gently massaging her wrists, and playing with her fingers.

Eventually she said: 'Albert, you give me such strength when things go wrong. If someone had shot at me six months ago probably I should have squealed and had the vapours and demanded everyone's immediate sympathy and felt exceedingly sorry for myself, but having you beside me, and seeing how you tried to protect me, gave me some of your courage.' She pressed his hand again. 'So you see how much I depend on you.'

Being so stubbornly independent by nature, he knew she did not find it easy to admit her dependence, even on him, and he appreciated it.

'I too depend on you,' he told her softly. 'More and more, each day.'

Victoria felt closer to him than she had for a long time. Facing the same serious danger seemed to have put their quarrels and the cause of them into perspective.

Being so close to losing his wife, Albert discovered how

much she meant to him, how the respect and affection he had always held for her had grown into something far more tender. He understood now how self-centred he had been to quarrel with her when she was carrying a child, and, without raking it all up again, he managed to apologize for his insistence on his rights as her husband. Victoria was touched. She realized, perhaps for the first time, how cut off he must feel in his peculiar position at her Court. She, too, apologized, and she begged that in future he would take his proper place as her confidential adviser in state affairs.

For a fraction of a second he hesitated. Proud by nature, and not always forgiving, he was tempted to be spiteful and refuse outright but, although a little time before he might have done it, his growing devotion to Victoria put it out of the question. He thanked her, and accepted her offer.

She had held her breath when he hesitated. Now joyfully she took his face in her hands and kissed him again and again.

'Perhaps,' suggested Albert through her kisses, 'we ought to be grateful to our would-be assassin for bringing us such great contentment.'

On their way back to the Palace, they were astounded to be met by a huge crowd of loyal subjects who cheered and waved hats and handkerchiefs and ran alongside the low carriage. Ladies and gentlemen stood in their carriages and bowed and afterwards clapped as the Queen and the Prince drove by. As if from nowhere there appeared dozens of horsemen who took position in the van and the rear and on the flanks as an unofficial bodyguard. It was a little late of course, as Albert wryly remarked, but the gesture was a token of their high regard and the bodyguard appeared for weeks afterwards whenever the Queen drove in the Park.

Victoria felt herself invigorated by their affection. She beamed at her people, returned the waves, and loved the way they showed their loyalty. In particular she was delighted because that evening for the first time she heard many cries of 'Long live the Prince' amongst the more usual 'God bless your majesty' and 'Long live the Queen'. Word had already got round how the Prince had tried to protect her. It swept him to a position of popularity he had never enjoyed before.

That evening, alone with Anson, the Prince confessed how affected he had been by the people's demonstration of affection.

He was not generally accepted in society; being shy and awkward made him seem standoffish. Despite all Anson's efforts to persuade him to visit the grand houses in London, he never did; or, if he did once, he never did again. He spent his time instead looking at architectural features, or visiting places of artistic and scientific interest accompanied by a single equerry and a groom. He might have won the land-owning Whigs and Tories in the country, for he loved farming and landscape gardening and country sports. But they did not care for his continental *battue* of driven game in which hundreds of pheasants were slaughtered, and they drew the line at his dazzling thigh-length shooting boots of soft red leather. Nor did the Prince get on well with nabobs and great industrialists. They disliked him for associating with slave abolitionists, social reformers, and other people of that kidney. As for the artisans and the labouring classes, he was foreign. That was sufficient to make him unpopular. Had it not been for Anson's friendship and the acquaintance of a few savants and courtiers, he would have been very lonely as well as very disillusioned about his position in England. Now, he told Anson, the people's cries in the Park that evening, had been like long draughts of champagne. Accepted at last, he felt soothed and enlivened at the same time.

Anson, who understood the vagaries of his countrymen, tried to warn the Prince not to count on too much, but at the same time, he did not want to spoil his present happiness.

The next day and the days following there were still louder and more extravagant proofs of the people's loyalty. The youngster who had made an attempt on the Queen's life turned out to be a half-witted potboy named Oxford. Victoria and Albert almost had cause to be grateful to him for starting such a rush of affection for the throne. Both Houses of Parliament moved votes of congratulation to the Queen on escaping the assassin's bullets and they went to Buckingham Palace in person to express their sentiments. The Speaker's carriage was followed by one hundred and nine other carriages crammed with members; and afterwards over eighty more, packed with peers. The Queen and the Prince received the barons first, then the viscounts, the earls, the marquises, and the dukes. They all wore their Orders, Stars and Garters which was inconvenient to Wellington who had far too many to carry in comfort. Last of all came the royal dukes, deaf Uncle Cambridge making loud personal comments about his fellow peers, and Uncle Sussex beaming and nodding and thoroughly pleased. While the Chancellor delivered their congratulations, the uncles stood on either side of Victoria and Albert, as tall and striking as janissaries guarding royal Ottomans.

At a humbler level there were continuous demonstrations. Whenever the Queen and the Prince drove out they were met by hundreds of cheering people, and they were escorted everywhere.

Londoners vied with each other in showing their loyalty. Triumphant arches of tree branches and flowers were erected. Many private houses flew flags. Traders sent congratulatory gifts. They varied from a bullet-proof parasol-cum-umbrella for the Queen and a swordstick for the Prince, to gifts of cherries and violets from the costermongers near the Palace gates. Some sects held thanksgiving services. A few lucky schoolboys were given extra holidays. Permission was asked by and refused to the Keeper of the Royal Menagerie to name a German bear Albert the Brave. Poets and ballad writers commemorated the event. At the opera and racecourse the Queen and the Prince were hailed with wild enthusiasm.

The Queen's postbag was packed with letters of congratulation. Though he saw her every day, sometimes twice or three times, the Prime Minister wrote to say, with great sincerity, how very providential her escape had been and how he shuddered at the thought of it. All the Queen's ministers wrote, as did the ambassadors accredited to St James's. After a short time letters began to come in from the continent as well.

'Old Louis-Philippe, once a tutor in Switzerland and exile in America and Twickenham, now elected King of the French, seized the opportunity to write a perfervid letter to his royal sister and cousin.

> ... *Je rends grâce du fond de mon coeur à la Divine Providence qui les a miraculeusement conservés, et qui semble n'avoir permis qu'ils fuissent exposés à un si grand danger, que pour faire briller aux yeux de tous, votre courage, votre sang-froid, et toutes les qualités qui vous distinguent.*

From the royal palace at Laeken, Uncle Leopold wrote that he was surprised such an attempt had been made. He could have understood an attack on George the Third, or even George the Fourth, but Victoria had been extremely liberal.

Victoria thought this just; but she did not altogether care for his sermonizing:

> *In your good little heart I hope that it may make you feel grateful to God for a protection which was very signal.*

'Pish!' she said when she read this. It was a word Albert disliked, but the habit was on her at present, and sometimes it exactly expressed her feelings. When Uncle Leopold reminded her of her duty to be grateful she felt like saying pish.

She also felt like saying it when Lord Melbourne brought her the news that her would-be assassin, Oxford, was not to be punished. A jury had found him insane and he was condemned to a criminal lunatic asylum for life.

When she taxed Lord Melbourne with this, and said it was a disgrace that young men who fired pistols at her should go scot free, he was inclined to agree. 'Though mark you, Ma'am, a lifetime in a criminal lunatic asylum if you

58

do not happen to be insane could be counted a very considerable punishment. And,' he added, 'though I believe the boy knew what he was doing, it's as well the jury disagreed. If they'd found him guilty of treason we'd have had to hang him, Ma'am, then draw and quarter him.'

She looked at him in horror. Her Evangelic tutor had had a Foxe's *Book of Martyrs* and she had once peeped at the engraved illustrations. The whole process whereby a condemned man was disembowelled and chopped up while still alive had terrified and disgusted her.

'It would not have been possible just to hang him?' she asked.

He shook his head. 'No. As the law stands, the grisly performance would have had to be carried out.'

'Then the law must be changed,' she said with spirit.

XI

Albert proved his worth again and again as Victoria's confidential political adviser. Lord Melbourne had gladly arranged for him to see all state papers, and he was out of bed and sitting at his desk reading them by the light of a green student's lamp long before Victoria was up. Quickly she felt the difference. He was not in the least baffled as she would have been by the complexities of such matters as the Irish Municipal Corporation Bill, and in no time he knew so much of the wars Britain was waging in China and Afghanistan that she doubted if anyone at the Horse Guards knew more.

Then his claims as her consort were recognized in a splendid manner.

Impressed by the public's regard for the young man who was the Queen's husband, the Ministry recommended that he should be sole Regent of the kingdom in the unlikely event of the Queen's death in childbirth.

There was a single objector to the proposal.

Got at by his sister-in-law of Cambridge, who never would forgive the snub of being uninvited to a Court ball, the Duke of Sussex said in the Lords he thought the old royal family ought to be involved in any regency; but their lordships recalled that though a few members of the old family were scholarly, pious and respectable, by far the majority were wildly extravagant, amiably stupid, and astonishingly debauched, and Sussex was the only member of either House to vote against the Bill. This provided that if the Queen should die and her child live, the Prince would rule for eighteen years without any controlling council.

It was a triumph of reason against bigotry, of her dear deserving Albert against those who made no attempt to understand him, yet, when she gave the Royal Assent and the Bill became an Act of Parliament, Victoria experienced a temporary low. The actual need for such an Act reminded her that she lay in some danger, and for a time she was exceedingly depressed. She was sure, she said, that she would die in her confinement just as Princess Charlotte had done, and she made the morbid decision to let it happen at Claremont where Charlotte had died. She sent orders that the rooms there were to be rearranged so that they were as they had been in 1817, and Baron Stockmar, who had attended the Princess on her deathbed and who had heard her very last words – 'Stocky, they have made me drunk!', was asked to make himself available towards the end of November. Several times she went herself to Claremont to brood there and weep in her deep dejection; and when there was a great to-do at Court because a brutal caricature had been published showing the Queen lying dead in bed with a dead child in her arms and the word 'November' printed beneath, she was not in the least angry and said it was only to be expected.

To add to Victoria's misery her dog, Dash, took a turn for the worse. He now stank so disagreeably that it required an effort of will to go near him and the Queen mortified herself to look after his needs. Then one of her favourite aunts, Princess Augusta, fell ill, and it did not seem likely that she would recover. Then, just when she was feeling so unsure of

60

herself, there was another treacherous stab at the heart of the *status quo*, this time in France. Prince Louis Bonaparte made a bid for the throne in Boulogne. Though the coup was a ridiculous failure (he had only fifty-three followers and a tame eagle) it frightened Victoria.

Albert was sufficiently concerned to consult her personal physician, Sir James Clark. Sir James was not sanguine. The Queen's lowness would not harm the child, but it augured badly for the future. He concluded with a Scotch proverb absolutely unintelligible to the Prince.

It was Lord Melbourne who began her cure. He felt deeply for Victoria and their daily consultations on affairs of state, while she sat listless and desolate, upset him a great deal. Characteristically he tried to discover what would please her most and he went to great lengths to make it possible. Precedents were looked out and when the crown lawyers were certain of the rights of the case, and not before, he told her that when she prorogued Parliament in state, the Prince could drive with her to the Palace of Westminster. Moreover, though not a peer of the realm, he could take her on his arm into the Lords and there sit on a throne, a little behind hers but beside it.

As he had hoped, Victoria was entranced. People had made so many difficulties about the Prince that she hardly believed it possible he could take his place in public beside her. Momentarily she frowned. Was Lord Melbourne absolutely sure? she asked. Could either of her uncles, Sussex or Cambridge, make a fuss and botheration? He assured her they could not. The Prince had his place beside the Queen on state occasions and that was that.

From the day she prorogued Parliament with Albert beside her the Queen began to lose her depression. The cure was completed when her quarrel with the Cambridges sparked into life again.

The circumstances were these. Albert was given the Freedom of the City of London and afterwards invited to a banquet at which, promised the Lord Mayor, 'the turtle soup and venison would astonish the company'. The Prince excused himself. With the Queen in her present condition, he did not like to leave her for too long. He had to return to Windsor. The Duke of Cambridge was present. As his hearing was almost totally eclipsed Albert found difficulty in making him understand why he could not stay for the banquet. When the reason was made clear the old Duke did not like it, and he said so. He grumbled and went on grumbling out loud at the banquet. But the family was family and he determined to cover up, as he considered it, Albert's apparent indifference to public feelings, and said he would reply on his behalf when the company toasted the Prince. The next morning the Queen read in her newspaper the following:

> *In reply His Royal Highness, Field Marshal the Duke of Cambridge said – "The illustrious Prince was not present at the Banquet, and his absence was a disappointment to many, but in fact Prince Albert had lately married a very fine girl, and they were somehow very fond of each other's society. (Laughter and immense cheering.) He perceived that the Prince was readily excused . . ." '*

The Queen was furious. She was prevented from sending off a very rude letter to her uncle reproving him for lack of respect in his speech and for the coarse hint which was shocking. But she let it be known that for the time being the Cambridge family would not be welcome at Court.

Her aunt replied by letting it be known that ostracism from the most shallow and tedious Court in Europe was a profound relief, and she wished that others could enjoy it with her.

The brisk exchange with Aunt Cambridge was very good for Victoria. She mastered her lowness and made a private resolution not to give way to it again if it was at all possible.

Feodore helped her to keep it. Of all her relations Victoria's half-sister was the dearest. Married to the German Prince of Hohenlohe-Langenburg, and herself the mother of a boy and a girl, she was perfect company for Victoria at this time. She came over from Germany with her children and stayed for a little more than a fortnight. In their long sisterly talks she was able to tell Victoria certain things about bearing children which she had had to learn from her own hard experience. They both deprecated the new fashion for keeping young women ignorant of such things. Victoria in particular thought it shocking. It was all very well knowing how children were conceived, but not of a great deal of practical use unless one knew precisely how they were born. Their mother had at least not had to face her first confinement in ignorance.

King Leopold and Queen Louise were also guests at Windsor that summer, as were the Queen Dowager, Adelaide, and the Duchess of Kent, and the house party was completed by three German princes who had been students with Albert at Bonn. Inevitably the more insular of Victoria's English courtiers frowned on the young men's singing and their passion for beer and radishes. Even Lord Melbourne found it hard going at Court because ninety per cent of the time everyone spoke German, and in the remaining tenth, French. But he was delighted to see how wonderfully Victoria responded to the affection of her family and how much she loved to show them the fruits of Albert's work at Windsor.

He had already started a stud of Arab ponies sent, with a naïve plea to protect his slave trading, by the Imaun of Muscat; and he was busy reordering the farms and parks. It was high time. Neglect had begun to show. Victoria had a particular love for George the Fourth's Gothic *cottage orné*, and for the Chinese fishing temple beside which he and she had angled while a band played Handel, Gluck and Mozart. Both buildings had fallen into a bad state and had been condemned. Albert just managed to save them. On the farms he planned to breed stock and was buying in bulls which he named after the Queen's Hanoverian uncles. Close to the Castle he was laying out fresh grounds, doing a good deal of the surveying himself. That summer he and the King of Belgium, accompanied sometimes by the singing princes, were often seen out on the terraces with builder's tapes and boning rods, measuring poles and a theodolite.

In the evenings there was dancing, not, of course, for the Queen, but she loved to watch, her small foot tap-tapping on the floor to the time of the music, following Albert with adoring eyes. She thought him by far the handsomest man in the ballroom, though Uncle Leopold, despite his rouge and high heels, came a close second. And uniform suited him so well, especially the gold-fringed cape and the cherry-red trousers of the Eleventh Hussars. Quite recently he had been given the Colonelcy, and Prince Albert's Own, as it was now called, was a dashing and highly-regarded regiment despite the violence and eccentricity of its commanding officer, the Earl of Cardigan.

So the summer passed -- good days with her family, long talks with Feodore, Uncle Leopold and Queen Adelaide; quiet times of sewing with Lehzen and Skerrett, sketching a little, reading a lot; making music with Albert, dispatch boxes with Albert, occasional drives with Albert; daily consultations with dear Lord M. and sometimes other ministers; tap-tapping with her foot each evening because she wanted to dance as well; feeling the child move and turn inside her, a comforting, exciting feeling.

When Princess Augusta died Victoria took it well. She had loved her aunt, but Albert had kept from her the distressing details of her disease and death. Nor would he allow her to go to the funeral, and took her instead to Claremont where now she could laugh at her morbid fancies of three months before.

Albert was adept at managing Victoria, but in the last weeks before her confinement he rather overburdened her with affairs. Some interested her. She was quick to agree that her mother should have Aunt Augusta's grace-and-favour houses at Frogmore, near Windsor, and Clarence House in London. And she was enthusiastic about Albert's plan to buy one day a country property as their own private home. But politics at home and abroad she found very wearing, especially a long-drawn-out crisis in the Near East which threatened to put her people and the French at each other's throats. She could not follow all the details despite Albert's careful tuition. Names like Mehemet Ali, Ibrahim and Apponyi buzzed about inside her head like angry wasps, and she came to the conclusion that her baby when it was born ought rightly to be called 'Turko-Egypto'.

Stockmar conceived it his duty to tell the Prince that women in the Queen's condition ought not to be over-pressed with problems. But Albert nonplussed him with Stockmarian logic. Victoria, he said, was no nitwit. Stockmar agreed. Indeed, continued Albert, considering she was a woman, her abilities were surprising. Therefore, whatever her physical condition, robust intellectual exercise could only do her good, and at the same time prevent her from dwelling on what lay ahead. Stockmar left it at that.

Lord Melbourne saw the way of it and he, too, thought the Queen ought not to be overtaxed. He dealt with the problem in a subtle way, by arranging privately with Archdeacon Wilberforce, the Prince's chaplain, to play chess with him each evening after dinner. In this way the Queen would be given at least a little time free from affairs of state.

The Archdeacon was dutiful and chess was played as often as possible until the Queen's child was born.

XII

Victoria Adelaide Mary Louise, the Princess Royal, ever afterwards called Pussy or Vicky, was born at two in the afternoon on November 21st.

The event took place earlier than was expected and in the lying-in room only a doctor and a midwife were present besides the Prince. In the next room, and within earshot as the laws of England required, were the Archbishop of Canterbury, the Bishop of London, the Prime Minister and Foreign Secretary, the Lord Steward of the Household, and the Master of the Horse. Beyond this room in a small ante-chamber, were several ladies and gentlemen of the Household.

Even while the guns were booming out in the Park and at the Tower, there was already a good deal of gossip.

Mrs Brand had seized on Miss Skerrett in a corridor and told her in shocked tones that the Prince had witnessed the birth of his daughter. 'He was there. Skerrett, throughout it all. Now, have you ever heard of anything more indelicate and disagreeable?'

To her surprise Skerrett made light of the matter. It was unusual, she said, but characteristic of the Prince who in all things was thoroughly scientific. He could not see any objection himself and the Queen would have been glad of his company. Surely it did not matter? He was the child's father.

Mrs Brand drew herself up. She was already irritable. Nurse Lilly, the midwife, had made it clear she ruled the roost at present. Now Skerrett was defending something which she herself found utterly shocking.

'Why, I declare,' she said, breathing heavily through her nose. 'You are quite *advanced*, my dear!' She said it as though Miss Skerrett had contracted a contagious and repellent disease. '*Immensely advanced!*' she said again.

The Duchess of Kent had at first decided to take offence for not having been specifically invited to her daughter's lying-in. For an hour or more she had been inveighing against Victoria and Albert – her rage largely put on for the benefit of her only son, Prince Charles of Leiningen, who was over in England to see her. She said they were thoughtless not to have asked her – ingrates, unfilial.

Now, when the news came and the guns boomed and the church bells rang, she forgave them and instead she was vexed with fate for giving them a girl. 'Too cruel,' she cried. 'A princess, not the prince she longed for, and I not there to comfort my poor darling.'

Prince Charles was vastly amused by this unusual description of his half-sister. She had never been their mother's favourite and the cordial relationship now between them was simply because both had learnt tolerance. But he did not show he was amused. He was only too aware of how his mother could whip herself into a frenzy if she thought people were being disagreeable. He tried to soothe her. 'They will be calling her after you, Mamma.'

'No,' she declared. 'Victoria after her mother. Her mother.' She took a large pinch of snuff.

'But she was named for you,' he said. 'Now there will be three Victorias!'

She was mollified. Suddenly, as sometimes happened with this mercurial lady, she altogether lost her fit of vapours. She listened to the peal of bells ringing out near Clarence House. She hummed their notes, went to the piano and began a tremendous improvisation in honour of her grandchild, thumping at the music and the rhythm of the bells beneath a fanfare of her own making.

Prince Charles chuckled. He had a deep affection for his mother. He went to the piano bench, flicked back his tails and sat beside her, caught her improvisation and joined in with a series of tinkling arpeggios.

The music of bells was merely a vexatious noise to Mr Greville. Tired from waiting the twelve long hours of the Queen's labour, he was now trying to get on with his work. The peals distracted him and there was much to do. He muffled his ears with a scarf while he made a memorandum on the proclamation of the birth of a Princess Royal. For the first time the Prince would be presiding at the Council and, unless he had everything thoroughly prepared beforehand, there were bound to be holdups and mistakes.

The scarf partially kept out the bells, but could not prevent him from being interrupted. A forefinger prodded his arm. He looked up to see Baron Stockmar smiling at him.

'Upon my word, Mr Greville, you look very strange.'

Greville mustered his dignity. He unwound the scarf and laid down his pen. Refusing to mention his appearance he said stiffly: 'How, Baron, may I serve you?'

'With a moment of your time,' replied Stockmar suavely.

'But no more, I beg.' Greville tapped the papers on his desk. 'A royal birth is always an event. The first child of a reigning sovereign even more so. I have much to do.'

'Of course,' said Stockmar with sympathetic understanding. Nevertheless he sat down and began to speak of the Prince's position as father of the child.

'The Prince,' cut in Mr Greville, 'has a recognized place. He will be presiding at a Council in lieu of the Queen within the hour. Indeed far less.'

'Yes, yes,' murmured Stockmar. He knew all about that, he said; he had come about something else.

'Truly, Baron, I lack the time. You must excuse me.'

But Stockmar either did not hear the protests or he paid no attention. With his fingers pressed together and gazing at a point one inch above Greville's head, he continued his speech. The Queen was desirous, he said, that the Prince should be prayed for by name at Divine Service, and he was sure Mr Greville would agree it was fitting that while mother and child were publicly prayed for each morning and evening, day by day, the father should be prayed for too.

Mr Greville was not a praying man, nor was he the slightest interested in the claim of Prince Albert to be the subject of praying Englishmen. And he was very busy. 'You should speak first,' he cut in again, 'to the Prime Minister.'

Stockmar finished what he was saying before he replied. 'But, dear me, I have, fifteen minutes ago.' He laid a sheet of paper on the desk. 'Lord Melbourne desired me to put the request in writing as from the Queen.' He tapped the paper. 'And he mentioned that he would bring the matter up at the Council this afternoon.'

Greville looked at his pocket watch. In barely fifteen minutes. And his work as Clerk was not yet done by any means. Drawing up a formal draft to include Prince Albert in the State Prayers would take a long time.

'It would have been considerate,' he said severely, 'to have given more notice.'

Stockmar stood up. 'It was her majesty's first wish after

seeing her child. I know, Mr Greville, that you will make it possible.'

Greville stood politely while the Baron bowed and left the room. Then with an exclamation of annoyance he sat at the desk and drew a fresh sheet of paper towards him. Another salute of guns had begun somewhere downriver. Now there were thuds as well as bells. It was intolerable. Once more he swathed his ears in the scarf. Concentrating was extremely difficult but eventually he was able to write:

> By an Order in Council dated November 21st, 1840, the following changes in the Book of Common Prayer were prescribed ...

Two gentlemen were eating luncheon together not far from the Tower. One was thoroughly enjoying the racket of the guns. To the other they were a faint popping in his damaged ears. Even if their height and the fact that one wore a black skullcap, had not made them easily recognizable, the way they tackled their food identified them immediately as the sons of George the Third.

The hot luncheons demanded by their nephew by marriage would not have suited either, and before them was laid out the remains of a fine English luncheon; a dozen or so oysters, boiled eggs and cresses, a basket of breads, cold roasts of mutton and beef, boiled silverside, cold shin pudding, cuts from the chine of a pig, a galantine of peppered veal, and cold game pie.

'So she's done it,' shouted the Duke of Sussex into his brother's ear. 'It'll vex Ernest badly. Put his nose out of joint.'

The Duke of Cambridge missed most of this. His brother repeated it. Both had had enough wine, which each dearly loved, to be delighted at the thought of the King of Hanover's nose being put out of joint. They rocked backwards and forwards.

Then Cambridge stopped laughing suddenly and inquired in the mighty voice of the deaf if Victoria were to nurse the child. 'Very important, that. Nothing like it. Nothing at all.'

Still at the top of his voice and in a manner which would have outraged his duchess, he expatiated on the large blessings given his own children at nature's founts, how George had been a pigmy feeder, Augusta less reluctant, and Mary Adelaide thoroughly greedy.

Despite his speech and vote against the Regency Bill, the Duke of Sussex was still received at Court, and he was in a position to tell his brother that the Queen had already decided not to nurse her child. She thought it unwise for reasons of state. This provoked an explosion of disgust from Cambridge who, again at the top of his voice, and above the noise of cannon and of bells, continued to expatiate on the benefits of breast-feeding.

The Duke of Sussex smiled. The smile broadened when the flow of words drew to a conclusion. 'There's a tail to our niece's decision,' he roared. 'As neat a tail as any I've heard. A wet nurse has already been engaged.'

'Yes, brother? Yes?'

'From Cowes,' roared Sussex.

They chuckled and chortled together.

Laughter, shouted the Duke of Cambridge wiping his eyes, always gave him an appetite. Would his brother care to join him in another slice or two of shin pudding? He would? Excellent!

Lord Melbourne met the Baroness outside the Queen's room. They walked together down the long gallery. The Palace was being altered in many ways. Soon it would be more suitable both for a family and for the sort of splendid entertainments the Queen was required to give. They discussed the alterations, keeping to small talk so that they did not betray their real feelings.

But they knew each other very well.

Even while Lord Melbourne was mentioning the incredible number and unsuitable shade of the strawberry-coloured columns in the Palace, Lehzen could tell how deeply he was feeling the birth of the Princess Royal. She did not guess at the extent; how distressed he was because the girl he learnt to admire and love had matured so far beyond his reach. Victoria as a bride was less estimable to him. As a mother she was even less so. And now the child would be a third person between them.

Melbourne, on his part, could spare a good deal of sympathy for the Baroness. She still had the reins of the Household in her hands but he knew she would have gladly exchanged them to have been with Victoria when her baby was born. But no one had suggested she should be there. In fact, because she had recently had jaundice, Baron Stockmar thought she ought to stay right away, and she had remained at some distance in the corridor, twisting her fingers in apprehension, trying to feel for Victoria every pang and pain she suffered in her long labour. Her position in the corridor, and standing not seated, was significant. Very slowly, so slowly as to be barely perceptible, she was being prised from her beloved Victoria. The Queen's young ladies who once had regarded her as their second mother already felt the difference, and they showed it. They were no less affectionate, but they were less in awe of her as the Queen's confidential friend. One had teased her in public for her habit of chewing caraways. Another, just after the attack of jaundice, had referred to her as the Yellow Dragon. Lehzen had pretended not to hear, but the girl's boldness told her that her worst fears were being realized. Victoria as a child had been obstinate and lovable. As a young woman she had been the same – always needing Lehzen. As a bride, inevitably, she had altered. And as a mother she would alter even more.

It was a sad couple who walked quietly past the strawberry-coloured columns while cannon fired salutes and the bells of London rang.

Part Two

I

For the life of her Victoria could not understand why her own mother spoke with such enthusiasm of the joys of motherhood, and she wondered cynically if it might be because she had been so conspicuously unsuccessful as a mother herself. But Lady Lyttelton, too, and Mrs Brand and the other matrons of her Court, appeared to think it a marvellous thing. They all doted on her baby girl, dandled her, cooed over her, and competed with each other in finding new superlatives to describe her beauty and intelligence. Victoria tried her hardest to do the same, but it seemed too stupid for words and she gave it up.

Uncle Leopold made her irritable by extolling the virtues of children and saying he was sure she would one day be a happy mother surrounded by her numerous children.

I think, dearest Uncle, [she wrote] *you cannot really wish me to be the 'Mamma d'une* nombreuse *famille', for*

I think you will see with me the great inconvenience a large family would be to us all ... Men never think, at least seldom think, what a hard task it is for us women to go through this very often.

Albert read what she had written and smiled, and persuaded her that it was likely they would, in fact, have a large family. He tried to reconcile her to it; not by insisting on her duty to England, nor by trying to share his own romantic feelings about big families; but by spinning dreams of the dynasty they would make together, how they would marry a son here and a daughter there until they were closely related to everyone of moment in Europe. She was not impressed.

She was very relieved when she confessed to Lord Melbourne that she thought her baby was ugly, and he chuckled, and adjusted his eye-glasses, and agreed wholeheartedly.

'In my private opinion, Ma'am, the majority of babies look like withered monkeys, and the rest resemble wrinkled frogs. But don't worry or fret. The Princess will improve. Believe me.'

She hoped he was correct and that she herself would improve and become like other mothers.

Lehzen gave her the greatest comfort. It was not often now that Victoria spontaneously went to her for advice, but Lehzen had brought her up and, though unmarried, she knew a great deal about children.

'There are wifely women,' Lehzen said, 'and there are motherly women. Very probably you are the former.' And that was all she would say.

Victoria thought she was right. Twice a day the baby was brought to her to be kissed and played with. But invariably Albert was at the centre of her thoughts and in the event of any danger she immediately feared for him more than anyone else.

One night not long before Christmas, the door of her dressing-room was opened with an alarming squeak and hurriedly shut to again. Lights were called for, servants summoned. The Prince, who was still playing chess with the Archdeacon, was asked to come at once. One of the pages,

Kennaird, examined the room, looked under the sofa, and turned white. He was too frightened to do anything and it was Lehzen, always quick to appear and act whenever she felt Victoria needed her, who bravely seized the sofa and dragged it away from the wall to reveal a boy.

Victoria was convinced he had come to murder Albert and had no thought for the safety of her child in the nearby nursery.

When the Prince arrived she burst into tears of relief and threw herself into his arms.

Lehzen calmed her down and put her to bed while the Prince interrogated the intruder. It turned out he had, in fact, come to see the Princess Royal and had already been in the Palace for several days. It turned out, as well, that he was the same boy, by the name of Jones, who had broken in to Buckingham Palace before the Queen's marriage and had lived there under the furniture. Afterwards he was sent to prison for his trouble, while the Prince set about trying to make the Palace boyproof, and Victoria, conscience-stricken because she was so unmaternal, tried to cultivate a real interest in the nursery where the Poet Laureate's sister-in-law, Mrs Southey, presided with great charm and, as they were to discover later, with great inefficiency.

But it was no use pretending. As Lehzen had said, she was a wifely woman and that was that. When Vicky had the croup Victoria accepted it with so calm a resignation that the nursery officials thought her the bravest possible mother. And yet, when Albert went through the ice while skating on the Palace pond, although he was only up to his knees in water, she was beside herself with anxiety. Her distress, and her attempt to help him out with a walking stick, were reported by toadying newspapers on the next day. He resented it, feeling that they were making a fool of him and his male dignity was affronted. 'What,' he asked in irritation, 'did they expect? That you would push me under?'

Having decided that maternity did not suit her, Victoria was not at all pleased when just after the baby's christening she found she was going to have another.

God's will be done, [she had written to her Uncle Leopold] *and if He decrees that we are to have a great number of children, why we must try to bring them up as useful and exemplary members of society.*

It was a drab, unenthusiastic way of putting things. Now, finding herself so soon in the same condition, she was exceedingly put out.

In the following days she complained so often and so long to Albert that one afternoon he lost his customary patience and told her quietly that she was behaving like a spoilt child. Her temper flared. Forgetting or paying no attention to the fact that the doors were open and some members of his Household were in the anteroom beyond, she scolded him in a loud voice and then ran from the room banging the doors behind her.

In the privacy of her own room, she sobbed and cried until she recovered her temper. Then she began to feel remorseful. Perhaps Albert was right. She did sometimes behave childishly when she was tetchy. Lehzen had often told her about it. So, once, had Lord M. Clearly it was her fault and she had to go back and apologize.

She had her hair seen to, and her face carefully powdered. Then, trembling a little but determined not to show it, she returned to Albert's apartments.

The anteroom was empty, and the doors she had slammed to were still shut. But when she turned the handle she found they were locked. She rattled the handle. Who had dared to lock the doors against her? Her chin set obstinately. She had been prepared to admit her fault, but if Albert was to do this to her in her own Palace he would learn very quickly who was its mistress. She rapped imperiously on the door.

'Who is there?' asked the Prince. His voice was calm and even.

'The Queen of England,' Victoria's reply rang through the anteroom. But it seemed to have no effect. She knocked again, louder this time. Once more Albert politely inquired who was there.

'The Queen of England,' she cried.

She bit her forefinger. There was the same red fury rising inside her. How dared he insult her so? A subject could not be insolent to his sovereign. He must learn. He must learn.

'The Queen of England,' she cried, and again: 'The Queen of England. The Queen of England.'

There was a silence from the room beyond. Victoria began to panic. What was Albert doing to her? Why was he being so obdurate? Why was he humiliating her? The dilemma was too much for her and she burst into tears. She could not leave, not now, not having insisted on her absolute right to enter the room. Nor could she bear to be treated like this. She wrung her hands, and leant her head against the door. 'Oh, Albert,' she pleaded. 'Please, please open the door.'

As calmly as before the question came: 'Who is there?'

For a moment she clenched her fists. She wanted to fight him. She wanted to insist for ever and ever and ever. But he had broken her.

'It is I, Victoria, your wife,' she said softly through her tears.

The door was immediately opened. His arms were outstretched to welcome her.

II

Prince Albert's popularity was ephemeral. It lasted briefly until he disastrously involved himself in what became known as the Cardigan Affair. Then, temporarily, it evaporated.

The Earl of Cardigan, Lieutenant-Colonel of the Eleventh Hussars, Prince Albert's Own, was a perfectionist. His turn-out in civilian or military dress was impeccable. His officers and men were held to be the best drilled and smartest in any regiment. He had large estates, a huge fortune, belonged to a great family, and was good-looking, dashing and brave. But these qualities were completely outweighed by his vices. The other side of the coin showed him as a martinet, a cruel bully, and one of the most disgraceful commanders in the whole of the British Army. At his whim and on the slightest pretext, his men were flogged, his officers broken, and a great scandal blew up when victimized officers managed at last to get their complaints heard at the Horse Guards. Cardigan was reprimanded by the Commander-in-Chief himself, and not once but several times, but, with astonishing effrontery, and to the rage of his many enemies, he simply refused to accept the reprimands. Letters of this kind from the Horse Guards were neither acknowledged nor answered, and, nonplussed, the Commander-in-Chief stopped writing them. Such lofty contempt for authority, and then his trial by the House of Lords for forcing and fighting a duel, in which he was acquitted on a technical point which hid from no one his obvious guilt, made Cardigan the most talked-about man in London. In many theatres and at the opera his box was booed and hissed and the performance prevented from starting until he left the house. Storms of public indignation led by the press attacked the Commander-in-Chief for not removing him from his regiment. Questions were raised in both Houses, and the command of the Eleventh Hussars was the subject of a long and heated discussion in Cabinet. If the Duke had not let his opinion be known nothing could have saved Cardigan from degradation. The Duke had a strong dislike of self-opinionated bullies, but he loved the Army too much to let it be subjected to popular and political control. That way he saw anarchy, an end of the proper discipline which made all soldiers from general officers to private men into fighting units. He would not sacrifice that discipline for the personal satisfaction of dealing justly with Cardigan.

Prince Albert's view corresponded almost exactly with that of the Duke. The Army had to be protected as much from political interference as the government had to be protected from the Army. The English, surely, had had enough of both in the Civil Wars? If he had simply agreed with Wellington and said nothing, all would have been well; but Albert believed it was his duty as Colonel of the Eleventh

Hussars to let his views be known. And unfortunately he said nothing specific to condemn Cardigan's behaviour but emphasized the principle that the Army should be left to look after its own problems.

His tactless intervention was not welcomed. It caused many people to turn against him. Perplexed and not a little indignant, he justified his point of view by insisting that it was precisely the same as the Duke's. This only made the case worse. He was informed, not directly, of course, but in a painful way nevertheless, that what the Duke of Wellington could do and what Prince Albert of Saxe-Coburg could do were very different things.

Anson believed it was still not too late to retrieve the situation if only his master would publicly condemn Cardigan's more obvious faults. But the Prince refused. By this time he was angry and hurt at being so much misunderstood, at being thought reactionary by liberal-minded people, and over-liberal by reactionaries. He was in an ill-temper about the whole affair. Wellington had come badly out of it. So had Lord Hill. And his own hard-earned popularity had vanished overnight. The only person to remain serene and imperturbable in the face of the uproar was Lord Cardigan himself. The English, said the Prince, bewildered him. They made no attempt to see his position or his point of view. Henceforth he would make no attempt to see theirs.

Because Anson was so devoted to his interests he persevered. Goodwill lost now would never be recaptured. For his own sake and for the Queen's, the Prince had to be persuaded to condemn the Earl of Cardigan in public.

He sought the help of three allies: Baron Stockmar, Dr Praetorius, the Prince's Librarian and German Secretary, and the Prince's tutor in constitutional law, Mr William Selwyn, the Treasurer of Lincoln's Inn.

Neither Stockmar nor Praetorius was of much assistance.

'Dear me, Mr Anson,' said the former, quite shocked by the proposal. 'I assure you the Prince's rectitude would never permit him to alter a convinced viewpoint.'

The latter, a little jealous perhaps of Anson's position as Private Secretary, merely said: 'You will know better than I how this can be done.'

Mr Selwyn, on the other hand, was eager to help. He was a distinguished barrister with a somewhat formidable appearance, being lame in both ankle joints, and as hairless as an egg. He also had a formidable voice. Usually he was silent. When he did speak he roared.

'Exactly!' he roared at Anson when the Private Secretary confided his anxieties. 'The Prince needs to change his mind. But he won't, you know. You'll never shift him.'

Anson threw his arms in the air. 'What can be done?' he asked.

'We'll change his mind for him,' Mr Selwyn roared in reply.

'You will forgive me, Selwyn. I do not follow you at all.'

The lawyer beamed from ear to ear and told Anson he was much too straightforward. Corkscrew thinking was required, some subtlety. He proceeded to explain. They had the wit between them to concoct and circulate appropriate rumours. It made no matter whether or not the Prince condemned Lord Cardigan in public as long as rumour said he had.

'Do I make myself clear?' he roared.

He did indeed. Limpidly clear. Anson gaped. He was remembering that the son of this scheming gentleman was the Bishop-elect of New Zealand and Melanesia. Mildly he suggested it wasn't quite the thing to do.

'Of course it isn't,' roared the other. 'It's damned underhand! But done well it will save the tattered scraps of Prince Albert's popularity, and his head's so high in the clouds he won't know anything about it.'

Anson hoped not, for he suspected that if his master did discover what had happened, his fury would be almost unbelievable.

'These are the essentials,' shouted Selwyn, telling them off on his fingers. 'Essentials for circulating. One, the Prince feels keenly the dishonour done to his regiment by Lord

Cardigan; two, he has always wished for something to be done; but, three, in his newness to the country and ignorance of English affairs, he thought it hardly his place to interfere. One, two, and three. Put those out, Anson, and the gossips will love him, and ten to one they'll say he could have done no better, really, than accept the guidance of the dear Duke. Well?'

'What a Machiavelli you are,' said Anson with a smile.

For a moment Selwyn looked solemn. 'I don't wish you to think this is the way I normally carry on,' he shouted. 'For I don't. But we need to look after the Prince, and this is the best way I can think of.'

Anson hurriedly assured him he was with him heart and soul. He thought it a marvellous plan, and had no scruples himself about using rumour to defeat rumour.

Mr Selwyn's plan was highly successful. His rumour was quietly fed to the benches of his inn of court. He also fed it to a group of port-drenched dons when he had occasion to visit Cambridge. Coming from so respectable and author-itative a source it was immediately accepted. Within a few days the story was being told back to him in professional confidence, suitably altered and embroidered. He was en-tirely satisfied. It would not be long before the ladies would be binding each other to eternal secrecy before passing on this new picture of Prince Albert, thereby ensuring its con-tinued repetition for at least a week. In that time he guessed a large number of people would adjust their view of the Queen's husband.

He was right. They did. Though the Prince did not regain all the popularity he had lost, in London, at any rate, people began to see his good points once again.

Down at Windsor the Prince was unpopular for another reason. There they cared little or nothing for the Cardigan affair. But the country people disliked the changes the Prince was making in the Great Park and on the three royal farms. They particularly disliked his new-fangled methods instituted in the cause of economy and greater efficiency. And the townspeople were as hostile, believing that he had infringed their rights by closing a number of footpaths and forbidding the taking of kindling and turf and rabbits.

The Prince found both points of view inexplicable and he was determined to ignore them. His Private Secretary, though, knew this would never do. After a lot of persuasion he made the estate workers see that the new changes would ultimately benefit everyone. Then he let it be known in the town that the Prince had infringed no one's rights. In the past people had been allowed to trespass on royal property and take what rabbits and firing they wanted. But this had been because of slipshod management. They had no legal and permanent right.

Ordinarily a clear explanation of the facts and the natural goodwill which the townspeople had for the royal family would have smoothed over the difficulties; but, just at that time, two court cases were heard in Windsor which aggravated their hostility.

The first was brought by a young woman named Maria Wells against one of Prince Albert's gamekeepers. She had been caught trespassing and collecting kindling on royal property and the keeper had set his bloodhound on her. She told the court that the dog had knocked her down and bitten her savagely in the back and the thigh. At the time she had been pregnant and although, fortunately, she had not miscarried, the mauling and the shock had made her very ill. The keeper's defence, that he had first warned the woman but she had taken no notice, did not get him anywhere. He was found guilty, fined two pounds and made to pay ten shillings costs. He was also dismissed from the Prince's service.

The second case was against an old man caught on royal property with four pheasants and six pheasants' eggs. As it was a small affair, the Town Clerk decided on his own initiative, and unwisely as it turned out, that it was not fitting for Prince Albert's name to be brought up as prosecutor in a police court, and he had the case heard privately by two magistrates in his own office. The old man was fined ten pounds with an alternative of four months in Reading jail.

The severity of the existing game laws accounted for the disparity between the two sentences, and until the laws were altered nothing could be done except to extract the old man from Reading jail by paying his fine anonymously. Anson was actually in the process of arranging this when, to his dismay, he learnt that the unfortunate facts were widely known. Windsor was seething with the story of how the royal keeper had been fined eight pounds less than the old poacher. Anson made inquiries. He discovered that only one parishioner had been perspicacious enough to know about the two cases. Only he had insisted on his right to be at the trials, and none of the magistrates had been able to persuade him to forgo it. And immediately Anson realized who had been salting the wound between town and Castle. He was not surprised, but his heart sank.

Jasper Tomsett Judge was the Windsor correspondent of a number of newspapers, chief amongst them the *Morning Herald*, and he was the sort of journalist who stated that anybody's privacy was of less importance than the public's inalienable right to information. In addition to holding this pestiferous doctrine he had a talent for aggravating people into angry indiscretions and for writing acidulous polemics, and he was an implacable enemy to the *status quo*. The perpetual man in opposition – at this time a Tory, of course, because Lord Melbourne's Whig ministry was still bumbling along trying to avoid any issue which might topple it – Judge was an idealist who believed, rightly or wrongly, that monarchs, courts, and all the apparatus of privilege and flunkeydom, were against the interests of the people, and he never missed a single opportunity to report activities at the Castle in an unfavourable light. Even this would have been bearable if he had not openly crowed over his victims. He relished the power of hurting, Scalding people's deepest feelings gave him great pleasure.

It appalled Anson to learn that he was behind the wave of hostility to the Prince and the Court. It was not simply a question of reporting the cases and local reactions and having done with it. He could sense that Judge was deliberately stirring up the townspeople. Within a few hours he had proof of it. Generally he judged it kinder and wiser not to show his master the journalist's most waspish criticisms. The Queen, too, was largely ignorant of the fact that such a man lived beneath her castle walls. Now, Anson feared, she would have to know, and both would have to be told what Judge was doing.

Victoria stormed up and down the room.

Anson almost regretted suggesting to the Prince that they take the problem to the Queen. She was exceedingly angry and had Jasper Tomsett Judge been before her at that moment she would have been tempted to box the man's ears.

Baron Stockmar, who had also supported Anson's suggestion, stood there looking anxious. Twice he begged the Queen to compose herself and be seated. Such an exhibition of rage was neither good for her nor for the child she carried. But he might as well have saved his breath. She walked up and down, fulminating against Judge. 'He should be punished,' she said severely. 'Heavily punished.' Her tone was explicit. Had she possessed the power he would have suffered for his insolence. And, for good measure, she would have dealt with that fool of a town clerk for holding the second trial in camera. By trying to toady to the Castle, he had laid the Prince open to the vituperative pen of Mr Judge.

Prince Albert interrupted to say it was well past their time for luncheon: 'The bell has sounded twice, my dear; and the Prime Minister and the Foreign Minister are here. They will be waiting.'

'Excellent!' The Queen immediately turned to go into luncheon. 'Lord Melbourne will know how to deal with this scribbler.'

*　　　*　　　*

As it turned out Lord Palmerston offered the more sympathetic ear. Lord Melbourne was far too preoccupied with

83

his ministry's delicate position in the Commons, and he wished they would allow him to eat in peace. But his brother-in-law, Palmerston, listened carefully as Anson, for the fifth or sixth time, retold the story of Judge's iniquity.

This surprised the Queen. In their previous dealings Lord Palmerston had given her the impression he had little interest in matters any less important than the policies and destinies of nations; but there he was listening to the details of their local squabble as though they merited the attention of international intrigues. How enigmatic he was with his reputation as an iron negotiator and as a terrible voluptuary. He womanized – Skerrett had whispered in her ear – which was why, perhaps, his colleagues called him Cupid. She peeped at him now beneath lowered lashes and found his youthfulness extraordinary. He could not be much more than five years younger than Lord M. and yet he looked much more. Vain of his appearance, his hair and whiskers were dyed a madder red, and his beautifully cut clothes were enlivened by a gaudy waistcoat . . .

Victoria suddenly realized her Foreign Secretary had caught her staring. She flushed. When Anson had finished she begged her guests to think of something, anything to control the odious Mr Judge.

Melbourne stopped wondering how the Whigs could escape political disaster. He hadn't heard a great deal of the story but enough to think they were probably making a great deal of fuss about nothing. Still, when the Queen used that tone of voice it showed she was upset and that would never do. He smiled at her encouragingly.

'A journalist, eh?' he remarked. 'Well it shouldn't be too difficult to settle this nonsense.' He looked hopefully round the table. Unhappily it seemed that everyone was looking to him. He turned to his brother-in-law. 'Well, Palmerston,' he said. 'Don't you agree?'

To his great relief Palmerston agreed; it should not be too difficult.

'Excellent,' said the Queen. 'He is a horrid man, and he must be . . .' She hesitated, searching for the right word: 'He must be *squashed*.'

84

To her surprise the Prime Minister shook his head. 'That'd never do. We mustn't make a martyr of him.' He looked again at his brother-in-law.

'Lord Melbourne is right, Ma'am. And squashed journalists have great powers of recovery. They rapidly resuscitate.' He laid down his fork and considered. 'Probably the best thing would be to bribe him.'

'Just so,' said Lord Melbourne.

Anson happened to be looking at Prince Albert when the Foreign Secretary came out with his fine eighteenth-century solution. The Prince started. A red blush spread from his neck up to his cheeks.

'You are serious, Lord Palmerston?' he asked.

'Indeed, yes,' he replied equably. 'He's very Tory so we'll try to buy his support for the Whigs. That ought to sheathe his claws. He'll not attack you, Sir, nor the Queen, if we buy his pen.'

'There is surely an alternative?' said Prince Albert stiffly.

'Not that I can think of,' said Lord Melbourne cheerfully. 'Bribery is generally better than constraint. No, I correct myself. Forgive me, Ma'am. An appropriate piece of *force majeure* occurs to me. If he's unbribable, we'll buy up his debts. He's the sort of man who'll have any number.'

Any number,' echoed Palmerston.

The Queen smiled at him. Lightly she touched Lord Melbourne's hand. The thought of Judge penniless, turned off from his work, driven from Windsor, his sting neutralized, was very pleasing to her. 'My dear and excellent ministers,' she murmured.

As it turned out Judge proved unbribable. He sent back the Whig messenger with a caustic and brave reply that not for five times the sum would he turn his coat. A week later he was approached again. His reply was the same. Then the Castle was unable to intimidate him by buying up his debts. As Lord Melbourne had suggested, he had a good many, but none of the Windsor tradesmen who supplied him would hear a word against him. Anson's messenger – a constable specially imported from London – brought back the surprising message.

Anson advised his master to be patient. Judge had been warned by events of the extent of power against him. If he wished to keep his position he would go more carefully for a time. Meanwhile they would watch him. The best cards were in their hands after all. All the Prince really required was patience, a good deal of patience.

As Anson had hoped, this message was passed on to the Queen. She accepted it because it was her dear Albert's advice, though being patient with a radical subject like the odious Mr Judge did not come easily to her.

III

That summer, when the Queen was carrying her second child, was as wet as any she had known. Miss Skerrett remarked that bad summers could always be measured by the number of Botany Bens who came over from the west country to sell baskets of wild ferns. The wetter it was the more there were, and this year the Queen saw quite a number travelling through Windsor on their way to London.

The weather was as warm as it was wet and in the humidity the Castle smelt so much that Victoria found it nauseating. When Uncle Leopold brought his family to Windsor for a visit she felt quite ashamed. He begged her not to be disturbed on their account. It had been far worse ten years before he told her, and Queen Adelaide, who was also staying at the Castle, agreed. Nothing, she claimed, and proudly – almost as if it was an achievement – nothing could have smelt more than the drains of Windsor Castle during the reign of her dear William.

It was barely surprising. Royal surveyors had looked into

the drainage system of the Castle, the nearby cavalry and infantry barracks, and Windsor town, and had reported that, while there was some sort of primitive system in the town, there was none at all either at the Castle or at the barracks. Like young Athenians into the Minotaur's maze, the drains simply disappeared underground.

Victoria was so mortified and so sickened by the smell that she begged some practical remedy should be found and as soon as possible. Albert agreed the case was urgent. He and King Leopold and Stockmar put their heads together and drew up a drainage scheme. But it was estimated to cost somewhere in the region of £17,000, and the Department of Woods and Forests, which looked after such things, jibbed at the expenditure.

Stockmar spoke solemnly of health. Albert spoke of efficiency. Leopold, more experienced in the myopia of household departments, merely shrugged his shoulders and accepted the inevitable. Victoria lost her temper. It was intolerable, she said, that the Queen of England had to bear the smell of drains because of some departmental economy. Nor was she consoled, in fact she was quite put out, when Queen Adelaide repeated her proud boast that in King William's day the smell had been far, far worse.

Just before her aunt and uncle left she apologized once more. Both assured her that the nuisance had not been as great as she feared, and Queen Louise took her on one side and suggested that her nose was so sharp and sensitive because of her condition.

Perhaps her aunt was right, considered Victoria after they had gone. Normally she was robust and not particularly fastidious, but in her present condition she did find the stench exceedingly unpleasant. What with that and the damp, and the trouble with horrible Mr Judge, and the vexation of a new and ridiculous rumour that to improve the amenities of the Castle the Prince wanted Parliament to move the whole of Windsor town a mile or two away, she was exceedingly glad to leave the place and begin on the first of her royal progresses with Albert.

Earlier in the summer they had been guests of the Archbishop of York at his manor of Nuneham on the Thames; a short visit which had reawakened her pleasure in staying at private houses. As a child she had been taken on progresses throughout the country by her mother and Conroy, and, hearing how much she had enjoyed the sightseeing, Albert proposed that they should make a small progress together.

Lord Melbourne had given his wholehearted support to the scheme and had inveigled them to accept invitations from two great Whig houses as well as his own invitation to visit his country seat at Brocket. He had particular reasons for this. His ministry had been twice beaten in the Commons and was tottering to a fall. And so, determined to try his fortune on one last throw, he had asked for a dissolution and was now appealing to the country. Perhaps there was an infinitesimal chance that a royal progress to Whig houses might help the party during the general election. Neither the Prince nor the Queen was taken in, though both politely pretended to be. Lord Melbourne played party politics too clumsily and too ingenuously to be offensive. Albert – while he did not altogether care for the idea of being used – was confident that their progress could in no way alter the certainty of a Tory victory at the polls; and Victoria thought that Lord M.'s plotting was really rather complimentary to her, and she was touched. She was right in this. He was not going to be overscrupulous if there was the slightest possibility of influencing the voting which would decide whether or not he could continue his daily consultations with Victoria. Occasionally, and the moments were rare because he firmly pushed the thought to the back of his mind, he knew that he was deceiving himself: that the future was already decided. The Whigs were out for the moment and though they would be back one day he feared that then they would no longer want his leadership. Therefore this was his last summer of high office and the inalienable right of access to the most inaccessible person in the kingdom, a woman whom he loved not with the grand passion of a youngster but with the melancholy and awe and gratitude which make up the love of an elderly man. And so he took his last opportunity to plan her progress to houses where he had a natural right to be himself: first to Woburn, thence to Panshanger and finally to his own beloved Brocket.

The country went to the polls when the Court was at Brocket and by common consent Lord Melbourne and his guests forgot about politics and enjoyed themselves. As if out of special consideration for their comfort the rain remained in the west and the sun shone brightly on the Brocket pleasure grounds. The Prince was much interested in his host's plantations, especially in the filberts which were grown in a vase shape, and he spent hours in the library where the writings of Greek and Latin philosophers, poets, historians and dramatists, and the works of the early Christian fathers, were as fully represented as in any major university. Melbourne was privately amused to notice that his interest did not appear to be in the contents of the volumes, but in their arrangement; and he did his best to explain why the works of Fronto, Herodes Atticus, Libanius and Themistius were grouped together, as rhetoricians and not under the letters 'F', 'H', 'L' and 'T'. They discussed the advantages and disadvantages of various systems. It turned out that the Prince and Stockmar planned to make a comprehensive catalogue of the royal possessions in all the royal palaces.

'Very useful,' he commented, 'for how anyone finds anything is a mystery.'

'It will also reduce thievery,' said Albert solemnly.

The Prime Minister nodded and said yes he supposed it would. The ponderous utterance had rather jaded him so he said nothing more.

The Prince was kindly and intelligent, undoubtedly an excellent husband for Victoria, and he managed his difficult position with great skill and patience, yet there was something solemnly worthy about him which made a certain type of Englishman feel uneasy in his company. Melbourne was no satyr like his brother-in-law Palmerston, but he liked things which would have shocked the Prince – to talk broad at times, to make himself comfortable by putting his feet on the table, to game a little, to eat well and heartily, and on occasions to drink into that dozy state where worries diminish. That was it, he decided, leaving the Prince to his study of cataloguing in the library, the boy's worthiness stood between them.

He found the Queen with Lady Lyttelton in the rose garden. Lehzen had been left at Windsor to keep a watchful eye on the royal nursery, and Lady Lyttelton was in constant attendance; but Prime Ministers have powers not possessed by other men. It was understood that the ladies and gentlemen of the Household automatically withdrew to a distance when Lord Melbourne approached.

'May I take your arm, Lord Melbourne?' asked the Queen.

Nothing could have delighted him more. He showed her the small Scotch briars, the cabbage roses from France, the whites and the moss roses. Together they smelt the sweet-briar which the Brocket gardeners had clipped into shapes.

Just for a time, not very long, but long enough to make a memory for them both, they were happy together as they had been before her marriage.

Victoria admitted her sadness to Albert that evening. 'I cannot bear to think of the dear good man being driven from office.'

Albert soothed her as well as he could. He told her that nothing yet was certain. Should the country return more Tories than Whigs Lord Melbourne would probably still remain as First Minister until his party was trounced in the Commons. If, then, he did have to go, why, few men had more interests and few men had such a house as Brocket Hall for their retirement.

Victoria still did not want to let Lord Melbourne go, but Albert's picture helped her to face the probability. She could imagine him settling comfortably at Brocket enjoying his plantations and pleasure grounds. She saw him as an old man shuffling from rose to rose, sniffing, plucking a petal here and there. She saw him in the library with all the time in the world to read his classical authors.

Albert was less concerned for Melbourne as a person. In many ways he admired the Prime Minister but he had come to the conclusion he was too old-fashioned to lead a modern Whig party. He also thought it a pity that he had clung so tenaciously to office. The country had been allowed to drift and hardly anything done in order that the Whigs could keep their place, and only because he was cornered had Melbourne agreed to a dissolution of Parliament. Privately he thought it would be better, perhaps, for everyone when the Tories took office. But he held his tongue. Brought up as the hope and champion of the Whigs Victoria would never easily bring herself to accept the Tories. There had been that quite dreadful scandal earlier in her reign when the Whigs had resigned office but the Queen had refused to give up her ladies. As a result, Peel had refused to form an administration and Melbourne had continued as First Minister. Albert was determined that there would be no repetition of this fiasco. Unknown to Victoria, he had already sent Anson to consult Peel as to how the difficulties were to be overcome, and Peel had suggested a neat compromise.

Albert stirred. Perhaps now was an appropriate time to mention it to her.

'Victoria,' he murmured.

She was not asleep.

He told her what he had done, and how Sir Robert had suggested a solution which would neither humiliate her nor appear to be a concession to principle on his part. If, before he took office, the three of her ladies who were most nearly connected with the Whig government, the Duchess of Bedford, Lady Normanby and the Duchess of Sutherland, gave in their resignations to the Queen, he would not ask her to make any changes at all.

To Albert's surprise Victoria accepted the scheme very gladly.

'You are not angry that I did this without your knowledge?' he asked.

She moved towards him. 'Once perhaps, yes I would have been. But not now. You considered it better not to worry me?'

He said yes, he had. It would not be easy for her, carrying their second child so soon after the first. The more he could take on his shoulders for her, the better.

She sighed. 'I shall not like it,' she confessed. 'Peel is too stiff. He is not comfortable like our dear Lord M.'

IV

The Houses of Parliament had been burnt to the ground seven years before and the members of the Commons were still in temporary quarters. But they carried their procedure, even their air, with them. Their hours were as outlandish, their method of showing approval or disapproval quite as noisy, their respect for one another was still more polite than real. In two particulars only were their habits changing. The Greek aphorisms and Latin tags which had once studded parliamentary oratory were less often heard; and the custom of wearing hats was falling into disuse amongst some of the radicals. As almost without exception the radicals were young and well crowned with hair, this party badge caused little inconvenience.

There was more hubbub than usual towards the end of August when the new Parliament met. The wet weather had returned. The atmosphere was humid. Only those who had faced the hustings with equanimity were unruffled. The tempers of the rest were edgy.

The Tories had won the general election but Lord Melbourne was determined to stay in office until he was voted out. The Lords had already done this, carrying an amendment on the Address against his ministry by seventy-two votes. Now in the Commons, where the Tories had a majority of eighty-two, the same amendment was being debated.

Palmerston watched the proceedings carefully. Lord John

Russell led the Commons, and reported daily to the Queen. Palmerston would report to his brother-in-law and tell him as gently as possible that no miracle on earth could keep him in power. He and Russell would be back again, that was certain, but his political sense told him that Melbourne's day was done.

He listened to a brilliant speech by the hatless and vigorous member for Stockport – a new member, he discovered to his surprise because new members were generally more reserved. But then his informant told him the speaker was Richard Cobden, the zealot for free trade in corn. He studied him carefully for he represented the new power, a man who by the steady application of his intellect to the dictates of his heart would work to build a heaven on earth. Once he had sold calicoes by commission. One day his sculpted figure would collect pigeon dung and grime in north country towns as the Apostle of Free Trade.

Palmerston also studied Peel. The Tory leader spoke little, but what he said was sound. He was one generation away from the manufacturing class. His father had been the nabob, a cotton man from Lancashire, with the usual fortune and baronetcy to leave to this brilliant son. Palmerston admired Peel. Few men were so intellectually clever in Parliament. Few had such integrity. Yet he did not envy him. To Palmerston politics were a pleasure. He enjoyed statecraft just as he enjoyed wine and plenty of meat courses at dinner, just as he enjoyed women, just as he enjoyed boating and hunting. Being Foreign Secretary was fun. But to Peel all responsibilities of office were a burden. It had been apparent during his short term as Prime Minister seven years before. It was apparent now. The Duke would be there to push and pull in Cabinet and give his immense weight to declared policies, but this was Peel's hour. And he looked, thought Palmerston, as glum and hangdog as if his fortune, position, party and policies all lay in the dust.

*   *   *

On August 29th Lord Melbourne went down to Windsor. It was a melancholy occasion. The announcement yet had to be made public but he had come to say goodbye to the Queen as her First Minister.

When he went to the familiar suite of rooms, numbered 343, in the Lancaster Tower he realized that it might be for the last time. Soon the rooms would be used by Peel and his ministers. As an occasional, very occasional guest at the Castle his room would be elsewhere.

Already dejected, he was cast down still further to see that someone had already made an innovation. On the mantelshelf of his sitting-room glittering offensively against a fine Reynolds portrait of the Queen's great-uncle, Edward, Duke of York, was an obelisk-shaped thermometer. On inquiry he was told there was now a thermometer in every room in the Castle. No doubt, he told himself, the Prince, Stockmar and Sir James Clark had been putting their scientific heads together. With an unusual show of stubborn independence, he put the thermometer in a cupboard. It should remain there for as long as he was Prime Minister. Afterwards Peel could do what he wished.

He was sitting hunched before the screened and empty grate, lost deeply in memories of the past, when Prince Albert was announced. It was unusual for him to visit number 343. Generally the Prime Minister went to the Prince's apartments or they met by appointment. Melbourne appreciated the visit for what it was, a token of the Prince's affection and respect. He rather hoped he would not notice the missing thermometer and make embarrassing inquiries. But either the Prince did not notice or he pretended not to. He was concerned, he said, to press on Lord Melbourne his own need and the Queen's for his continued counsel; not, of course, on affairs of state which would belong to Sir Robert Peel, but on private and family matters.

'We should value your wise advice,' he urged, and he went on to say that no doubt Lord Melbourne would feel easier if any communication on family matters was passed through Anson.

Once Melbourne had been wily, or, at any rate, shrewd enough not to take things at their face value. He would have translated the Prince's request as a polite, yet firm reminder that after his resignation he must not continue to influence the Queen politically. But he was so pathetically pleased to hear his advice had been appreciated and was still valued that he was incapable of swift and clear thinking. He accepted the Prince's request with tears of gratitude in his eyes.

'If I may help, ever, in any way, Sir. Simply call on me. Call. Depend on it, Sir. I am ever at your service. Yours and the Queen's. Ever. Depend on it.'

Poor Melbourne. Just for a moment he trembled physically. He knew that prickly, hot and cold sensation felt by people with sensitive skins when they are attacked by clouds of insects on a summer's evening.

Albert was embarrassed by such an uncontrolled display. Expressions of deep emotion always made him shy away. As a result he plunged rather abruptly into a subject he had hoped to approach with some delicacy. Bluntly he asked what could be done with Baroness Lehzen. He was being kept in a constant state of annoyance by her interference.

The unexpectedness of the question surprised Melbourne. Its seriousness jerked him from his temporary and pathetic state. Rapidly he pulled himself together.

More than most people he appreciated how important cabals could become at Court. He realized that Lehzen's nebulous position was a continual irritant to the Prince; that her supposed influence over the Queen, though it had been enormously reduced, was equally irritating. He also realized it was almost inevitable for Albert, the husband, to impute bad motives to Victoria's closest confidante; and perversely see her qualities of natural intelligence, candour and loyalty as base cunning, hypocrisy and the exploitation of affection. He knew, as well as Lehzen herself surely knew, that she would have to go.

Melbourne had all this in mind as he advised the Prince. Without appearing partisan he made a point of listing Lehzen's undoubted merits, and, while mildly suggesting the Prince be less stringent in his views on her, he said nevertheless that he saw the wisdom of certain changes being made.

'No one of sensibility enjoys changes if they are made irrationally,' he said, gazing at his mantelshelf where very soon the obelisk-shaped thermometer would no doubt take pride of place. 'But without her mother, without her old governess, and without, I might add, her old Prime Minister, the Queen will have new views to hear, new ideas to absorb, fresh air to breathe.'

'But how,' persisted Prince Albert, 'can the Baroness be removed?'

Lord Melbourne considered. 'I *could* press the Queen now, Sir, to remove her. Later, under a Tory Ministry, her known dislike of their policies would make her believe there was a plot afoot.'

'Now?' repeated the Prince.

Melbourne nodded. 'Yes. Now. But unless you are determined at all costs to be rid of the Baroness, I would recommend caution. Be patient, Sir. The Baroness herself understands that the present situation cannot last. But she would be loath to move before – how may I put it? – before the natural time.'

The Prince disliked his advice, but he accepted it. 'I am obliged to you, my lord, for your counsel.' He took Melbourne's hand. 'We shall be honoured to keep your friendship, and to ask for your advice from time to time on family affairs.'

Melbourne started to say again that of all things ... but the Prince wisely cut him short.

'Through Mr Anson, my lord,' he repeated. 'Communicate with us through Mr Anson.'

He left and Melbourne sat once more before the empty grate. He ran over in his mind their conversation. On reflection it clarified. He saw now what the Prince had meant, and chuckled when a few minutes later as if to underline the fact, Anson himself was announced.

'Now, George,' he said. 'There's no need to utter a word. Not a word. Like Bottom with his part as Pyramus, I have it pat.'

Anson smiled. He knew the Prince had been to see the Prime Minister and he knew why, but he quickly disclaimed any connection between their visits.

'I am here privately, my lord, not as Prince Albert's Private Secretary.' He did his best to explain that his high regard for his old master had in no sense waned when he had received his new appointment. His principal loyalty had had to pass to the Prince, whom more and more he found to be a noble, intelligent and kindly man, too much misunderstood; but he would always have the warmest recollections of his years with the Prime Minister. For this reason he had come to express his own private sympathy on an occasion which he knew must be distressing Lord Melbourne a great deal.

'Damn it, George,' said Melbourne, much affected. 'The thought is kind, my lad. I'll not deny, not to you at any rate, that it's a sorry moment.' He sniffed, blew his nose heartily, and to relieve his feelings blasphemed a little. 'But to have the friendship of good people, of men like you, why it makes a difference. Damn it! It's kind of you, George.'

On the next day, when Viscount Melbourne had his last audience of the Queen as her First Lord of the Treasury, he recalled something Anson had said to him and repeated it to Victoria.

'Depend as much as you can, Ma'am, on your husband. Lean on him just as in one sense you have leant on me. As for the country, Sir Robert and the Duke will serve you well, be sure.' He stopped for a moment as he noticed her cheeks were very red and the corner of her eyes puckered; signs that she had been crying. 'Ma'am,' he said a trifle huskily, 'I'll ever be your most devoted and attached servant.'

'We shall hope to see you often, Lord Melbourne,' she said. There were tears in her eyes.

'Thank you, Ma'am.' Tears call to tears. He could not help crying himself. 'And if I may add without presumption, Ma'am, I'll ever be your majesty's faithful and affectionate friend.'

She touched his hand lightly. He took it and kissed it. Then he bowed, kissed her hand again, and backed from her presence. Very often it was allowed to elderly men that they backed away for a respectful distance and then let themselves more comfortably out of the doors. On this occasion, with tears rolling down his cheeks, Melbourne backed all the way to the door. There he bowed once more and turned into the antechamber: no longer First Minister to the Queen, but plain William Lamb, second Viscount Melbourne.

V

It was all very well, said Victoria confidentially to Lehzen, for Uncle Leopold to say she would soon settle down well with her new Prime Minister. Settling down with shy and awkward Peel was as plodding as an exercise in algebra and made her itch with impatience and long to scream. She would persevere, of course, but the abrupt change from her dear Lord M. to solemn Peel was like changing from champagne to port.

This was bad enough, she complained, and now the Baron was saying Lord Melbourne should not be writing to her so often, that it was improper, quite shocking. She wanted to know why not, and why, simply because he had once been her closest adviser, Melbourne was the only one amongst her subjects who could not write to her. His advice on appointments and procedure was not partisan, in fact no more Whig than Peel's. And besides, he seldom wrote on political matters; more often on such harmless and diverting subjects as his travels from country house to country house, his distaste for methodistical and precatory preaching, the excellence of the Duchess of Somerset's cook, and light gossip about mutual acquaintances such as the lady who 'talks three or four times as much as she ought, and like many such women often says exactly the things she ought not to say'. Stockmar, thought the Queen, had no cause to be so disapproving; and she was delighted to hear, through Miss Skerrett who had it from the Duchess of Inverness who had it herself from a certain Mrs Norton, that when the Baron made his views known to Lord Melbourne, the latter had shown deep feelings, jumped from his seat and cried violently, 'God eternally damn it! Flesh and blood cannot stand it!'

'Such awful passion!' said Miss Skerrett, giving the appearance of being shocked by such language.

'Yes, indeed,' murmured the Queen, her tone completely concealing her delight. Excellent Lord Melbourne. How sorry she was that he had refused the Garter. He was her true knight.

One thing and one thing only could be said for the change of government which the Queen detested so much. It took her mind off her approaching confinement. So did the exercise of patronage, for Victoria thoroughly enjoyed making appointments. In this she was quite unlike Lord Melbourne who loathed it, and was so exasperated by the necessity to nominate bishop after bishop that he declared their predecessors had died merely to vex him. The more vacancies there were, the happier the Queen, and she busied herself with the vacant Governor-Generalships of Canada and India, and the Governorship and Captaincy of the Isle of Wight. Nothing was too small for her attention. She examined the qualifications of the three candidates for the Mastership of Trinity and agreed with Sir Robert Peel that Professor Whewell had the best claim.

Other less momentous happenings helped to keep her mind off the unpleasant fact that, no matter how her ladies contrived to disguise the fact, she was enormous, and she felt bloated and ugly. People who interested her were asked to dine and sometimes to stay.

Aunt Mary of Gloucester arrived with a pair of jelly dogs who set on Albert's greyhound Eos, and, instead of calling them off, she urged them on. The greyhound won, and the old lady did not mind in the least. She brought to Victoria's Court a teasing whiff of earlier, more rascally days; cursed roundly, took snuff from a spoon, displayed Amazon energy, wore a wig which occasionally she removed to cool her overheated head, ate and drank heartily, told salty stories, and spoke often and with great devotion of her dead husband who had been an amiable lunatic. Though she had no children of her own, she discussed conception and parturition with a gusto which her niece found encouraging. Victoria had always been fascinated by Aunt Gloucester and loved her dearly.

Dr Hawtrey, the Headmaster of Eton, dined at Windsor several times. His wit amused her. When she asked him to name the cleverest boy in the school he made a profound bow and asked to be excused from answering. Otherwise, he declared, he would make six hundred enemies all at once. He had the true teacher's gift for imparting confidence. He spoke with massive simplicity of complicated things, interesting the Queen a great deal and making her feel she was growing intellectually.

Then Victoria was told of a dwarf in Wapping who stood twenty-six inches high, and she invited him to tea.

In almost the same spirit she wanted to invite Dr Newman down from Oxford, the clergyman who had written her favourite hymn, 'Lead, kindly light', while becalmed in an orange freighter off Marseilles, and who had just fired a decisive shot in the warm battle between High Church and Low by publishing a tract.

Albert persuaded her not to. Newman's *Tract 90* made him far too controversial a figure to take tea or dine in royal palaces. And the same, he added swiftly when Victoria made her next suggestion, was equally true of Lord Cardigan.

Despite his notoriety Victoria had secretly nursed a good opinion of the Earl of Cardigan. Like many other women she found his good looks and dash and courage very attractive; and she also admired and envied his insouciance and imperturbability in face of the mob's hostility. But Albert was firm. The Lieutenant-Colonel of his regiment ought not to be given a single sign of royal favour. He was too brazen altogether, either that or too megalomanic, for, although his reputation was so unsavoury, he was at that very time applying to Peel for the Lord Lieutenancy of

Northamptonshire, emphasizing that he would be exceedingly hurt and angry if he did not get it. Victoria pouted. She liked Lord Cardigan. Albert found himself obliged to reveal what so far had been hidden from her, that even while he was insisting on his right to a Lord Lieutenancy, Lord William Paget was declaring his intention, through the extraordinary medium of a letter to *The Times*, of determining in a court of law whether or not Lord Cardigan had committed adultery with Lady Frances, his wife.

Victoria's eyes opened wide. 'Through *The Times*?'

Albert nodded. 'Through *The Times*,' he repeated. And he went on to say there was talk of Lord William pretending to go off to the country while skulking in a cab in Berkeley Square; of a hired witness named Winter who had spent more than two uncomfortable hours concealed beneath a sofa; of Lady Frances having a black eye shortly afterwards.

Victoria nodded solemnly. Albert was right. Until the Earl of Cardigan's guilt or innocence was proved his presence at Court would be objectionable. Secretly she was wishing Aunt Gloucester had not gone home. How she would have enjoyed that particular story.

Deprived of Newman and Cardigan – what a delicious combination at the tea table – Victoria's spirits might have fallen had she not been presented with a copy of a book about herself entitled *Victoria from Birth to Bridal* by a Miss Agnes Strickland. This was so full of errors that she spent a great deal of time scoring them out and writing 'NOT TRUE' in the margin, and when Queen Adelaide wrote to say she had been reading the book and, though wrong in many particulars, she found it amusing and very interesting, Victoria was not at all pleased. At her instigation a process was begun which eventually resulted in the book's suppression.

Family squabbles also kept Victoria busy at this time. Besides writing about the odious Miss Strickland, Queen Adelaide was complaining that King Leopold had not troubled to say goodbye to her when he left Windsor. Her mother, who had spent the spring and summer first at

Laeken and then with her son Charles in Amorbach, was complaining that on her arrival in Belgium King Leopold had ordered 'all civilities' for his sister instead of 'royal honours'. Aunt Sophia was complaining that more should have been done for her on Aunt Augusta's death as she was the family pauper.

Victoria dealt with them one by one, with great tact, and was glad to have her mind occupied. Not much else interested her. Visits to the nursery and Vicky and the Poet Laureate's sister-in-law were daily duties and, frankly, exceedingly boring. Albert was busy persuading influential people to have frescoes painted in the new Houses of Parliament. He was also organizing concerts, and interesting himself in mundane affairs like housing, sanitation and the condition of the working classes. She had heard that her own father had been the same, but she suspected both were more concerned to make people more efficient than more comfortable. She found the subject dull, and thanked God the working classes were remote. When they ganged together and burnt ricks and machinery and threw bricks at magistrates they were the mob she feared above all things.

She was exceedingly glad when the day she had wanted to postpone indefinitely arrived. At the beginning of November she experienced familiar pangs of the year before, and her labour and lying-in began.

VI

'It would have been better, dear, not to have insisted,' murmured Lehzen.

It was good advice, and Lord Melbourne not being to hand, no one had a better right to offer it.

Prince Albert Edward was Earl of Chester and Duke of Cornwall by birth, and Prince of Wales by his mother's creation. No subject could be higher and, in preparing his armorial bearings, the College of Heralds had not looked with favour on Prince Albert's request that his son should also wear the arms of Saxony. Indeed, Garter King-of-Arms had made a formal protest against quartering the Royal Arms of England with those of a minor state the size of Dorset. This slight to her husband had stung Victoria. She had insisted on the quarterings being made. And now quite ordinary people were shouting things at Albert when he rode out to visit museums and galleries, and society had made it clear that it considered England had been insulted.

Worried, feeling low after her lying-in, Victoria had taken her trouble to Lehzen, but she did not relish what Lehzen said.

'It was a reasonable request,' she claimed. 'A child naturally bears the arms of his own father.'

Lehzen smiled. 'You know what you English are,' she said. 'So touchy where your honour or your importance are concerned.'

'I had every right to command those saucy heralds to do as they were told.'

'Of course,' soothed her old governess, 'but was it wise to exercise the right?'

Victoria tossed her head. 'Lehzen, I declare you are as ungenerous to Albert as the rest of them. He should not be made to feel so small, so insignificant. No man can abide it.'

The Baroness looked reproachful. Recently she had had a recurrence of her jaundice and her own nerves were frayed. In justice to herself she wanted to remind the Queen that she had always been a strong supporter of Prince Albert, that she had never once passed a derogatory remark on him. But she held her tongue. She knew Victoria was being subjected to all sorts of pressures from the world beyond her Palace gates. Besides her anxieties for Prince Albert, she was being worried sick by a vile rumour circulating through the country that both her children were blind and deformed. She had even heard a loathsome suggestion that little Vicky should be publicly exhibited naked in a glass case each day

103

so that the common people could file past and see that she was a normal child. With all this added to her depression, Victoria thought and behaved with a degree of irrationality which did not brook any sort of argument, and Lehzen thoroughly understood.

Suddenly Victoria sobbed. 'Oh, Lehzen, dear, dear Lehzen. What shall I do? How can I . . .?'

Lehzen took her in her arms and prevented her from finishing. With her old skill she soothed Victoria until her tears dried and she wiped her eyes. She turned the subject to the new bonnet fashion, so highly decorated that they looked like Gothic corbels; and to the modish colours of tawny, violet and bullrush brown. It was not long before Victoria was relaxed and sufficiently calm to control her feelings.

Lehzen could not know that, ironically, she had cut short a plea for help, a sentence which would have told her Prince Albert was determined to drive her from the Court, because it was the realization of this which distressed the Queen so much. Perhaps it was better that she did not know.

The Prince had accepted Lord Melbourne's advice. Personally he found the Baroness trying but he was prepared to tolerate the nuisance just so long as only he suffered from what he considered her interference. But when it seemed she was interfering in the nursery he came to the conclusion he ought not to be patient any longer.

He was appalled by the state of affairs in the royal nursery. Vicky was jealous of the attention given to her little brother but no one made any sort of attempt to mollify her. And clearly there was something else the matter. She ailed and she lost weight. Sir James Clark put her on to asses' milk and chicken-flavoured gruel but this restrictive diet, somehow reminiscent of Imperial Rome as well as Scotch crofts, made little difference.

The Queen was unconcerned. Let the child be given plain nursery food and left alone to grow, she said. Her own harsh experience made her believe childhood was something to be got through – rather like an infectious disease – not something to be enjoyed. Its path could be sugared with rewards, treats, and appropriate gifts; and any difficulties of temperament overcome by whippings, purgings, and being sent to bed. With her common-sense, for she had more than her share of it in practical day-by-day matters, she saw at once that the nursery was badly run. Mrs Southey ruled her staff with little knowledge of what they were doing, and her responsibility kept her in a constant state of twittering nerves. Her nurses were an indifferent lot. Though given the matronly title as a courtesy they were single women, and were selected for their qualities of character rather than for any knowledge they might have of looking after children. One, called Ratsey, was as nervous as Mrs Southey and, holding her charges at arm's length, would gurgle and crow at them a baby talk the Prince found infuriating. He was equally incensed by her colleague, Mrs Packer, who had temporarily studied music at the London Royal Academy, and who sang arias in a deep contralto and with an Edinburgh accent as she supervised the ablutions of the Princess Royal. The Prince of Wales' wet nurse, Mary Ann Brough, had glaring, staring eyes, and Prince Albert was disgusted to notice that whenever the nursery was particularly warm, she always had dried saliva at the corners of her mouth. The only one who might have been called Stockmar-chosen, that is, was thorough and appeared to know what she was doing, was a Mrs Roberts; and Albert discovered that she was immensely resentful of any sort of criticism and moreover was hand in glove with the Baroness.

This at once made him suspect that Lehzen was influencing the nursery. He had regretted leaving her in sole charge the year before when he and Victoria had made their progress, and he had only consented because of the advantages of separating Victoria from her governess. Now he regretted it still more. Through Mrs Roberts she was directing the way in which his children should be brought up.

It was unjust of him to believe this as it was quite untrue. Lehzen's great love for Victoria did not extend to her children. She wished them well, and visited them occasionally, but she was not especially interested in them or in the nursery. But Mrs Roberts, who did not like the Prince, saw what he had at the back of his mind, and she aggravated the situation by encouraging him in his mistake. Halfway through January in 1842, he was absolutely certain that Lehzen was interfering in the day-to-day running of the nursery. So often did he denigrate her before Victoria, unkindly calling her the Yellow Lady on account of her jaundiced complexion, that she realized the time was drawing near when he would demand Lehzen's dismissal.

VII

On January 16th, the Queen and the Prince returned to Windsor from a visit to Claremont. Victoria was very tired. She was also extremely irritable. Why Albert had wanted to drag her to Claremont in winter time was more than she could understand, and she had been cold and silently angry for some time. Then, though he had not said a word either, Albert's gloomy air of disaster had been the equivalent of half an hour's invective against Lehzen. She had had to clench her fist and set her teeth for the past four miles in order to avoid speaking out and showing her anger.

Though she was still exceedingly low, she had her figure back and her strength. When the carriage stopped at the south-eastern corner of the great quadrangle where they used a private entrance to the Castle, she was quick to descend from the carriage. She swept up the two shallow steps and through heavy oak doors panelled with glass into the small octagonal hall which led to a staircase. Standing there was Mrs Southey. She had a report that Princess Victoria was unwell again. She had a mild fever and had been sick. Sir James was not concerned, nor was she; but she would feel more reassured if the royal parents would be so kind as to visit the nursery. Without removing their travelling clothes they followed her.

They found Mrs Roberts walking up and down the room rocking Vicky in her arms. Albert quietly suggested that being shaken up and down could not be good for a child who had recently been sick.

To his surprise Mrs Roberts took no notice. She showed the Princess to the Queen who agreed that there was nothing very much to worry about, and then continued rocking the child.

The Prince flushed with anger. Not only had the nurse paid no attention to what he said, rudely she had ignored his presence altogether. 'Mrs Roberts,' he said. 'I repeat, it cannot be good for a child who has recently been sick to be jolted up and down. She should be laid down to rest.'

Mrs Roberts curtseyed to the Queen and asked if it was her majesty's pleasure that the Princess should be rocked into comfortable sleep, or left flat on a bed.

Victoria, already peevish with Albert, was further vexed with him for being so petty and so prickly. He was for ever worrying about insignificant matters, and for ever defending his position. Surely Mrs Roberts ought to know what was good for a sick child.

'Do as you think best,' she said to the nurse.

Albert stared at her unbelievingly. Never before had she failed to support him in public, and to all intents and purposes this was a public place. Mrs Southey was by the door, Mrs Gow and Mrs Ratsey stood beside the nursery cupboard. Mary Ann Brough was rocking the Prince of Wales' cradle. There were lower servants in the room as well. Everyone found it difficult to credit that the Queen had opposed the Prince in their hearing.

Mrs Roberts took immediate advantage of the situation. Triumphantly she rocked the Princess up and down, while murmuring impatient asides which were meant to be heard. How, she asked rhetorically, could a foreign royal highness, and a prince at that, know what was good for an English princess?

Albert turned to Victoria. Although he was angry he spoke in a controlled and steady voice. 'This really is malicious,' he said so quietly that no one else would hear. He

107

was indignant that Victoria should appear to overlook the insolent remark, indignant that he should have to remind her of her duty to rebuke the nurse.

It was like lighting the fuse of a mine. Everyone was astounded at the frightening outburst which followed. Before them all Victoria accused her husband of such regular and mischievous interference in nursery affairs that she herself had no say there at all, and the life of their little daughter was in jeopardy.

What she said was irrational, unjust, and was shouted at the top of her voice. Of all those present only Mrs Southey and Mrs Roberts could recall how her blind old grandfather had shouted in the same way in this very castle.

There was a horrified silence.

The Prince, struggling to control himself, muttered a prayer for patience, bowed to the Queen and left the nursery.

Mrs Roberts sent a servant running for the Baroness; and removed the weeping Queen's travelling cape and sat her before the nursery fire. Lehzen arrived and quietly sent the servants back to their quarters and everyone else into the night nurseries.

Alone by the fire, she rubbed the Queen's hands and warmed her a glass of wine and asked what all the trouble was.

Being in her old governess' arms, safe in the aura of caraway and the metallic smell of the purple bombazine which Lehzen loved to wear, Victoria found it easy to be confiding. She told her of her private undertaking not to give way to lowness and confessed how miserably she had failed. Everything stemmed from that, she said; her jealousies, her nervousness, her bad temper.

When she had finished, Lehzen squeezed her lovingly. She said she could understand some of her motives and some of her feelings, but other people would not be able to do so, and if she behaved so stupidly again they might begin to fear for her reason.

Victoria's hand flew to her mouth. Her face was deathly white. Lehzen laid a finger against her lips.

'No one knows you better than I, dear, and never for one moment have I doubted you are as sane as anyone in Europe. But you must not give way so easily. Tantrums do not suit you ...'

'But, Lehzen!' interrupted Victoria. Then she stopped. She would not have taken this from anyone else, but Lehzen's rebuke was silky.

'Tantrums do not suit you,' repeated Lehzen, stroking her hair. 'Once, perhaps; but not now. You are a grown woman, a wife, the mother of two children. You have a crown, too. Tantrums no longer suit you. Queens do not make scenes. Nor do ladies defy their husbands in the public eye.'

Chastened, sobbing her gratitude to Lehzen, the Queen knew what had to be done. Leaving her old governess to persuade Mrs Southey and the nurses that a still tongue would be kind and to everyone's benefit, she left the nursery and went to apologize to Albert for her bad behaviour.

It was hopeless from the start.

Now that they were alone Albert could unbottle his anger. She found it terrifying. Twice, three times she attempted to make her apology. He would not listen. How dared she defy his authority? he thundered. How dared she allow Lehzen's friend to insult him in public?

She tried to stem the flood. 'It was Lehzen ...' she began, with every intention of telling him it was Lehzen who had reasoned with her, Lehzen who supported him, Lehzen who had persuaded her to apologize.

But he would not listen. Lehzen, he said, was her evil genius and she lacked the wit to see it.

Victoria lifted her head. He had touched a nerve which was sensitive.

Seeing it he hurt the nerve again. 'You do not have the intelligence to see what mischief she is causing in the nursery.'

Docility, obedience, patience; all the wifely virtues she knew she ought to show, flew off like windblown thistle seed. Suddenly she was as angry as he was.

They quarrelled violently. He was obdurate. Her repressive measures in the nursery, learnt of course from Lehzen and her own childhood, were harming the health of their child.

Her reply was venomous. He, of course, was clever. Moreover he was scientific, with a logical approach to problems. And he was a man, blessed with the enviable advantages and special powers enjoyed by his sex. All these were well known facts at Court – for did not he himself hammer them home each day? Why then, she asked, had Dr Clark and the nursery staff failed to avail themselves of the offer of such wisdom?

'Because,' he said harshly, 'because they are under your protection and that of Baroness Lehzen.'

'Rather,' she snapped back, 'it is because you have vexed them with your impatient interference.'

This made him storm at her in a way he never had done before. She became hysterical. Racked with sobs she flew from the room.

But he had not yet finished. Half an hour later, one of the Prince's pages brought a hastily scribbled letter.

I shall have nothing more to do with it; take the child away and do as you like and if she dies you will have it on your conscience.

Victoria gazed at the scalding words. Her capacity for anger had gone. Now she was frightened, very frightened. All her old feelings for Albert welled up inside her. She sobbed with the strength of them. How could he treat her so when she loved him from the bottom of her heart? If only he would be reasonable. If only he would take back the cruel words he had shouted at her.

In her misery she longed to send for Lehzen, but to do so would alienate Albert further. Given the choice there was no suggestion of hesitating between Albert and Lehzen. Lehzen was perhaps her greatest consolation in life, but her husband was life itself.

There was no bitter-sweet reconciliation that night, and early the next morning Albert went off to London to lay the foundation stone of the new Stock Exchange.

Lehzen paid her usual morning call during the Queen's toilette, and as nothing was said, she supposed Victoria and her husband were reconciled and the matter was being allowed to drop. Tactfully she did not mention it herself. Victoria, at first relieved, was afterwards puzzled why Lehzen had said nothing. Then she was a little indignant. Did her old governess think the terrible chasm which had opened between her and Albert was merely a lovers' tiff? It was on account of this small misunderstanding, and because the Queen dreaded making Albert any angrier, that Lehzen was no longer personally involved in an affair which concerned her most closely.

Victoria would have given a great deal for Lord Melbourne's honest advice just then, but he had been at Court for Christmas and the Baron had expressed the firmest possible opinion that it would be improper for him to be invited there again for some little time.

Cut off from Lehzen and from Lord Melbourne, Victoria turned to the Baron himself. Though he usually advised her in less intimate matters she felt she could count on his help now in her great dilemma. Kennaird, her page on duty, was sent off to summon the Baron from his tower.

He was a long time in coming, so long that Victoria's nervousness increased. He asked her forgiveness, made a mention of arthritis as the reason for his slowness, and kissed her hand. Though it was against Court protocol, she invited him to be seated.

'It was a coincidence, Ma'am, that you should send for me,' he said, 'for I was about to request an audience.'

The Queen caught her breath. In the balance of things Stockmar was more Albert's confidant than he was hers.

Guessing her thought, Stockmar tried to help. 'Yes, Ma'am, about the unfortunate contretemps which took place yesterday evening.'

His use of the word contretemps angered her because it so belittled that awful scene of hysteria and hate. 'You wished to see me on Prince Albert's behalf?' she asked.

111

'Upon my word, no,' he said. 'I had hoped as your mutual adviser to reconcile you both.'

In her agitation she jumped to her feet and the Baron was obliged to stand as well. She begged him to remain seated. 'I shall walk up and down. I find it relieves me. But you must rest your arthritis, Baron.' She stopped. 'Tell me, is the Prince very angry?'

His bulging eyes were kinder than she had ever seen before. 'Yes,' he said quietly. 'It would be wrong of me to say otherwise. And you will perhaps understand why. His position as a husband and father is overweighed by your own authority as his sovereign. Then there is the Baroness ...' He paused. 'I have the greatest admiration for all that Baroness Lehzen has been able to do for your majesty in the past ...' Once more he paused. 'But perhaps the time has come for her to pass her offices into other hands.'

Victoria looked out of the window. 'I cannot believe the Prince hates her so,' she said over her shoulder. 'He could not.'

'He considers,' said Stockmar, 'that the Baroness has never been a good influence on you, Ma'am; that she has brought you up in her own way for her own purposes.'

'I cannot believe it,' she said; more softly this time.

'He considers that a great deal of the ill will between your mother and yourself was caused and nourished by the Baroness.'

'No!' said Victoria sharply. 'No!'

She was remembering her mother's indifference to her for so long and her overfamiliarity and probably more with her odious Comptroller, their attempt to coerce her to give him a position of power when she came to the throne; and in all the loneliness and bitterness of her childhood only Lehzen had given her love and understanding.

Or was she wrong?

She put her hands to her ears for a moment.

Had she been mistaken all along? Was Lehzen really as wicked as Albert said?

Victoria turned from the window. 'Do you believe these things yourself?' she asked.

'Understand me, Ma'am. In this present conflict my opinion of Baroness Lehzen is of no account. The important thing, for the crown, for your family, and for you both is that a good relationship should be re-established between you and the Prince.'

'Oh, yes,' she cried. 'I agree, I agree.'

'The Prince's view of Baroness Lehzen stands in the way of it. He is implacably hostile to her.'

She shook her head miserably.

'I had hoped to persuade you,' he said, 'with my own advocacy. As I have failed, I shall read you a memorandum sent to me by the Prince.' He unfolded a letter. 'I have his royal highness' permission,' he added.

Lehzen [the Baron read] *is a crazy, common, stupid intriguer, obsessed with lust of power, who regards herself as a demi god, and anyone who refuses to acknowledge her as such, is a criminal.*

He looked up at the Queen. She was white faced and trembling.

'Please, Ma'am, sit down,' he urged.

She shook her head. 'I am quite well, thank you, Baron,' she said in a shaky voice. 'Please continue reading.'

'Dear me, surely you are persuaded, Ma'am?'

She shook her head again. 'Continue reading, please,' she ordered.

'Very well.' The Baron turned back to the memorandum, and hastily skipped two sentences which would certainly have persuaded the Queen but which also would have caused her great hurt. He selected a piece and read it out.

There can be no improvement till Victoria sees Lehzen as she is, and I pray that this comes. But it seems like a curse on our heads that the whole world sees the truth, and only the person concerned does not realize it, but regards the object of her infatuation as an angel and the world as suspicious, slanderous, envious . . .

113

The Baron stopped. He folded the paper and replaced it in his pocket and sat quietly, saying nothing for a time.

Victoria had returned to the window. She was trying to absorb the terrible things her own husband had written about Lehzen, trying as well to accept the fact that Lehzen would have to leave. It was inevitable. As Stockmar had said, the crown, her family and her marriage mattered more in the end than Lehzen.

Her eyes were blinded with tears, therefore she could not see Stockmar properly when she turned and said: 'I am persuaded, Baron, and would ask you to be good enough to tell the Prince that any arrangements he cares to make with regard to the Household or the nursery will be satisfactory to me.'

Stockmar bowed: 'It is for the best, Ma'am; believe me.'

VIII

Queen Victoria wrote to her uncle, the King of the Belgians:

> We think of going to Brighton early in February, as the physicians think it will do the children great good and perhaps it may me; for I am very strong as to fatigue and exertion, but not quite right otherwise; I am growing thinner, and there is a want of tone which the sea may correct.

She was over-sanguine. Brighton did them no good at all.

The Pavilion did not suit Prince Albert. He found the onion domes distasteful; the gilt lacquer and porcelain and glass lustres ostentatious; the Chinese dragons in the corridors disconcerting.

The Queen had once liked it, chiefly sentimentally because it was the fantastic creation of her uncle, George the Fourth, and she had fond memories of this extraordinary relative who wore corsets and scent and rouge. But now she was willing to agree that as a royal palace it was, perhaps too exuberant, too *outré* altogether.

Taste aside, as a palace it was too small. Some Coburg relations who had been at Windsor for the christening of the Prince of Wales went with them to Brighton, and there was insufficient room for everyone to be comfortable. Moreover it was noisy. In his middle age, Victoria's uncle had had a Latin taste for crowds, and his Pavilion was so much at the centre of things that she and Albert could not take the smallest walk out of doors without being mobbed. It suited neither of them. Both wanted peace. Both wanted privacy. Both on this occasion wanted to move carefully and gently through the uneasy period which followed their bitter quarrel.

When the Coburg cousins left for Germany, they went off themselves to London. Their short time in Brighton had turned them against the place for ever. The Pavilion belonged to a time and to a generation which both found alien. Talk turned once more to building a house in the country of their own and Victoria asked Sir Robert if he would kindly make discreet inquiries on their behalf about a reasonable estate in the country not too far from London and Windsor.

Albert set about the task of reorganizing the nursery. There were few objections, and almost everyone agreed that his arrangements were excellent. He worked quietly, taking the trouble to win over Mrs Roberts, trying with all the considerable charm he had at his disposal to persuade a certain lady to take over as nursery superintendent. At first he would not reveal her name. He could not, he said, in case, after all, she refused to be persuaded, but after a time he was able to tell Victoria that Lady Lyttelton had agreed to superintend the royal nurseries if she could be released from her duties as one of the Queen's ladies. He was triumphant, and she could see why. As a dowager free to do what she wished, a mother and grandmother with a large experience of children, and being a good and kind woman of common-sense and character, Lady Lyttelton was the ideal person to look after the royal children. She agreed at once, although she would feel the lack of Lady Lyttelton herself. Without her and without Lehzen, what would she do?

A family tragedy made her forget her self-pity. After her accession Victoria had volunteered to continue the places and pensions of King William's bastard children. They had been touched and grateful, and two especially had attached themselves to her Court and were amongst the most loyal of her subjects: Lord Adolphus FitzClarence who was a rear-admiral and had command of the royal yacht, and his elder brother, the Earl of Munster. Munster was a sad figure ruined by his shrewish wife, and in March Victoria was brought the news that she had driven him so distracted that he shot himself. The suicide worried her conscience. Not long before he had written to her explaining his wretched-ness and giving his reasons for it. Could she not have pre-vented the tragedy in some way by sending for Lady Munster and reasoning with her? Or by giving her half-cousin a foreign appointment to separate them for a time? She was so horrified at what a woman could do to her hus-band that her resolve to control her own temper with Albert was enormously strengthened. She sent her condolences to Lord Adolphus and assured him that his brother's pension would be continued.

The loss of her half-cousin sent her into a temporary low, and her dejection was increased by reports from Sir Robert on the state of the country. Parliament was attempting to help trade and lessen the suffering of the labouring classes. Bills were passed for imposing duty on imported corn, for imposing income tax at sevenpence in the pound, and for the relief of the poor. There was even one prohibiting women and young boys from being employed in the mines.

Victoria watched the passage of these bills with close at-tention. People whom she admired told her they were good and necessary pieces of legislation. But she was not so sure herself. There were signs of serious unrest in the north country, and agitators were gaining ground politically. This frightened her. She was in great dread of people who manipulated mobs, and it seemed to her that the more concessions they were given, the greedier they became.

Nevertheless, conscious that many of her subjects were in need, she did what little she could. To encourage trade she asked that all ladies attending her drawing-rooms, should wear dresses of English manufacture, and she decided to give a *bal costumé* at which all guests were asked to wear fourteenth-century dress made of English materials.

But the reformers and agitators would not give her any credit. They did not even acknowledge her good intentions. They said she was frivolous, and that for her to wear a costume with jewels worth over £20,000, was an insult to the hungry poor. A public speaker went so far as to call her 'a dawdling useless thing'.

Theirs was a bigoted, short-sighted policy. If the Reformers had won the Queen whole-heartedly to their side she would have brought her great influence to bear and the future passing of progressive legislation would have been much easier. But she resented their sneers at her attempt to do some good. She also despised their bigotry. They never had a single generous word to spare for her or the class they regarded as oppressors. In this they were like the self-righteous Jasper Tomsett Judge.

The remains from her ball had hardly been cleared away before she found Lord Cardigan at the centre of affairs again. Having been refused the Lord Lieutenancy of Northamptonshire for reasons which ought really to have been obvious, he was now applying for a Garter. His cool demand for entry to the oldest, noblest and by far the most exclusive order of chivalry in the world made even the Queen think Albert's lieutenant-colonel was being a little presumptuous. It was unheard of. Her previous good opinion of Lord Cardigan cooled rapidly. But she was still doubtful when both Peel and the Commander-in-Chief recommended that something constructive should be done to disassociate Cardigan from the royal family. As he could not easily be removed from his command, it would be as well for Prince Albert himself to move. Would he accept the Colonelcy of Guards in lieu of the Eleventh Hussars? Eventually the Queen was persuaded and the change was made; though she warned Peel that Lord Cardigan would very probably be angry, and some sort of gesture from the government might placate him. She was right. This time Cardigan was not insouciant. He was beside himself with rage, and so outspoken in public places that Peel seized on his indiscretion as a good reason for not giving him any sort of honour or promotion.

Cardigan's complaints and claims fell upon deaf ears. The Queen was no longer his champion. Her uncle, Count Mensdorff, had arrived at Court. He had with him his four handsome sons, and brought news of the Hereditary Prince Ernest's wedding. Victoria enjoyed long family gossips. She enjoyed taking them sightseeing in London, and she found them a great comfort when at the very end of May a second attempt was made on her life.

They were returning home from Church on a Sunday, and driving down Birdcage Walk when the Prince noticed a swarthy young man step out of the crowd on his side of the carriage and point a pistol at the Queen. Before he could speak or move or do anything the man pulled the trigger. By an extraordinary chance the pistol misfired, but the flash in the pan was not especially noticeable and the man was able to slip away in the crowd. Barely anyone had seen what had happened. There was no fuss. The Prince told the coachman to carry on. Even the Queen's ladies in the following carriage were unaware of what had taken place.

On their return to the Palace an agitated group discussed what had happened. Conditioned by the reports she had received almost daily from the Home Secretary about unrest up and down the country, Victoria said she was not in the least surprised to be the victim of an assassination attempt but, from the Prince's description of his manner, the swarthy man appeared to be a madman. If so he would probably try again. Ideas for her extra protection she brushed aside. Until the man was caught she would be in terror of her life. He must be tempted to try again in the same place the next day. Until then it would be wiser not to mention what had happened to anyone. Reluctantly the Prince agreed with her.

On the following afternoon the Queen sent a message to her Lady-in-Waiting. Her attendance would not be required that day. The Prince's equerries stationed themselves not far from the open carriage. Victoria, her small hand gripping the handle of her bullet-proof Parasol, showed a smile to the world and felt sick with apprehension. She was a marvel of composure, Albert whispered out of the corner of his mouth as they turned into Birdcage Walk, but her scalp tingled with fears as the carriage rolled towards a mad marksman who might kill or maim her.

Her gasp of relief when the weapon was fired was louder to Albert than the report of the pistol. Only then did he realize what she had gone through. Her plan had worked perfectly. His equerries and a few police who had been mingling in the crowd had a swarthy man by the shoulders. After all they had gone through it was ironic to discover that his pistol had not even been loaded.

He and Uncle Mensdorff and their cousins were solicitous of Victoria that evening, and said they were enormously proud of her. They were consoling and she was grateful but every so often, when she remembered the look she had seen in the assassin's eyes, she trembled from head to foot. It appeared he was not in the least mad or even mentally deficient as the potboy Oxford had been. And yet he had made two cold-blooded attempts to kill her. The mob she had feared from her childhood was at last being personified. Her frayed nerves now made her see the mob not only as a destructive force goaded on by agitators, but as something ugly in itself, composed of vindictive, cruel and unrelenting people.

The assassin's name was John Francis. He was condemned to death and this time Victoria made no plea to her Prime Minister that the savage laws of treason might be changed. She was even mildly shocked when he was reprieved by the Home Secretary and transported because the pistol had not been loaded. An execution, she said, might have discouraged other assassins.

Only two days later her opinion seemed to be borne out. Another attempt was made on her life, this time by a hunch-back named Bean who presented a pistol at her and tried to fire it. She had the terrifying experience of seeing him press the trigger and hearing the hammer click. Nothing had happened. He threw down the weapon and bolted. With the same outward appearance of imperturbability the Queen ordered the coachman to proceed, but her nerves were ragged. It made no difference to the horror she had endured to know that the case had ludicrous aspects; that the pistol was a three-shilling toy with a weak lock and had been stuffed with a mixture of paper and tobacco as well as gun-powder; and that, to make sure of getting Bean, the police had rounded up every hunchback in the area, and no less than sixty had been packed together in the local police station. Then they had quarrelled and fought and tried to make each other confess so that they could go home. She was not pleased when Bean was given a short sentence of eighteen months' imprisonment. It hardly compensated for the severe fright he had given her. Temporarily she had lost her confidence in people and, apart from notable exceptions, she never afterwards gave her affectionate trust to members of the lower classes. From that time no lower servant was ever allowed to look her in the face. She did not want to meet their eyes nor for the rest of her life did she ever do so.

Victoria's two escapes – if not from a violent death, then certainly from nervous collapse – seemed all the more providential when news came from France that Louis-Philippe's eldest son and heir had been killed in a carriage accident. His horses had bolted and he had fallen from a phaeton on to his head. Shocked letters passed backwards and forwards between Victoria and her Uncle Leopold. The Queen's condolences were sent to the French Court. She was quick to point out to those of her ladies who were nervous of the railways that riding in carriages was equally dangerous. That summer she had taken her first ride in a railway train,

120

an event which had terrified her ladies and caused consternation in the department of the Master of the Horse who was responsible for her transport. The Earl of Albermarle had gone down to Slough station to satisfy himself that the locomotive, tender and state-carriage of the Great Western Railway Company looked and were safe for the Queen. The royal coachman, insisting on his rights, had travelled on the footplate of the pilot engine which preceded the royal train; but it had been for the first and last time. Coal smoke in his eyes, smuts all over his scarlet livery, and the gaping of by-standers as he was chugged ridiculously through the countryside, quickly made him relinquish his rights. In neither horse nor railway-carriage, said the Queen, could one be absolutely sure of being safe; but one could reduce the chances by taking care. She ordered that her stables were to be reviewed. Any beast which showed the slightest irregularity in temperament or a disposition to nervousness was to be separated from the rest and if necessary sold away. As for the railways, she ordered an extraordinary precaution to be taken whenever the royal train was used. At her expense there were to be men stationed all along its route at half-mile intervals.

IX

Prince Albert gradually brought pressure to bear on Lehzen. It was not in his own interest to be bludgeoning and direct. Being gentle and subtle was the surer method of getting rid of her; and he saw all her particular friends in the household, and the people she most admired, one after the other, and he made them realize that the situation as it existed was no longer tolerable, that for the sake of their Queen, even in the end for the sake of Lehzen's own peace of mind, she ought to retire. Baron Stockmar, Lady Lyttelton, Miss Skerrett and Mrs Brand, Sarah Mary Cavendish and Caroline

Cocks her two favourites amongst the Queen's young ladies, Lady Palmerston, even Lord Melbourne and his own Private Secretary George Anson were asked to help; and because they agreed with his conclusions, though not always for the same reason, they undertook to speak to the Baroness or hint what was in their minds.

In the event, not one of her friends said anything direct, but shrewd old Lehzen saw at once what was happening. Since January 16th there had been no appreciable difference in her friendship with the Queen. She still looked after the most private correspondence and acted as Privy Purse and general superintendent of the household, but Victoria no longer spontaneously went to her old governess with her troubles. Lehzen guessed she was doing this in order to avoid vexing Prince Albert, a guess which seemed to be borne out when, just after Francis' attempt on her life, Victoria had been so frightened that, despite herself, she had rushed to Lehzen for some sort of comfort.

With each of her friends she was courteously understanding. Yes, she told them, as soon as someone could be trained to take her place she would retire to live with her sister in Germany. This, she considered, would be wiser and perhaps pleasanter than living in England. After such a long time she would feel the break, of course, but there would almost certainly be opportunities to keep up old friendships by correspondence and by occasional visits.

To Lord Melbourne, and to him alone, she opened her heart. She realized, she said, that the separation would be permanent. In far-off Germany she would be as completely cut off as though she and the Queen lived on different planets. She would feature less and less in Victoria's thinking until she became just a memory. Perhaps, she added with a smile, self-cautery was good for her. For a long time she had dreaded this moment but now it had come it did not seem to be too painful. The old viscount took both her hands and pumped them up and down. She said little else and he said hardly anything at all; but there was a depth of understanding and feeling between them which both found helpful. Afterwards he was amazed to discover that the talk had been so moving, to both of them, that she had offered him a caraway seed to chew, and he had accepted it.

On July 25th Prince Albert told Victoria that Lehzen would be leaving her service in two months' time. She had not wished to cause the Queen distress by offering her resignation personally and had gone instead to him. He, on the Queen's behalf, had been pleased to accept her resignation and release her from the royal service. She had recommended that Miss Skerrett be appointed to replace her as copyist of the Queen's private papers and to undertake other small matters of a confidential nature and had offered to train that lady in her duties. Again on the Queen's behalf, he had accepted both her recommendation and her offer.

He was extremely careful how he said all this, avoiding any suggestion of triumph, and trying very hard as well, not to appear too nonchalant as though he was speaking of very ordinary affairs. Either might have angered Victoria.

Her reaction surprised him. She had already faced the fact that Lehzen was going. Hearing it, even from Albert, could not upset her much more. Curiously, at this important moment, she found her mind flying off at a tangent. Her minister at The Hague was obstinately prejudiced against her Uncle Leopold, and was being dismissed. He, too, would be leaving. Her thoughts came back to Lehzen. Two tears stole from the corners of her eyes. One she decided was for dear, good Lehzen. The other was shed out of relief because at last the triangle was broken.

If her mother had publicly celebrated Lehzen's decision to retire, Victoria would not have been surprised. Though never open enemies they had been antagonistic to each other for years; and had it not been for the special protection given her by King William and the Duke of Sussex, Lehzen would have been packed off back to Germany long before. But the Duchess had mellowed. Her comfortable life at Frogmore House and Clarence House, and her opportunities for visiting relatives in Europe, made her more kindly disposed to people. This included Victoria and even, in some degree, Lehzen. Instead of crowing over Lehzen she did something which Victoria found very touching.

Many years before one of her Ladies-in-Waiting, a Madame Späth, had trod clumsily on delicate ground; that is, she had somehow interfered in the Duchess' private relationship with her Comptroller, and she had been summarily dismissed. Späth had been a great friend of Lehzen, and one of the few grown-ups to whom Victoria had taken a liking. Both had felt her dismissal keenly and had cried as much as she, when bewildered and sobbing she had gone off to live with Princess Feodore in Germany. Now the Duchess made an adequate apology and invited the old lady back into her service again. It would oblige her enormously, she said, if Madame Späth would consent to be her Lady-in-Waiting.

Lehzen appreciated this gesture. It could not be made to her, but the offer to Späth was the next best thing. And Victoria appreciated it as well. When Lehzen had gone, Madame Späth would be close at hand to talk over her nursery and schoolroom days at Kensington.

Beyond this barely anyone appeared to notice that a radical change was about to take place right at the centre of royal affairs. Perhaps, thought Victoria, people were being kind. She hoped so. The alternative, that they were actually indifferent, was painful to consider.

It was fortunate that during Lehzen's last weeks in England, when she was training Miss Skerrett to take her place, the Court was mostly away from Windsor. It was doubly fortunate, too, that the Queen made a progress in Scotland from one great house to the other, and fell in love with the country. The phrase accurately described her depth of feeling.

Itinerant agitators were stirring up the north country, and though a battalion of Guards had been sent up by train, the Queen was advised to skirt the unruly areas and travel by sea. She did, particularly regretting the decision when, in the second night out, head winds delayed them and made her sick. She and Albert remained all day on deck, lying on sofas, and longing for the end of the voyage. But her spirits returned two days later when Lord Adolphus FitzClarence commanded the royal yacht's anchor to be let go in the Firth of Forth, and from the moment she and Albert stepped ashore at Granton Pier her enthusiasm for Scotland was unbounded.

Edinburgh she found enchanting. She was pleased to hear it called 'the modern Athens'. Albert agreed. The Acropolis, in Periclean times, he said, could not have been finer. Scotland made Albert feel very much at home. The people, he told Victoria, looked like Germans, and many views and towns reminded him of places he had lived in or visited in Europe. With Albert happy, Victoria was happy. In her journal she recorded his successes in shooting grouse, blackcock, and capercailzie and deer, and mentioned how he cheerfully crawled on all fours and plodded up to his knees through bogs to get his stag. She recaptured her love of simple things: enjoying the sight of an old woman washing potatoes by a river, and drinking milk in a clean, cool dairy; and she took unbounded pleasure in everything which was essentially Scotch from examining the royal regalia to eating porridge and smoked haddock. She was especially delighted by the Royal Company of Archers, composed entirely of noblemen and gentlemen, by her Highland Guard in constant attendance with drawn claymores, and the nine pipers of Lord Breadalbane who played before and at all meals and whenever she went in or out of Taymouth Castle.

When she returned to England she was full of praise for her northern kingdom and wrote to Lord Melbourne saying how beautiful she had found the country, and how in the clan system there were fascinating historic remains of feudal times and institutions. He replied dryly from Brocket that it was as well for the monarchy that the clans were but historic remains, and that the only thing which detracted from Scotland was 'the very high opinion that the Scotch themselves entertain of it'. But Melbourne realized just as Peel realized that the Queen had done a great deal to restore cordial relations between the two peoples. It was little more than a hundred years since the arrogance of the MacDonalds and the savagery of Butcher Cumberland had made the battle of Culloden Moor a hateful memory to the Scotch. Now Cumberland's great-great-niece had wiped away some of the bitterness. Peel was quick to suggest that, in the event of her wishing to make royal visits north of the border, the Admiralty should provide a royal yacht driven by a screw. This would ensure a more comfortable voyage than the paddle steamer at present in use. Gratefully she accepted. She had every intention of returning to Scotland.

Madame Späth arrived from Germany. Once she was comfortably installed at Frogmore House Victoria invited her to take tea in the Castle. It was a special occasion, Lehzen's last day. She had handed in her keys and her bags were packed. The next afternoon she was sailing from Gravesend.

There were just the three of them and they were happy in one sense because neither Victoria nor Lehzen had seen Späth since the Coronation and there were messages from Feodore.

Späth appeared to be no older. Her round spectacled face had a rosy, ageless quality, and out of an inordinate fondness for dark grey she seldom wore any other colour. A glove or cuff, fichu or pocket handkerchief of a different colour would set it off but the permanent impression was grey, and, always appearing the same, she never looked older. And Späth's extravagant respect for royalty, which Lehzen well remembered, had in no way abated. Sitting in the presence of the Queen of England seemed to paralyse her. She could hardly manage her teacup, and contributed little to the conversation until talk of the days when Victoria had been a little girl in Kensington Palace gradually unfroze her and she began to relax. Soon her eyes were glistening behind her gold-rimmed spectacles. She was chuckling into her teacup, and capping each 'Do you recall?' with another memory of her own.

That was all any of them could manage – to recall the past.

Späth took her leave first, promising to be a faithful correspondent to Lehzen, and promising the Queen that from time to time, when the Duchess could spare her, she would propose herself for a visit. Victoria kissed her and said she would appreciate the kindness. She repeated, it really would be a kindness.

When she had gone Victoria and Lehzen both started talking at once, stopped, waited for each other to begin, and once more began at exactly the same moment. They laughed but Lehzen realized it showed how nervous they were, how, for the first time, they were actually uncomfortable in each other's company. Their talk was constrained. Now that Späth had gone neither wanted to go on talking about the past. Nor could they bear to mention the future. They discussed the most jejune matters until very sensibly Lehzen stood up to go.

Victoria kissed her. 'Until tomorrow,' she said softly, 'when we say goodbye.'

Victoria could not sleep that night. Albert guessing why could think of no way to comfort her. She turned restlessly from side to side, crying as quietly as she could so that Albert would not be disturbed; wondering how she could say goodbye to Lehzen, what words to use, how best to express her devotion and affection and gratitude.

When she got up the next morning, she was steeled for the pain of saying goodbye and giving Lehzen a last embrace. It was unnecessary. Knowing the distress it would cause them both, Lehzen had already gone, leaving a tender message of farewell.

Victoria read it through tear-filled eyes. 'Oh, Lehzen!' she sobbed. 'Oh, Lehzen!'

X

To begin with time dragged without Lehzen. Victoria felt her absence as realistically as if she had had a tooth pulled. There was a jagging emptiness and soreness to remind her constantly of what she had lost. She bitterly regretted the missed opportunities for being with her old friend. But then time accelerated, and her sense of loss was soothed by suddenly having a great deal to do.

The serious state of affairs at home, territorial squabbles with America, and the end of the wars in Afghanistan and China multiplied the number of dispatch boxes which followed her everywhere, and it was difficult to find time for anything else. But Albert persuaded her to read constitutional history with him, and he was for ever proposing small trips, and treats, and diverting her with surprises. Really he had never before been so thoughtful and considerate. When the Duke offered them the use of Walmer Castle, his official residence as Lord Warden of the Cinque Ports, Albert insisted that they accept. The change of air would do them all the greatest good, he said. Victoria found he was right and she would have thoroughly enjoyed her stay if she had not been so concerned about poor Lord M. who had had a paralytic seizure. But, again, time scuttled so quickly by that it seemed but a moment before he had recovered sufficiently to send her a bouquet of daphnes from the garden at Brocket, and soon afterwards he was enjoying a daily half pint of dry champagne and re-reading Cicero.

As Lehzen herself had predicted, she featured less and less in the Queen's thoughts as week chased week and month chased month.

Time brought its harvests. In fairly rapid succession she presented Albert with another daughter and another son. Alice and Alfred, neither very easily born, but both perfect, without a blemish, were given into the care of the excellent

Lady Lyttelton. Victoria had infinite confidence in the new nursery superintendent and was intrigued by the way she treated the children as small adults. Her own method of treating them, like animated dolls, made Lady Lyttelton frown. That was not the way, she scolded. Children were not toys. Although they were so little they could be cruel and jealous and vain and abject, and share almost all the emotions of grown-up people. Victoria also found herself being urged by Lady Lyttelton not to spoil the children. In that wise lady's opinion they were given far too many honours and dignities. What, she asked, was the point of making the Prince of Wales a governor of Christ's Hospital? And why had the Queen allowed a steel engraving to be published and sold entitled *The First Prayer of HRH Prince Albert Edward, Prince of Wales, Duke of Cornwall, etc, etc*? This showed the infant Prince lying on a cushion, surrounded by the emblems of sovereignty, and gazing into a blaze of light, while repeating the prayer: 'Oh Lord God Almighty, graciously condescend to hear my first prayer; may Old England, my beloved and noble country, be always powerful and happy.' This, said Lady Lyttelton severely, was improper. Victoria was quickly persuaded to agree though privately she thought the sentiment less offensive than the flattering portrait of her son and heir. It was easier and pleasanter to agree with Lady Lyttelton who had a formidable manner when defending her charges from the mistakes of their parents. How dearly she loved them, and how exceptionally reliable she was as a royal foster mother. Incomparable Lady Lyttelton.

When the Duke of Sussex fell mortally ill with erysipelas Victoria was very distressed. Since her marriage they had not always been friends but she would never forget how he had stood up for her in her dingy and isolated childhood. Now her uncle was dying and Victoria grieved.

He was nursed devotedly by the Duchess of Inverness and by his faithful page, Mr Blackman. To give the old man peace they removed his caged bullfinches and stopped all the clocks in his apartments, but this only agitated him and the birds were returned and the clocks started again. There he lay for a few days, growing weaker, saying little, feeding exclusively on turtle soup and orange sorbets, until he judged it was time to take formal leave of his household and servants. He could not complete the ceremony. As he struggled to say goodbye he died. Simultaneously his bullfinches were piping, all the timepieces in Kensington were chiming the hour, and his musical clocks were playing martial airs and the National Anthem.

Victoria had just been confined and though she sincerely mourned her uncle, the child helped her to accept his death philosophically. The Lord had given, the Lord had taken away. She was moved by his bequest to 'my dearest niece', and delighted that he had not overlooked Albert who became the owner of a macabre gold watch which had a miniature of Princess Charlotte's eyeball painted on the back. Nevertheless she was startled and a little put out by the Duke's direction that his corpse should be opened up and examined in the interests of scientific inquiry, and his remains afterwards buried in the public cemetery at Kensal Green. Kensal Green barely seemed a fitting burial place for a Prince of the Blood and a Knight of the Garter, and the Lord Chancellor, the Archbishop, the Prime Minister, and even the Duke of Wellington were consulted. The last said that not to bury the Duke at Windsor was a regrettable concession to radicalism but it could not be helped. And so Uncle Sussex was laid to rest in Kensal Green and a space reserved nearby for his morganatic wife.

Victoria sent her condolences. Had she not been lying-in she would have called on the Duchess of Inverness herself. As it was, Queen Adelaide went to Kensington on her behalf, and because the Duchess, though twice widowed, seemed to be singularly ignorant of what should be done, she helped her with practical matters. Amongst other things she had arrangements made for a sale of the Duke's library, and it never occurred to her to have the books examined first. As a result, one lucky gentleman who bought one of the Duke's annotated prayer books found himself the owner of a unique royal curio. Against the Athanasian Creed was a beautifully-drawn pointing hand and, in the Duke's familiar handwriting, a laconic note: *'I don't believe a word of it'*.

Victoria's distress at losing a good uncle seemed aggravated when Uncle Ernest behaved badly at Alice's christening. Though invited to be a sponsor, he deliberately arrived just too late for the ceremony, made no apology, and immediately put in a formal claim for those of Victoria's jewels which had belonged to his mother and sisters. Rudely he told her that England not having Salic law gave her a right to the crown, but it gave her no right to his diamonds.

Victoria had a natural gift for checking insolence. Her turn to quarter-profile and her look were generally sufficient to quell anyone. But her regal manner made not the slightest difference to the King of Hanover. Tall, gaunt, bald, with straggly white whiskers drawn over the sword gash on his cheek, he was equally regal, and he still tended to regard his niece as a chit of a princess and her husband as a paper royal highness. 'On her high horse, eh?' he said, quite loud enough for everyone at the christening to hear. 'As high as a horse can be, by God!'

He was so insistent in his demands that Victoria turned the matter of the jewels over to the Prime Minister and he appointed a commission of three to look into it. Uncle Ernest then took his seat in the House of Lords as Duke of Cumberland, used his apartments in St James's, visited old friends, and announced his intention of staying in England until the commission decided in his favour. Albert advised her to capitulate and hand over the jewels, but Victoria stubbornly refused to consider it. With her little jaw set firmly in Hanoverian pugnaciousness she said the jewels were hers and she was going to keep them.

Uncle Ernest made her pay for her obstinacy. He joined the Cambridges in their cabals against the Palace.

There had been a truce of sorts when the Duke of Cambridge sought and obtained Victoria's permission for his daughter Augusta to marry a prince of Mecklenburg-Strelitz, and the Court ban against the Cambridges had been withdrawn. But since then a salacious piece of tittle-tattle had rumoured that the Duke of Beaufort's daughter, Lady Augusta, was carrying a child, and rumour added that Prince George of Cambridge was the father. Unwisely Victoria had held her tongue. If she had spoken out and declared her faith in the young people's innocence, the weight of her opinion would have told. But she said nothing and the Duke of Beaufort and Lord Adolphus FitzClarence on behalf of Prince George, felt obliged to publish a denial in *The Times*. Understandably the Duchess of Cambridge was exceedingly cantankerous. She tried to force the Queen's hand by taking the maligned Lady Augusta on a visit to Court. In this way she hoped to demonstrate the young lady's virtue and her own son's innocence. Victoria was disobliging. Furious at being manoeuvred into a false position, she told her ladies to ignore Lady Augusta, and as soon as she decently could she intimated to her aunt that her suite of rooms was required for another guest. That evening the Duchess of Cambridge and Lady Augusta left the Court.

At Cambridge House members of the anti-Palace party put their heads together to study their revenge. At length they decided that Albert's precedence was the Queen's most vulnerable spot and the King of Hanover had consistently refused to give way. So far it had only aggravated the Queen in theory because her Uncle Ernest had avoided public functions where the issue might cause trouble. But now, he said, he was prepared and very happy to press his claim and assert in practice the rights of his rank. And where better than at a royal wedding, full in the public eye? Delightedly they set about preparing an announcement to be published in the London newspapers that the King of Hanover had accepted his brother's invitation to be a principal witness at the marriage of Princess Augusta of Cambridge in July.

'That,' said the Duchess in the greatest satisfaction, 'will torment her beyond description.'

It was a skilfully chosen revenge. Victoria was aghast when she saw the announcement. It had been understood that Uncle Ernest would return to Hanover before July as he had a strong distaste for weddings. Now that he was to be a principal witness she immediately realized the possibilities.

They made her terribly anxious, and as time passed her apprehension grew. When both she and Albert caught influenza a little time before the wedding she was almost thankful. But they recovered too soon.

The day arrived.

Enfeebled and worried and, in the July heat, feeling the weight of the clothes and jewels which such a ceremony required, Victoria began to panic when she found Uncle Ernest was next to her at the altar steps in Albert's place. How he had got there and what had happened to Albert she did not know, and tears of weakness filled her eyes at this public display of rudeness to her husband. But neither she nor Uncle Ernest had counted on Albert's dogged persistence. Finding himself edged out of his position he took the only course open to him and he forced his way back into it again. He realized it was unseemly to jostle Victoria's uncle off the altar steps, but he was determined and he managed it with the minimum of fuss. The King of Hanover, already replete with satisfaction at having gained his precedence before the altar, suddenly found himself treading on other people's feet and being trodden on. Angrily he planned that whatever happened he would keep next to the Queen when she was signing the register so that he could seize the pen from her and sign before Albert. But he was outwitted in this as well. He and the Cambridges hemmed the Queen in, cutting her off from Albert who was at the other side of the vestry table, and there was such a crush he could not get to her. With great presence of mind she made her way round the table to where he was. No one could bar the Queen's passage, and she had the register handed to her across the table and had signed it and passed the pen to Albert long before Uncle Ernest could find a way to get there himself.

Afterwards he was so disgruntled that he repeated his threat to stay in England until the commission had decided in his favour. But Victoria considered that he could not make much more of a nuisance of himself than he had already, and in any case she and Albert were planning to be away for some time on the trials of the new royal yacht. She wrote a letter to Sir Robert Peel about the work of the commission, and desired a copy to be sent to Uncle Ernest.

> *The Queen* [she wrote] *is desirous that whatever is right should be done, but is strongly of opinion that the King of Hanover's threat (for as such it must be regarded) not to leave this country till the affair is decided upon, should in NO WAY influence the transaction, as it is quite immaterial whether the King stays longer here or not.*

Affairs in Hanover persuaded Uncle Ernest at last to return to his kingdom. This he did in a great bad temper. In equally great relief Victoria and Albert began their sea voyages.

XI

Prince Albert's chief interest over a long period of time was in putting certain domestic reforms in hand. It was really a crusade against muddle, waste, inefficiency and sloth, and, armed with the Queen's *carte blanche*, he began correcting abuses with his customary thoroughness.

He quickly discovered that at the heart of the trouble lay the conflicting responsibilities of the Lord Chamberlain, the Lord Steward and the Master of the Horse. Each had a department and by tradition each department had certain privileges and duties in the household. The result was confusion; as when, for example, a fire was laid by a servant belonging to the Lord Steward but could only be lighted by a Lord Chamberlain's man. Albert came to the conclusion that one person only, a Master of the Household, ought to have complete authority over the inside of royal palaces.

And there was evidence of cupidity and waste which badly needed stopping. There were literally dozens of abuses, but three were grosser than the rest. Albert discovered that because Victoria's grandfather had once had a cold in the nose and at that time the burning of tallow candles was thought to be an efficacious cure, fifty pounds weight of them had been ordered each month. They were still being bought twenty-three years later, and the candles sold as a perquisite. Then there was a rule that wax candles were never to be lighted twice. Hundreds a day were therefore wasted and became another perquisite. And there was a dreadful state of affairs in the royal stables where there were so many unused horses that the head-stableman doubled his income by hiring them out as common hacks.

Equally reprehensible was the idleness and inefficiency of so many royal servants. Footmen failed to show guests to their rooms, and strangers wandered helplessly along badly-lighted corridors trying to find their way downstairs. Looking vainly for his own room, the French Foreign Secretary once entered the Queen's room while she was dressing. As bad was the inefficiency of royal carpenters and builders. They were notoriously lazy and their work makeshift. Simply to save the trouble of finding or constructing a down sewer, they actually attached a lavatory to a rain pipe at Buckingham Palace so that it emptied itself on the leads just outside the Queen's dressing-room window.

The Prince's crusade made him hearty enemies. At least ninety per cent of the royal servants were virulently opposed to his reforms because the old system had meant light work and rich perquisites. But he persevered, and was very encouraged to find that his one-time critics on the royal estates had become his staunchest supporters. They had begun to feel the benefits of his original improvements and now they were proud of him when he won a first at Smithfield with his prize pig, and took medals with the great royal bull, Fitz-Clarence. Now they were willing to fall in with his new-fangled ideas, even when he asked them to wash down the dairy cows once a week with mops and buckets of sweet disinfectant. The lodge keepers were even prepared to do something which, two years before, would have been unthinkable – walk proudly into Windsor in uniforms designed by the Prince: a green plush coat and waistcoat with brass buttons, black trousers and tall hat.

But, without doubt, the most potent and most constant of the Prince's supporters was the Queen. She gave whole-hearted approval to everything he did, and said publicly that had she been properly served before, the need for such reforms would never have arisen.

Albert was touched by her attitude. It moved him to approach his work from a different angle. He found himself working in order to please Victoria, doing something not for its own sake as in the past, but for hers. And nothing was too small for his attention if it could possibly please her. She had a hearty appetite and therefore her food became the subject of a detailed scrutiny. She was particularly fond of chicken, but Albert believed that with a certain amount of trouble and care a fairly ordinary table pleasure could be made into something much grander. And so he bred pens of splendid poultry for the royal table; eighteen different breeds altogether, including Silver-spangled Hamburghs, Black Minorcas and Andalusians. His care for her even went to the lengths of experimenting with the eggs of different breeds until he found the one she most preferred. Thereafter, for the rest of her life the eggs of White Dorkings always appeared on her breakfast table.

Sensible of Albert's attentiveness and of their very real closeness to one another, Victoria wanted him to share in every facet of her life. Gone and forgotten were the days when jealousy made her keep him ignorant of affairs of state. Now she depended on him to such an extent that he had considerable political power.

The Prince's admiration for Sir Robert Peel made the Queen change her mind about her new Prime Minister. She became less critical of his awkward manner and she tried to be more understanding and helpful when shyness made him appear off-hand and rigid. As a result Peel lost a good deal of his timidity: his whole attitude to his attendance on the Queen underwent a radical change. On taking office he had reverted to the habits of King William's ministers, writing letters and memoranda each day, and visiting the sovereign once a week. But soon he found himself so comfortable at

Court that he surprised his followers by the regularity of his attendance.

Patiently Peel continued the Queen's political training, acting on Melbourne's advice and reducing everything to its simplest terms; and he found her affectingly concerned about the welfare of her people. She wanted the poor fed and clothed and housed, and she was exceedingly angry when she discovered that their distress could not be relieved simply because agitators were demanding unacceptable political power on their behalf as well as bread. It seemed to her that the distressed had a wrong spokesman, villains who confused votes with loaves, and for this very reason she had not much sympathy with the bands of rioters in Wales who, dressed in women's clothes, demonstrated against toll gates and were known as 'Rebecca and her daughters'. 'Tolls!' she said, when she heard of the serious disturbances in Wales. 'Have they nothing more urgent to riot about? Their families' bread matters more than tolls.' Peel liked her naïvety and rather agreed with her. So did Lord Melbourne who confessed he was concerned at the lawlessness being worked up by radicals.

When such things begin [he wrote] *nobody can say how far they will go or how much they will spread. There are many who expect and predict a general rising against property.*

The Prime Minister did not mind that Melbourne still wrote to the Queen. Stockmar had finally tried to silence the old man with an enormous, carefully-reasoned memorandum, and had received a three-line acknowledgement, and nothing else, for his pains. But to Peel's mind there could be no harm in the correspondence provided that the Queen showed him Melbourne's important letters, and this she did. Moreover, it was becoming obvious, even to the Queen, that Melbourne had never fully recovered from his stroke. Quite often he repeated himself, and he imagined things – that he was very poor, for instance, a conviction which drove him to ask her for a loan – and that he was no longer wanted at Court, a conviction which made him write pathetic, scolding letters. Victoria bore it patiently. She owed him a great deal. And she wrote to him as regularly as she could. But politically she depended entirely on her new Prime Minister.

Peel led her through the intricate paths of reform and anti-reform; of free trade and protection; and she grew very fond of him indeed. Therefore she was horror-struck when, in mistake for Peel, his secretary was murdered in Whitehall by a lunatic Scotsman named Macnaughton. Though the assassin was mad, his reasons were political. Victoria was appalled, and deeply thankful that Sir Robert had been spared to guide the country in such lawless times.

Both Victoria and Albert were anxious to be of service in any way they could. Peel emphasized the importance of maintaining stability. By going about their ordinary duties in a calm and purposeful way their example would do much to steady the country.

The royal routine was generally tedious, and holding drawing-rooms and levées and making official visits consumed an enormous amount of time. But there was a satisfaction in feeling their work was useful, and quite often unexpected compensations enlivened the round of duty. In France, for example, when they paid a state visit of notable diplomatic importance, Victoria's chief recollection was of a basket of cakes. It was sent by an admirer for the Queen of England and, as she happened to be sitting on the deck of the royal yacht when the special messenger arrived, she said she would take the basket herself. The messenger looked doubtful. They were cakes for the Queen, he told her, and obviously he was very reluctant to hand them over to someone who, from her drab gown, bonnet and shawl, might well have been the ship's laundress. Before he would part with the basket he instructed her to take great care of the cakes, not to eat them, nor squash them, but see that they reached the Queen. This sort of thing delighted her. So did the romantic behaviour of Trinity undergraduates when she and Albert went to Cambridge to exercise her prerogative of using the Master's Lodge as a royal palace. The young gentlemen emulated Sir Walter Raleigh and made a path of their gowns for her right across the Great Court. Then there was the gala day when she drove in state through London to open the new Royal Exchange. Many people recalled it because though it was an October day the weather was bland. Others remembered it as one of the finest pieces of pageantry ever seen in the city. A few gourmets never forgot it because the vintners had surpassed themselves at the banquet, and the livery cooks produced a notable dish of salsify and pike. Victoria and Albert remembered it because of the Lord Mayor's boots. Because of mud underfoot he wore jackboots over his dress pumps while waiting for the procession at Temple Bar. As the glass coach approached carrying the Queen and the Prince, he quickly began to remove them. One came off. The other obstinately refused. Furred aldermen, mace bearers, even the chaplain tugged at his jackboot without success while the Lord Mayor hopped on one leg. In the end he was obliged to replace the other over his pump; and jackbooted like a bandit he joined the royal procession and presided at the banquet.

Victoria was more worried than pleased by the necessity to entertain foreign monarchs.

Nicholas the First, Autocrat of all the Russias, was her most unprepossessing guest. He proposed himself for a visit in a June so dry that the grass at Windsor had turned brown and only two months before she was due to be confined. Feeling very huge and very hot, Victoria was in no mood to entertain anyone. Moreover because of his ruthlessness with the Poles she felt certain he would be assassinated on his visit, an event which would have deplorable political consequences but which privately she would not have minded a great deal. On the Tsar's arrival he sent to the stables for a truss of straw on which to sleep, and with the effrontery of an Italian he ogled her ladies all of whom knew that in Poland he had had women knouted and that he had handed over a convent of fifty nuns to the caprices of his wild Cossacks. The Duke was called in to help entertain him, but in some ways it was a mistake. He was growing deafer and

139

deafer and could not make much of a conversation with strangers. At a military review the artillery blundered and, though instructed not to fire until the Queen had left the ground, for she could not abide salutes, they advanced and fired not very far from her. This resulted in the Duke making an exhibition of himself. He was livid with anger. The Queen, the Prince, even the Russian Autocrat all tried to appease him at the top of their voices, but he paid no attention at all. 'By God! By God! By God!' he raged. 'They shall go to the rear, damn it. Damn it! They shall.' He as good as told the Tsar not to interfere with English military affairs, summoned up the trumpeter and had him order the artillery into a position of disgrace at the rear. That evening he had recovered his temper and found himself sitting opposite the Tsar at dinner. Lady Lyttelton was beside him and, to her great embarrassment, he began talking about the royal visitor in the penetrating voice of the deaf. 'Very good-looking man that,' he shouted in her ear as though he had never seen the Tsar before in his life. She managed to make him realize who it was. This irritated the Duke and he pretended to have known all along. 'Always was so,' he bawled, pointedly. 'Scarcely altered since I last saw him. Rather browner. No other change. Very handsome man now. Don't you think so?' Poor Lady Lyttelton. With the Tsar's wild eyes not five feet from hers she was obliged to scream into the old Duke's ears: 'Yes, very handsome indeed!' In fact the eyes made her shudder, as they did the Queen; and both were paralysed with fright when he bounced the Prince of Wales up and down and persuaded Vicky to kiss him. At his departure everyone was vastly relieved. His stern, melancholy look, and his smile which Victoria said was more bloodcurdling than the worst sort of frown, had been very offensive.

Another royal guest, the King of Saxony, was altogether different; quiet, unassuming and eager to please his hostess. Victoria found him charming. But she was less enthusiastic about a visit from Louis-Philippe who invited himself to Windsor as soon as he knew his enemy the Tsar had been there. By the request of his daughter, the King of the French had to be denied a reasonable breakfast and given a horse-hair mattress on a plank of wood in lieu of a proper bed. These mortifications were not so much for the good of his soul as to prevent him from gormandizing and doing himself some sort of physical mischief. Moreover, because of the incompetence of his secretaries, Victoria found herself rewriting her own guest's English speeches of thanks.

Official visitors were too grave a responsibility and too taxing altogether. Victoria and Albert far preferred entertaining their own chosen guests, cousins from Coburg, the Queen's half-sister Feodore and her husband, Felix Mendelssohn, Aunt Gloucester, a group of Red Indians who arrived over Christmastide wearing beads and full war paint, and, when she was not junketing in Paris or in Switzerland travelling incognito as the Countess of Dublin, Victoria's mother with dear Madame Späth.

Victoria also gathered fond memories of their own visits to private houses: vignettes, which faded into a glittering background of display and comfort.

She saw herself at Sir Robert Peel's, dressing by candlelight for dinner, wearing the pink silk gown with three flounces which became Albert's favourite.

At Chatsworth there was the Grand Banqueting Hall prepared for a ball; outside the windows, shrubberies, coverts and waterworks brightly illuminated. Yet at breakfast the same scene bore no signs of the festivities. Two hundred men under Paxton the head gardener had worked hard and silently in the dark to clear everything away. And at Chatsworth, too, she saw Albert in the lily house designed by Paxton for the great Amazon water lily. They had their heads close together, the Prince and the gardener, as they examined the structure of the lily-leaf. There was talk of horizontal and vertical thrust, and stresses; and Paxton demonstrated the strength of the six-foot leaves which surfaced the pool like papier mâché tea-trays. He put a criss-cross of wood on a leaf to spread the load and then triumphantly lifted his daughter Anne on to it.

There was a picture of the whole house party at Belvoir

receiving Albert in from the hunting field. He had distinguished himself by his gallant riding. They crowded round congratulating him; the Duke, the Palmerstons, dear old Lord M.; so many people.

At Burghley there was the memory of Lord Exeter's stupefaction when he was showing the royal party round his house and threw open the door of one of the most historic rooms to reveal an elderly and hairless cousin carefully dressing his wig and whiskers on a chestnut block.

True to her promise, Victoria returned to Scotland as the guest of Lord Glenlyon, and she filled her journal with affectionate descriptions of all she had seen and all she had done. But the vignette that stayed in her memory was of Vicky eating broth in an inn parlour at Dunkeld. The child was away from the nursery and travelling with her parents for the first time, and she behaved beautifully. When the townspeople outside called for a sight of her, without any prompting she put down her spoon, walked to the window, bowed to her mother's subjects, and returned to the broth.

The Duke of Buckingham's place at Stowe was too Augustan for Victoria's taste. Palladian temples, prospects gazebos and lakes were soon forgotten. There remained the picture of a young Jewish gentleman talking in the Grand Saloon. He wore the brightest of clothes, the most sparkling of rings, had long oiled curls, and spoke far too much for a young man. Yet her first sight of Benjamin Disraeli was the one she remembered as an old woman.

Stratfield Saye, the property given by a grateful nation to the Duke of Wellington, was a remarkable place. It was the warmest house Victoria had ever stayed in. She recalled visiting a boiler room where the Duke proudly showed her his new apparatus for heating by tanks of hot water. It was a dark, gritty place, uncomfortably hot, and the Duke's loud voice echoed louder as he bellowed instructions to his gardener-boilerman. His deafness was aggravating because Albert had a naturally low voice and the strain of shouting in the Duke's ear began to tell; but no host could have been more attentive. At luncheon he served them a jumble of puddings and tarts with his own hands, and each evening solemnly lit the Queen to bed by walking before her with a branched candlestick. When she confided in him that they were thinking of making a private visit to Coburg that summer he at once had his librarian look out maps of Europe. Nothing could persuade him that the journey would not be in the least difficult. He insisted on showing them a travelling sleeping bag he himself had invented to defeat the vermin of European posting inns. It was made of silk because in his opinion fleas and bugs found this a difficult material to penetrate, and was of a light colour so that their number and disposition could be seen at a glance.

Visits to other people's homes increased their desire for a country house of their own, and they were overjoyed when, after their visit to Stratfield Saye, Sir Robert announced that he had been able to buy a property on their behalf on the Isle of Wight. Victoria liked the island, it had memories for her of her childhood. Albert enjoyed sea-bathing and boating, and considered the property an excellent place in which to bring up children. He began designing their new home at once. It was called Osborne House.

XII

Victoria was superstitious. On the actual day they planned to leave for the continent a disaster took place. She was proroguing Parliament in person and the Duke of Argyll, who carried the crown on a cushion, missed two steps as he backed from the throne and landed painfully on the floor. The crown bounced and bounced, clattered like a spinning trencher and came to a rest at the foot of the throne. Some of its jewels had been jerked from their settings. The Queen begged the Duke not to be distressed and yet she was horrified. Afterwards she told Albert their journey would have to be postponed by a day. He laughed until he saw that she meant it, and then he was incredulous. To pay superstitious attention to omens was nonsense, irreligious and unscientific. Still protesting vigorously, Victoria found herself boarding the royal yacht which sailed for Antwerp at the scheduled time. She really was concerned by this accident to the crown and any political crisis or upset in the following twelve months she tended to attribute to the accident; but secretly she enjoyed Albert being masterful. It was the proper thing, and made her proud of him.

He was masterful for most of the journey. Uncle Leopold and Aunt Louise joined them for the holiday, but Albert remained in charge of everything. When they were met by the Crown Prince of Prussia and afterwards by his father the King, it was Albert who greeted them aboard the royal train. Then at Friedrichsthal when an equerry reported that a Baroness Lehzen had come to greet them, Victoria immediately looked to Albert to see if he favoured the plan. He considered for what seemed a long time and then said yes, the Baroness might be admitted.

It was a sad little meeting. Lehzen, trying to be brave, said hardly anything. Victoria was concerned to see how old she appeared, and how drab; how very different from the pert, sparrow-like figure in violet bombazine who had played such a large part in her life. Albert did not withdraw, as both expected him to. Instead he made pleasantries and talked of the growing children until the train was signalled to proceed. Then he nodded to Anson to open the carriage door. Lehzen and Victoria embraced. How small she is, thought the Queen. The Prince bowed and Lehzen curtseyed. Anson, in helping her to the platform, managed to squeeze her arm. Why he did it he did not know. Nor did Lehzen. But both found it comforting. There was a lingering scent of caraway in the carriage until the Prince declared it was stuffy and threw open a window.

The Queen was silent for a time, but not for long. That part of her life was over, and Lehzen was being well cared for by her sister. Or was it the other way about? She realized, guiltily, that she had not asked after the sister at all; nor even after Lehzen's own health.

The Prince gave her a glass of Apollinaris water. It was lightly flavoured with whisky, a spirit she had tried and grown fond of in Scotland. He kept her from brooding by speculating as to why the burghers of Cologne had sprinkled eau-de-cologne before their royal carriage. Had it been an advertisement, or was it to hide the city's notoriously faulty drainage system? In this way he put that sad little meeting with Lehzen to where he considered it properly belonged, to the back of Victoria's mind.

Victoria much enjoyed the journey through Germany, although she was offended when on a roundabout way through Prussia, and merely because Albert had been given no title or precedence by the English, he was placed at some distance from her at a state banquet.

Coburg delighted her. She thought the little duchy fascinating and the welcome they were given was kind beyond belief, but unfortunately, no less than sixty-one relatives had gathered there to greet her. She found it a little too much and, being less patient than usual, she made the mistake of criticizing some of them to Albert. There was the King of Bavaria, for instance, who had the objectionable habit of talking to people with his eyes tightly shut. Immediately Albert was on the defensive. 'If,' said he, 'we are reduced to being personal about Coburg friends and relatives, may I say that they compare very favourably with the house of Hanover.' He began to count them off on his fingers: 'There is the King of Hanover, Princess Sophia, your aunt and uncle of Cambridge . . .' She stopped him with a little shriek. What he said was a reflection on her dear, dear father. Edward of Kent, he replied, had been as bad as any of them. The quarrel enlarged a little more; then blew cold, and ended in tears of reconciliation.

Almost everything about Albert's old home and his family pleased Victoria, but one event threatened to spoil the whole of her holiday. Unfortunately, as it had been specially arranged in her honour, she could neither criticize nor avoid it. Ordinarily she was not squeamish. Without any trouble

145

she could watch the gralloching of a deer or a fox being rent by hounds. But the Coburg *battue* of driven deer was a different matter.

It was held on the edge of the huge Thüringian forest. Victoria sat with the other ladies in a temporary pavilion decorated with flowers while deer were driven into a fenced enclosure by beaters dressed in white. When the best part of fifty deer had been driven into the enclosure, they were gated in and Albert and the other guns shot the trapped beasts down.

Victoria sat with clenched hands, her knuckles white, staring straight ahead while the dead and dying deer had their throats cut at her very feet. It occurred to her that the *battue* had more in common with the Roman circus than with deer-stalking as she knew it in Scotland – for, throughout the whole performance, a Pomeranian band, in scarlet uniforms and large whiskers, played lively polkas one after the other.

She felt very ashamed when, on their return home to England, she found the story in the English papers. Generally she was impatient with reporters and journalists and held some, like Mr Judge, in great contempt; but, in justice, nothing could be said or done to condemn or contradict what her people said about that afternoon of butchery. A newish weekly, called *Punch*, published a satire which made her hang her head.

Sing a song of Gotha – a pocketful of rye,
Eight-and-forty timid deer driven in to die;
When the sport was open'd, all bleeding they were seen,
Wasn't that a dainty dish to set before a Queen!

146

XIII

The Queen had thoroughly understood when the Prime Minister came to her and said he had been persuaded to change his mind about free trade so far as corn was concerned.

Her people in Ireland were starving. Politically the country had been a festering sore for years, and she was not lightly disposed to give sympathy to people who affected to take in sedition with their mother's milk, but the failure of potato crops, the literal starvation of hundreds of thousands of her people, affected her profoundly.

With a woman's instinct she cared not a pin for laying blame. Food was the important thing, and it incensed her that so much energy was spent in hunting for scapegoats. While some found fault with the fiscal policies of the government, and others with the bleeding of Ireland by absentee landlords, and others with the indifference of a Protestant ascendancy to a Catholic peasantry, and others with the gombeen men, and others with the priests, and others with the improvidence, stupidity and ineptitude of the Irish, and others with the greed and malice of the English, her people were dying and being driven to emigration.

She asked why Ireland could not be given a temporary dictator to deal with the problem. There was the Duke – an Irishman himself, a superb leader, strategist, and administrator. But Peel would not hear of it. Constitutionally it was impossible. Nor would the Duke agree. The Irish, he bellowed at her, were a very different kettle of fish from the Greeks and Romans who chose to subject themselves to such leaders as Solon and Cincinnatus. Show them a dictator and they'd fight like the devil. Either that or despair. 'It's the way of the Irish, Ma'am. They fight or they despair. Out of the question, Ma'am. Never do at all.'

It had proved absolutely indispensable to open British

ports to foreign grain, and Peel had done it despite Whig taunts that he had changed his policy. He learnt from it. Whenever he had had to relax the sacred protectionist policies, the measures had been successful. Eventually he had announced his determination to abolish permanently the duty on imported corn.

His cabinet, all save Lord Stanley who was a diehard protectionist, stayed with him. So did the Queen. But he was placed in an impossibly difficult position. The diehards, and in particular wasp-tongued Disraeli, were ranged against him. As soon as his Corn Importation Act had been pushed by the Whigs and his own followers through Parliament, the diehards crippled his government. On a small bill he was defeated and forced to resign.

Victoria was tearful. Less than a month before this Princess Helena had been born – a child conceived in the mock medieval palace of Rosenau set in green German meadows and surrounded by the nests of storks – and she was suffering from the usual bout of lowness after her lying-in. Albert who by now had learnt each facet of this kind of depression, and could judge to a nicety when and how to give her bad news, told her of Peel's fall from power.

Considering the circumstances, she took it very well, but she bewailed the fact that no sooner had she grown to know and admire a minister than the absurd processes of party politics removed him.

Temporarily she brightened at the thought of Lord Melbourne returning to office, but it was made clear to her that the Whigs would not accept his leadership any longer. And on talking the matter over with Albert she was bound to agree. Poor Lord Melbourne could hardly manage to look after himself, let alone Great Britain. At once she wrote him a soothing letter and was glad she had done so when she received his reply.

He intimated that during the political crisis he had sat at Brocket waiting to be sent for. She could imagine his nervous expectation as he looked out from his library windows searching for any sign of a courier; a royal estafette in the Queen's livery, or messengers from his fellow Whigs.

To do this for days and see nothing, nothing at all, must have made him feel entirely unwanted and old even beyond his years. But bravely he hid his hurt and his disappointment by pretending that he had decided, in any case, that his health would prevent him serving her. She had sent a warm invitation for him to propose himself for a visit. He thanked her. This would please him a great deal. But even this acceptance was touched with pathos. He so looked forward to seeing her, he wrote, though his frailty made him dread the weight of Court dress.

She cried over his letter, and even more when she heard that Sir Robert had been invited to write to Prince Albert from time to time. It was ironic after all the moral indignation worked up about Lord Melbourne's letters to her.

Lord John Russell became her First Minister and she found him disconcerting because he was bald, had massive whiskers, and was so very small. She was tiny herself, and Prince Albert was not much taller, but, secretly, her confidence was most easily given to tall men. She disliked Lord John's bigotry in Church affairs for he was a stern Evangelical, and she was dismayed by his devotion to party politics. She considered that doctrinaire squabbles were all very well for backbenchers but in her ministers she required a breadth of vision which put the country first. Lord Melbourne had been quasi-Tory; Sir Robert, quasi-Whig; but Lord John was the Whiggiest of all Whigs.

She tested him out. 'Is it true, Lord John,' she asked, 'that you hold a subject is justified in certain circumstances in disobeying his sovereign?'

His reply was cryptic. 'Speaking to a sovereign of the House of Hanover, Ma'am, I can only say that I suppose it is.'

She screwed up her eyes and sighed. She thought she knew what he meant, and she thought he had been rather impolite. But, sensibly, she did not take offence. Instead she made it clear to him that in her experience she and the Prince could best serve the state in two ways. The first had been Peel's recommendation, though, of course, she did not say so. They considered it their special duty to steady the country by showing imperturbability and going about their ordinary duties in a calm and purposeful manner. The second, which was the Prince's idea, though again she did not say so, was equally important. Owing to their unique position as relatives by blood and marriage to so many European sovereigns, they would continue to hold a general supervision over foreign affairs.

'The last Foreign Secretary, dear Lord Aberdeen, agreed that our splendid opportunities should not be wasted,' she told him.

Lord John did not argue. The thought of these two young people, prompted by their Merlin, Baron Stockmar, poking their fingers into the foreign policies of Great Britain and Ireland was offensive to his Whig soul. But he did not need to say so. His Foreign Secretary Lord Palmerston was quite capable of dealing with their notions of family diplomacy.

Initially the Queen was pleased that Lord Palmerston had returned to office. As Lord M.'s brother-in-law he was very welcome and, secretly, she was fascinated by the stories of his gallantries. He still managed to look youthful, and he still had the same forthrightness and bounce and love of freedom. Little did she realize how provoking he was to be in the very near future. As for Albert, he was made very uneasy by Cupid's return to the Foreign Office. He had not forgotten his unscrupulous eighteenth-century way of going about things, and he disapproved profoundly of his puckish lack of respect for authority. He foresaw the storms ahead from the moment Palmerston bounced into the audience chamber to kiss hands on his appointment; his baby face wreathed in smiles, his hair and whiskers dyed redder than ever, his waistcoat more gorgeous. With a sinking heart he realized that here was the *enfant terrible* of the new ministry, and within a few days he was proved right.

As the young Queen of Spain was growing older her marriage had been at the centre of high international diplomacy for some time. Both Albert and Victoria enjoyed matchmaking and at a family level had done all they could to promote the suit of England's candidate, Prince Leopold of Saxe-Coburg. His chief rival was the Duc de Montpensier, a son of Louis-Philippe; and quite recently the Spanish marriage had been thrashed out personally by Victoria and Louis-Philippe with their Foreign Ministers in attendance. They had reached a deadlock. Neither could or would give way because of the balance of power, and there being no alternative, each country had agreed to withdraw its candidate. Now Palmerston had returned to the Foreign Office, and far from honouring the agreement, and without a word to anyone, he sent off a meddling dispatch to Madrid which included Prince Leopold's name amongst the list of candidates.

Louis-Philippe immediately declared that England had gone back on her word and he made plans to the advantage of his country. As it turned out they were frustrated by events but Victoria could not look into the future. She and Albert were exceedingly angry with France. In some degree this tempered their displeasure with Palmerston for his impossible meddling, but they still made their feelings plain. He tried without success to justify his action, and made Victoria's eyes open wide when he suggested that the end result had really been a kindness to the Queen of Spain. International rumour had it she so hungered for marriage that an heir would arrive before a husband unless the powers moved quickly.

Within six months he had managed to provoke the royal wrath again. Portugal was on the brink of civil war between the Junta, a group who wanted constitutional government, and their obstinate, reactionary Queen.

As Victoria wrote to Lord John Russell, *the Sovereigns of that country are her near and dear relations*', and, with the government's approval, Albert sent an equerry with a private family message urging them to concede terms and negotiate. It might well have been successful but for Palmerston's interference. All this time he was urging the English diplomats in Lisbon to show sympathy with the Junta.

Happily civil war was averted by a conference of the Powers in London, but this in no way mitigated Victoria's exasperation with her Foreign Secretary. Nor was it lessened when in defence of his opinions he wrote her a succinct description of the Court of her near and dear relations:

The Court is guided, I might almost say governed, by a pedantic and bigoted tutor, by a furious political Portuguese Fanatic, by a newspaper Editor, a vulgar man suddenly raised to power and full of low resentments, and by a gambling, drinking, unscrupulous Priest.

To relieve her feelings Victoria slowly dictated to Miss Skerrett her own private views of Lord Palmerston. The new confidential secretary's pen scratched and scratched. But this only gave Victoria passing relief. The memorandum had to be thrown away. It could never be used or seen by anyone. And such an ebullient, apparently impervious man as Lord Palmerston would cause trouble and vexations as long as the Whigs were in power. From that time she and Albert called him Pilgerstein. It was a simple German adaption of his name, but it seemed to suit him perfectly. Pilgerstein the bumptious. Pilgerstein the braggart. Headstrong, pugnacious Pilgerstein, Secretary of State for Foreign Affairs.

XIV

It was comforting to escape from international politics to those of the University of Cambridge. Not that they were a great deal less heated; but they made less noise.

Prince Albert had made an excellent impression on the occasion of their first visit to the university and now he was to be elected Chancellor. That, at any rate, was how Victoria viewed the events; and, as a consequence, she was startled to discover he had an opponent. It was hardly seemly, she thought, that the Queen's consort should be voted for or not voted for like any other man. Albert agreed with her, and refused to stand; but the Vice-Chancellor and by far the majority of the Heads of Houses were with him, and they persuaded him to change his mind. The other candidate was Lord Powis, a strong Tory and strong churchman. Unlike Oxford, where the recent election of a Professor of Poetry had developed into an internecine contest between High Church and Low, religion had very little to do with the election of a Cambridge Chancellor. But it did have something. The Prince was known to be forward-looking, scientific, a lover of crafts, and there was a hint, no more, that he was inclined to tolerate all Christian religions except, of course, the Roman Catholic. Country clergymen who detested Protestant dissenters even more than the Pope of Rome, would only vote for a sound Church of England candidate. But the country clergy and their squire cousins could not muster the following of a progressive candidate. Though Lord Powis ran special trains to Cambridge for his supporters, he lost the election by eighty votes. The total poll of 1791 votes showed how close a thing it had been. The Queen noted in her journal that 'all the cleverest men were among those on my beloved Albert's side', and was forced for a moment to concede her gratitude that Pilgerstein had voted for him too.

There was a preliminary installation ceremony at Buckingham Palace which she thought it prudent not to attend. She was right. Drawn from their learned courts, the reverend gentlemen who governed the university were unused to entertainments in royal palaces. The Master of Sidney Sussex drank a great deal of cold punch and turtle soup, and, gorged to stupefaction, had to be carried from the dining-room. Afterwards, the Master of Caius refused the proffered claret or sherry and in stentorian tones demanded port. It appeared he spoke for all. Once it was on the table and, to the Prince's amazement, tried and pronounced excellent, it began its round as solemnly as a liturgical function. In a desultory discussion which followed, he mentioned his work as Chancellor. It seemed a pity, he remarked, that the curriculum was confined to mathematics and classics. Ought not modern languages to be represented? And the history of art and aesthetics? Immediately there was an icy silence. Uncomfortably he tried to continue. 'And there is geography,' he said, and stopped.

'Geography!' repeated one of them, as though it was an obscene or blasphemous word. 'Bah!'

Alarmed by this experience Albert was not very enthusiastic about going up to Cambridge for the official installation, but his Private Secretary persuaded him that all would be well. Academic oligarchs, said Anson, showed better in their proper environment of dark combination rooms and dusty sets of rooms.

The occasion was to be made a royal visit by the Queen as well as the installation of the Prince as head of the university and the colleges prepared themselves with slow but adequate thoroughness.

Miss Skerrett, as royal ambassador to art and letters, went ahead with a few other officials of the Royal Household. The Master's Lodge at Trinity was dusted out, refurnished, and filled with flowers. She thoroughly enjoyed herself, walking with her page all over the college, prying into the kitchens as well as the libraries. Porters with centuries of tradition behind them which forbade the entry of women to certain places, watched helplessly. They feared that she would tread on the shaven lawns in the Great Court where only the Master and Fellows had a right to walk. She did. And they had a great dread that she would penetrate unasked into the chapel for morning prayer, sit in an impossible place, and then refuse to move when asked. She did all these things. But though she threw the porters into dismay, Miss Skerrett was very much admired by everyone else. She was the toast of the undergraduates who liked her independent spirit, and two middle-aged dons found their hearts fluttering in a way they hadn't for twenty years. Even the Master, vexed because he had to turn out of his Lodge, was pacified by her wonderful tact.

To all intents and purposes by the time the royal party arrived from the station Miss Skerrett had taken over Trinity, but when she saw the Queen descend from the carriage she wished that, after all, she had been allowed to remain at home to advise her mistress on her wardrobe. Without Skerrett there to act as a brake the Queen's doubtful taste in clothes was allowed too much licence. And there she was, about to be formally greeted by the university, dressed in a medley of predominant colours – black, white, amber, lilac, green, and radish red.

But Miss Skerrett had little time to grieve. The Queen and her ladies and gentlemen in attendance were led directly to the Great Hall while the Prince was taken aside, and dressed in a heavy black and gold gown with a train. He then led an enormous throng of dons into the Hall to welcome the Queen, where he read out a prepared speech.

Both maintained the solemn face which was necessary for the occasion, though the Queen found it difficult. She found it more difficult still when the Heads of Houses came forward to kiss her hand and then back away, for it was obvious no one had advised them to practise. Tall and gaunt or round and chubby, bewigged and heavily whiskered, and all encoiled in cassocks, gowns, scarves and academic hoods, they made a terrible spectacle of themselves; one tugging on the Queen's hand to lever himself upright again; another kissing her with such wet lips that it felt as if a slug had been laid across her fingers; another so nervous and trembling that his spectacles slipped from his nose and he had to grovel at the Queen's feet picking them up; another with a large walking-stick which, to get rid of while he knelt, he simply gave to the Queen to hold. As for backing away, wound up as they were in black and crimson cloth, and not having rehearsed this unusual mode of locomotion, not one of them managed it with the skill of their royal Chancellor. Though he had a train and two bearers, he backed away with elegance. The others were in confusion. One walked crab-wise. Two stumbled and had to be helped up. Another fell off the edge of the dais, fortunately into the arms of Trinity undergraduates. Yet another stared at the Queen with fixed, glassy eyes and retired backwards stamping his feet like an infantryman on parade. Seeing their fate, the last few very sensibly decided to make only a token. They backed for two steps or more then turned. How Victoria kept a straight face she did not know. Those of the old gentlemen who did not make her want to smile made her want to grimace, but throughout she maintained an even and calm composure.

Afterwards in her dressing-room at the Master's Lodge, she was gratified to find Skerrett so much in command and at home. It made everything easier and more comfortable.

'Dear Skerrett,' she said, immediately and thankfully accepting a cup of tea. 'I have rather dreaded this man's world, and your welcome has made a great deal of difference.'

Skerrett took her bonnet and travelling shawl, and rang for the tiring-maid to help the Queen change. A less startlingly indiscreet dress was looked out, approved of by Miss Skerrett. Then the Queen's hair was combed.

The tea, the combing, a touch of Portugal water at her temples, and a comfortable chair soothed away the strain of being formally received by the oligarchs of Cambridge and the tiredness of her journey.

'Mr Hudson travelled with me from Tottenham,' the Queen told Skerrett. 'Such a big man. So confident. Which is barely surprising. The Prince mentioned that a whole railway carriage, perhaps two, would hardly be sufficient to carry his private fortune. It seems scarcely credible that anyone could be so rich.'

Being the daughter of a West Indian nabob Miss Skerrett did not really care for industrial *nouveaux riches* – of whom Hudson, the railway king as he was called, was supreme and chief.

'Surely, Ma'am, he did not travel in your own carriage.'

'Skerrett!' Victoria's eyes opened wide in amazement. 'How could you think, even think such a thing? Now that the manufacturing people have been given a certain position, the Prince thinks it right to be agreeable to new men. The prosperity of the country, he says, lies in their hands. And so Mr Hudson was presented before we left Tottenham, and we saw him directing his railwaymen at various halts on the line. But where he travelled I have not the least idea.'

Her tone told Skerrett that had Hudson travelled on the

footplate it would have neither surprised nor interested the Queen.

They began to speak of the events which would take place on the following day. Her reception had made the Queen nervous. She feared there might be a repetition of the scene in the Great Hall.

As it turned out all passed well enough. The Senate House where Prince Albert was installed was packed to capacity. The July day was warm. Never before had Victoria felt so crowded in, so distinctly oppressed by the heat and the dust and the stuffiness. But the ceremony was not overlong and she was truly proud of her husband. No robes or uniform suited him better than academic dress; it became his wisdom and his years, his status as a husband and father. The sight of him standing there, Chancellor of the University, while a choir sang an ode in his honour was worth all the discomfort of the Senate House.

The new Chancellor was reminded of his family's concern for the Protestant cause:

> Albert, in thy race we cherish
> A nation's strength, that will not finish
> While England's sceptred line
> True to the King of kings is found . . .

A touching, fine sentiment, thought the Queen; recalling that one of Albert's forefathers had been called 'Praying Ernest'. There was also a pretty compliment to her:

> Resound, resound the strain
> That hails him for your own!
> Again, again and yet again,
> For the Church, the State, the Throne!
> And that Presence fair and bright,
> Ever blest wherever seen,
> Who deigns to grace our festal rite,
> The Pride of the Island, Victoria the Queen.

As the music died away, Victoria had tears in her eyes.

*   *   *

157

After the ceremony there was a reception and a banquet.

Considering he could have no better advice, Albert outlined the plan for the education of the Prince of Wales and asked for the counsel of the Heads of Houses seated closest to him. He and Stockmar had laboured on it for days, and its curriculum contained the essence of everything they thought the boy needed to know. The dons eyed one another. Such an elaborate scheme might have been appropriate for a royal genius and from all Prince Albert was saying, his son was something of a dolt. Nevertheless it was better to talk of the rearing of a five-year-old than discuss in public that other subject close to their new Chancellor's heart, university reform.

The Queen gave half an ear to what was being said and dearly wished that little Bertie was not so stupid and that he would try harder to please his father. Half the time he was being obstinate; the other half dreamy, and when dreamy he wore a vacant expression which irritated Albert beyond description. For a moment she listened to the Provost of King's rumbling on about intellectual disciplines and seizing the bones of a subject, but she seriously doubted if great scholars knew much about the education of little boys. Lady Lyttelton knew more than any of them.

Her appetite had been blunted by the press and the heat in the Senate House. She refused three courses, played with her rings under the tablecloth, and kept her eyes down. Feeling inadequate herself amongst so many men of academic distinction, she could hardly bring herself to say a word. Then an elderly clergyman, swathed in crimson doctor's robes and with a face to match, who obviously knew nothing of protocol, conceived it his duty to draw her out. She could not remember his name but she was grateful for his kindness as he spoke of the Prince's reputation as a scholar and scientist, as a patron and encourager of the fine arts, as the ideal amateur of music, director of Antient Concerts and a talented executant and composer. Music was an absorbing interest in Victoria's own life, and she was herself as talented as Albert, but no music was so sweet to her as to hear such good and obviously sincere opinions of her husband. No

158

doubt, said the red clergyman, the Prince would have modern ideas for reforming the curriculum which would provoke adversaries in all sections of the university, but, for his part, he was exceedingly glad to welcome their royal Chancellor.

Encouraged, the Queen murmured that the installation ceremony had been very fine, very fine indeed. And she had particularly liked the choral poem. Who, she wondered, had written it? With consternation she saw a frown appear on the reverend gentleman's brow.

'It was written, Ma'am,' he said, evidently having a struggle to control himself, 'by your new Poet Laureate.'

'Oh!' Victoria said nothing else, deeming it wiser.

'By Mr Wordsworth, Ma'am, who on occasions, rare ones, turns out a sort of English verse which England may be proud of.'

'Just so.'

'But his ode they sang at us today was cant, woolly, the thinnest of gravy . . .' He became so violent and puce in his search for metaphors to express his disgust at the Installation Ode, that the Queen feared he might have a seizure. She tried to mollify him. At the same time she wondered how academic clergymen managed to work themselves into such states. There was that terrifying don at Albert's preliminary installation, the subject who had shouted 'Bah!' in his sovereign's dining-room simply because the word 'geography' was used. Perhaps this was the same volatile man. It was all so curious that for a second she was tempted to say 'geography' to see if anything happened, but the temptation passed. Instead she spent a lot of her time and a good deal of her persuasive skill in quietening him down. He still mumbled through the beginning of the musical entertainment provided by the Vice-Chancellor, when Albani and Salvi sang, as well as her dear old singing master to whom she had once given her adolescent heart, Luigi Lablache.

The atmosphere became as stuffy as the Senate House had been and the noise increased minute by minute as the Vice-Chancellor's college provided its finest wines for the occasion. The Duke was there, not as Chancellor of Oxford, but as an honorary doctor of the university, and he was shouting at the top of his voice. Peel was there as well, and Pilgerstein. The company was a heady mixture and at the drawing of the covers, the Queen was greatly relieved to take her ladies off to the drawing-rooms in Trinity Lodge and leave the university to the solemn circulation and swilling of port. An hour of this was enough for Albert. He begged leave from the Vice-Chancellor, and joined Victoria in an informal stroll along the Backs.

It was the sort of thing they loved to do and Victoria was delighted when she discovered they were lost in the gardens of St John's. Such small adventures were usually denied them. They were put on their way again and walked, arm in arm, talking over the day's events. He was glad to have an opportunity to tell of his plans for the reform of the university curriculum and she was glad to describe to him the extraordinary behaviour of the clergyman who detested the Installation Ode.

He sympathized with her. The academic world was evidently an unusual branch of the clergy. 'But perhaps he was right about the poem,' he suggested.

'Oh, no!' protested Victoria. 'Surely not?'

'Its faults were rather strident.' He smiled. 'You will forgive me, my love, if I go so far as to say that one of the verses sounded less like a compliment to you than the naming of a tugboat or barge.'

'Albert!'

' "The Pride of the Island",' he repeated. ' "Victoria the Queen".'

She smiled. Then they both laughed together. After two days of July heat and university solemnity it was good to laugh.

To Victoria this was the best part of their visit to Cambridge. People knew quite well who they were, but were sufficiently civilized and considerate not to interfere with their privacy. Yet even the memory of this evening stroll along the Backs was later spoilt by a reporter who was looking for copy beneath the St John's limes. Either with plain stupidity or with malicious sarcasm he repeated that her majesty and his royal highness were pleased to walk incognito after the day's celebrations, she wearing a shawl over her diamond diadem, he wearing a mackintosh and his Chancellor's cap.

XV

Because the mobbing of subjects and the impertinence of journalists made privacy so important, both Victoria and Albert were deeply appreciative of their country estate on the Isle of Wight. Moreover as it was their own property they could do what they wished with it. It was a blessing, wrote Victoria to her Uncle Leopold, to be *'free from all Woods and Forests, and other charming Departments who really are the plague of one's life'*.

Osborne she had known as a child. Her mother's Comptroller, the hated John Conroy, had owned a cottage there and she had stayed at nearby Norris Castle, riding and studying the botany with Lehzen, and collecting seaweed and other trophies from the rocky pools on the shore. Now she had the delight of seeing her own children doing the same.

Albert was equally happy there. His curious penchant for making comparisons caused him to admire the place largely because it reminded him of Naples, and the house which he designed to replace the smaller, original house was cast in his idea of an Italian mould with arcades, sculpted gardens, a loggia and two campaniles. The rooms had low arched ceilings and were much smaller in size than the rooms they were accustomed to at Buckingham Palace and at Windsor. Far more than the other royal residences it was the Prince's idea of a home.

Though progressive in a number of matters, Albert was not in accord with those advanced thinkers who championed the individual above all things. To him the community was more important and, exalting the idea of the family with the zeal of an ancient Roman, he made the whole of Osborne a temple for the *lares et penates* of the house of Saxe-Coburg.

There was a remarkable hotch-potch of mementoes, furnishings and decorations: wallpapers, tapestries, and chintzes designed by the Prince himself, old masters, imitation marble columns, portraits of relations in pencil drawings, oils and sculpture, ornaments on revolving bases, statuettes and sketches of favourite dogs and horses, chairs made of coal, framed photographs, the carved hands and feet of the royal children displayed on cushions of crimson velvet, stacks of albums and folios, royal relics in bijoutery cabinets, collections of minerals and dressed dolls, an *hortus siccus*, German porcelain views painted below glaze on plates, teapots and knick-knacks, and above each doorway the entwined initials *V* and *A*, except that of the smoking-room where there was the single initial *A*.

Fresco had never been considered entirely suitable to the draughts, damp and darkness of the British Isles, but Albert thought it the noblest form of painting and two large frescoes decorated the family home at Osborne. The largest was on the walls of the main staircase and showed Neptune giving his empire to Britannia; a happy compliment to Victoria and a golden opportunity for William Dyce the painter to enjoy himself with waves, crustaceans, shells, fish, seaweed, salt plants, waders and gulls. Still better painted was his fresco in the Prince's dressing-room and bathroom which the Prince called the marriage of Heracles and Omphale.

Dyce considered it a curious choice of subject, especially as the liaison between the two had hardly been a marriage in the generally understood sense of the term; and he recalled what he supposed the Prince and Mr Anson must have forgotten, that Heracles had actually been sold to Queen Omphale for a year's slavery and had been forced to do women's work while she assumed his lionskin and club. Looked at allegorically, such a scene painted in the Prince's private rooms would give rise to all manner of unpleasant interpretations and so Dyce decided on his own initiative to modify the legend, painting an ordinary enough classical wedding, without slave irons or spinning wheels, and with the lionskin on Heracles not Omphale. The Prince was delighted with his work.

Albert never pretended that the house was worthy of an architectural prize. It was a pretty piece of domestic architecture but that was incidental to its main purpose. He made it to be a home to be lived in and enjoyed. The views from the flat leads and from the windows was superb, and the house was so comfortable in comparison to the royal palaces that it invited informality.

At Osborne the Queen felt it proper to wear aprons and galoshes. There for the first time she helped Lady Lyttelton and Miss Hildyard, the governess, and the nursery staff with her children. She bathed them and kissed them and spanked them. She took them to the fruit gardens to pick strawberries, raspberries and currants. She went with them on their shell-gathering expeditions. When they went sailing with their father she agreed to be at a certain point on the shore at a certain time so that they could all wave at each other. She did not mind in the least when they draped festoons of seaweed over the statues in the hall; a performance which shocked the Prince until he discovered the seaweed was to be used scientifically, as a natural barometer or weather-prophet. It was she who, because of her own frustrated childish longings to play house, persuaded him to have a special hut built for the children. The result was a Swiss chalet, complete in every detail, erected at some little distance from Osborne House, where make-believe was easy and the children gave them tea parties.

Albert ensured that they had their own small gardens where they could grow simple vegetables and plants, a plan which appealed to all save the Princess Royal. She frowned on the easy cultivation of sunflowers, cress and lettuces and longed for gardenias and pomegranates. Such a liking for the exotic sometimes worried her father whose Lutheran up bringing made him suspect luxury. But she could charm away his frown with a single smile. He tried to show no partiality but it was obvious that he loved her more than all his other children and that he found her so much better company than his son Bertie.

Victoria talked this over with Lady Lyttelton, and wondered if anything could be done for Bertie. He seemed so wilful and so stupid. Lady Lyttelton had her answer pat. He needed a companion, someone who would neither bully him nor tease him. And to the Queen's delight she was able to provide exactly the right companion. Her younger sister was married to a Mr Gladstone, one of Peel's younger colleagues in the Tory ministry, and they had a son of the Prince's age. Neither Stockmar nor the Prince, nor even Victoria herself, really approved of the Prince of Wales hobnobbing with a subject but it was impossible to find a child of his own rank and the Gladstone boy was at least related to Lady Lyttelton. And so William Henry was invited for Osborne holidays; a solemn little boy who liked what he called nasties – bettles, toads, earthworms, wasp grubs, and almost everything the princesses found frightening and disgusting. Bertie rather agreed with his sisters, but he shared William Henry's other interests. Both liked dressing-up, eating, drinking sherbert, making secret hiding places, playing soldiers, and challenging each other to do difficult, embarrassing and degrading things. They got on well enough, though when they lost their tempers they would hammer at each other mercilessly, and sometimes, when they fought duels with wooden swords or quarter staves, they began quietly but ended by hitting each other as hard as they could.

Lady Lyttelton was overjoyed. It did not seem to make any difference to her charge's stupidity in the schoolroom, but William Henry's companionship certainly made him happier. The Queen was equally pleased. Bertie was seldom sulky with his father when William Henry was at Osborne, and the young Gladstone became so much a part of the summer scene that one day she found herself inadvertently smacking him for something he had done wrong as though he were one of her own children.

Osborne did Victoria a great deal of good. She saw more of her family, but she also learnt there the value of tranquillity and solitude. She had seldom experienced either during the whole of her life. By her mother's special order she had never been left alone for a single moment, day or night, all through her childhood; and though Lehzen had sometimes contrived to wink a blind eye at the rule, it had not been often. Then since her accession and her marriage, it had hardly ever been possible to be alone in the sense that many of her subjects could be alone. There were always people about. At Osborne a new pattern of daily life gave her more solitude. It was understood that neither her attendants nor the children should disturb her. If she wished, she could go to them, or ring a handbell for a servant and ask for them to be sent to her. Only the Prince had the liberty to break her solitude but as Osborne grew he was generally too busy in his workshop, the library or his writing-room to be with her very often.

She spent most of the day out of doors. One of the particular delights of her girlhood had been tea on the lawn at Kensington. Her mother and Sir John might have been present or absent; it made no difference, she always pretended they were not there. But Lehzen was there tatting or crocheting and popping caraway seeds into her mouth; and generally Aunt Sophoa joined them, to embroider and sigh and sigh and sigh; and sometimes Uncle Sussex, with the black page behind his chair to run in and out fetching books or pen and ink or brandy and water or a straw hat or a mathematical instrument. Tea on the lawn at Kensington had been wonderful. At Osborne Victoria repeated it, breakfasting and lunching as well as taking tea under the great cypress on the lawn, or in the summer-house, or in the park, or down by the Solent in a retreat designed by Albert, shaped like a lemon wedge, with a cool mosaic floor and a moulded ceiling painted pink and blue and gold. And in one or other of these outdoor rooms she worked at her papers, or sketched, or relaxed with needlework and reading, or simply sat back with her eyes half closed to enjoy the view.

To the pleasures of solitude and tranquillity at Osborne she added the pleasure of bathing. Sea-bathing was exceedingly fashionable. Many years before physicians had prescribed it as remedial for certain ailments and generally beneficial, and the Prince Regent himself had bathed at Brighton, a function attended by some pomp as brass bands played the National Anthem at the precise moment the royal toe touched the English Channel. Sir James Clark had recommended it to Victoria as salutary and particularly good for the nerves; but she had a certain bashfulness about bathing naked in the sea even from the Osborne beach, and a secret fear that she would make herself ridiculous. For these reasons, and also perhaps because of a fear of the sea itself, she postponed bathing until after their return from the Prince's installation at Cambridge, and then, driven to be adventurous by the unusual heat, she sent orders to the royal bathing woman to prepare the machine. Not mentioning it to Albert, and attended only by her tiring-maid, she went down to the beach.

The royal bathing machine, painted in red and white stripes like a barber's pole and surmounted by a gilded crown, had been run down a sloping wooden pier to the shore. The horse which would pull it back again was cropping samphire grass. Mary Rush the bathing woman swept a large curtsey. She looked formidable and was of Amazon proportions, dressed from top to toe in a tent-like garment gathered at the waist, and with her hair snooded back and partially covered with a floppy, rimless hat. She saw the Queen was nervous, and did her best to be reassuring. Hardly ever before, she said, had the sea been so glossy, the sun so high, the breeze so warming. It was inevitable that her majesty should enjoy her bathe.

'Thank you, Rush,' said the Queen. She signed to her tiring-maid to lead up the steps into the machine.

The interior was crypt-like because it was lighted by two tiny windows of frosted glass, but they soon became accustomed to the gloom and the Queen undressed. The maid slipped a voluminous bathing robe over her head, a shapeless garment gathered by tapes at the waist and throat. This was topped by a floppy cap. Conscious that she looked more like a minor version of Mary Rush than Victoria, Queen of England, she allowed herself to be led through a door at the sea end of the machine. There was a half platform with steps which led down into the sea. Round it were long drapes of soft leather. She steeled herself against the cold, and found the water warm. It came exactly up to her chin. Presumably bathing women were like undertakers and had an eye for their clients' height. The tiniest of waves lapped around her. She made a movement to lift the leather drape and look out to sea, when the deep voice of Mary Rush came from the other side. 'Your majesty is ready?'

'Thank you, Rush, yes I am.'

'Then if your majesty's maid will remove your bathing robe, I'll see to Dobbin.'

This was the point Victoria disliked, but she had no time to be over-modest. Her tiring-maid rang a small ship's bell attached to the machine and the bathing woman clapped her hands and shouted. The horse left off cropping and slowly trundled the machine up out of the sea. Victoria was left to enjoy herself. She did. She could not yet swim but she delighted in rolling about and scrunching the sand up with her toes. It was exhilarating to feel that something recommended by the doctors could be so pleasant. But she did not enjoy the experiment of putting her head under the water. Her eyes were screwed tight so she saw nothing, and then the stifling, enclosed feeling became too much for her and she opened her mouth. Red faced and gasping, with water streaming from her nose, she jerked her head out again. The horrible sensation of drowning decided her to make no more experiments. Always after she sponged her face with sea water in the bathing machine and then 'plunged', as she called it, with her head erect.

She waved to her maid who rang the bell, and the machine came down into the water again. The leather drapes hid her from sight so she wondered why it was necessary to put on a bathing robe again. Nevertheless she did. It was part of the procedure.

Osborne was never finished in the sense that a church or a museum or a railway station could be finished. Because the family grew, and because the Prince was imaginative, he was always adding or subtracting, or altering in some way. But from the time they began to make it their home, it was his favourite, and Victoria's and the children's. Then something quite unforeseen took place which made it no less desirable but distinctly less peaceful.

Mr Hudson's railway engine altered the face of England. He himself was not able to enjoy it, as he was found guilty of peculation and fraud, and ruined for ever; but the money of speculators made it possible for most of the country to be served by railways. The Irish railway navigators who wore a distinguished uniform of white tall hats, red waistcoats, and square-tailed coats of velveteen, were in evidence everywhere except the remote shires. But with the benefits of more comfortable travel, cheaper coal and cheaper food, the railways also made places too accessible.

The Queen's privacy at Osborne was threatened. Victoria was assiduous in her duty to the state, and she knew she must hold herself available in London and at Windsor as the fountainhead of patronage and the leader of society, but she did not feel she had any particular duty to satisfy the curiosity of newspapermen, social reformers, and idle gazers who could so easily take a train from London and a steamer from Portsmouth. The most stringent precautions had to be taken against peeping toms and trespassers. And when it became possible to travel from London to Portsmouth for a penny a mile, a special police guard had to patrol the grounds at Osborne whenever the royal family were in residence.

One young policeman, newly arrived from Ryde, arrested a man who he considered was stealing stealthily through the park. He took him round to the great kitchen where the police had their headquarters; and was dismayed to see everyone suddenly scramble to his feet and learn that he had laid hands on the Prince. But the Prince did not seem to mind. He had not explained himself, he said, to see how the police went about their business and he was satisfied that Osborne was being well taken care of. He congratulated the abashed constable on his zeal and continued his evening walk.

Nevertheless people did slip through the patrol. The

Queen's mother and Madame Späth were almost frightened out of their wits by a young man who leered at them from round a tree. Twice the children met total strangers down by the shore. Happily none of them was as frightened as their nurse-maids who screamed and screamed, and William Henry distinguished himself by hitting one of the strangers with his wooden sword. Then Miss Skerrett, mistaken for the Queen by a female fanatic reformer, was asked to grant the six points of the People's Charter, and to get rid of the nuisance said yes, of course she would. Later the Queen's own sketch book was stolen from where she had left it in the summerhouse and the contents sold by an unscrupulous dealer in London. On this occasion the press came to her defence. The Queen ought to be allowed, it said, the same privacy and protection from petty thieves enjoyed by the meanest of her subjects. Victoria was not grateful. Such newspaper reports merely put wicked ideas into the minds of people who otherwise might not have thought of them. Soon, no doubt, the cross-Solent ferry would be packed by sketch-book thieves.

Osborne she loved dearly, but not even for strawberry picking with the children, hornpipes, breakfast under the cypress, and sea-bathing superintended by Mary Rush could she stand the constant and impertinent intrusion of complete strangers into her privacy. They would have to have a second home to use as an alternative on occasions, and she and Albert set about looking for one where their privacy would be assured.

Victoria explained the situation to her Prime Minister. 'We are thinking,' she said, 'of Scotland.'

Lord John temporized. His own views on the northern kingdom were Johnsonian, but if the Queen made regular visits there it would certainly maintain good harmony between Edinburgh and London. Yet, buried in North Britain, escaping from the accessibility of Osborne to inaccessibility north of the Border, would not make government any easier. She had to be within reach, especially as she was so insistent on seeing the major foreign dispatches before they were sent out.

'Holyrood Palace, Ma'am, is barely fit at present.'

'Holyrood!' she repeated. 'We certainly have no intention of living in a low lying situation. The Prince already has a great affection for the Highlands.'

'It is important to be in touch with the central government,' he reminded her.

'Of course, Lord John. We realize it to the full. But there is the electric telegraph. There are railway locomotives. There are fast sloops and frigates.'

– And there are balloons and pigeons, he added peevishly to himself, or runners like those who carried Apennine snows to cool the imperial wine on Capri. She was becoming too grand altogether, expecting the resources of the kingdom to be placed at her disposal simply because of a whim to live in the godforsaken wilds of nowhere. His Whig soul was affronted by her regal manner. It made him play an unfair card.

'It is my duty to advise you, Ma'am, that necessary government expenditure obliges us to be cautious. I doubt if in this year especially any sort of parliamentary grant could be raised even if it were debated.'

But even this had little effect on her. 'We intend, Lord John, to buy a property outright. It will belong to the Prince. No grant is called for, nor, if it were offered should I be inclined to accept it.' She held out her hand to signify the audience was over. He kissed it. 'We shall be up there very soon,' she told him, 'as guests, with Prince Leiningen, of Lord Abercorn at Ardverikie. The gentlemen will enjoy the stalking and we shall have an opportunity to look about for a suitable property.'

The trip to Ardverikie was not as successful as the Queen had hoped.

For remoteness they could hardly have chosen a better place; no village, house or cottage within four miles, and only accessible by ferry across Loch Laggan. Moreover, as the ferry belonged exclusively to Lord Abercorn, the journalists sent north to report on the royal holiday could not get across. This was a distinct consolation but, for the first time, the royal family was exposed to the real malice of Highland weather.

In 1842 and again on their visit to Blair Athole in 1844 it had, of course, frequently rained – but never with such force and persistence as it did at Ardverikie. For days at a time there was a sustained downpour only relieved by either violent August storms or impenetrable fog, and on the rare occasions when a watery sun made a brave attempt to light up the hills, it was still extraordinarily cold.

The house was a stone-built shooting lodge, decorated with antlers in the corridors and over the entrance to each room, and with large frescoes in two of the larger rooms. They were by Landseer. The Prince could not have been more delighted, and dinner was postponed on the night of their arrival while he examined the paintings in detail. On the dining-room and drawing-room walls were the originals of 'The Monarch of the Glen', 'The Challenge' and 'The Sanctuary'. It appeared that Landseer was a friend of the Abercorns and a frequent guest at Ardverikie. On one occasion, complaining of the glare of whitewash, he had set himself to remedy it with a pair of stepladders and a box of paints. Albert was enchanted. This was proof of the painter's sensibility, of his feeling for colour. Victoria was equally fond of Landseer's stags and dogs though, after three days virtual imprisonment in the house, she began to think his frescoes were more probably a *passatempo* which owed their origin to the lonely situation and intolerable climate of Ardverikie.

If anything the weather made the house seem smaller. Certainly it was packed. Very few of the Household were in attendance and Victoria's half brother Charles of Leiningen had only one gentleman with him. The children, Vicky and Bertie, had their governess Miss Hildyard. As for the servants: tents and a distant inn had to be pressed into service.

Lord Abercorn was a considerate host. To make as much room as possible he turned out his own children to confined quarters on the home farm. All save one were very content. It was an adventure to be at the home farm, but little Lord

Claud Hamilton objected to being turned out for the Queen's elder children. When his mother presented him to the Queen he made his displeasure clear by refusing to bow. Instead he stood upside down – a trick he had recently learnt – and affronted his sovereign by showing her he wore nothing under his kilt. He was taken away and scolded and told to be a good boy and give his bow to the Queen. Chastened he returned, but the Queen appeared to be scowling. He promptly stood upside down again, his kilt flapping against his face. He heard the cross lady say: 'Marchioness, I do not wish to see that naughty boy again unless he is in breeches.'

Albert's unquenchable high spirits kept Victoria's from falling too low. Unnecessary business, he said, should not be allowed to obtrude on their holiday. When government estafettes arrived he quickly went through her state papers and selected those which needed her personal attention. The remainder he dealt with himself. He did not altogether approve of novel-reading, but held that holidays provide a welcome exception to most rules and kept Victoria and her ladies spellbound with readings of Moir's study of the Scotch in *The Life of Mansie Waunch, Tailor in Dalkeith*. Then afterwards he terrified them with a chilling ghost story published that very summer, *The Story of Lilly Dawson* by Catherine Crowe. When the steady rain turned to drizzle he took her for long drives in a pony carriage or for rows on the loch. And he was indefatigable in the pursuit of game.

You can only have two words today [he wrote to his brother] *to tell you that we are well, that whenever we stir out we come home almost frozen and always wet to the skin, that grouse are wild, and the deer very hard to get at, despite all which we are still very happy.*

The chase took Albert away from Victoria for she could not take an active part and in such abominable weather she could not follow; and his long absences might have made her a little fractious had it not been for Sir James Clark's insistence that the holiday must undoubtedly be doing her good.

172

Once again she was carrying a child, and bearing the last, Princess Helena, had been a long and painful labour. Sir James, an acknowledged expert on the influence of climate on health, had promised her that the pure and peaty air of Inverness would give her resources of strength which would be invaluable in six months' time. Nevertheless as day succeeded day of steady, sheeting rain, he began to change his mind. Few in that packed, damp household avoided rheumatic pains. The Queen's were pronounced. And the air was too heavy with moisture to be as beneficial as he had hoped.

When he confessed this to the Queen she tried her very best to be patient with him. He had been her medical adviser for as long as she could remember; had seen her through childish ailments, typhoid and childbirth, and only once – and that was in the case of one of her mother's Ladies-in-Waiting – had he ever let her down. But enduring the cramped conditions and awful downpour at Ardverikie tested her patience to the limit, and she found it hard to be polite to Sir James when he said that perhaps they would have been more comfortable after all on the other side of the Grampians. The storms spent themselves on the mountains and to the east there were sheltered valleys. His own son John was convalescing there beside the river Dee at that very moment, and his letters praised the dry sweet air and the amazing amount of sunshine he had been enjoying. On the strength of John's reports Sir James was prepared to alter his mind about Inverness. No doubt it would be better for the Queen's health if they found a property over on the eastern side of the Cairngorm mass.

The Queen agreed. Vexed by his bumbling she could not prevent herself from saying that there was hardly any alternative, for what Christian soul could go out in Inverness weather to find anything suitable there?

When she told Albert what Sir James had said he showed great interest and took an opportunity to talk to the doctor himself. Though refusing to be dismayed and dejected by the weather he shared Victoria's view that Ardverikie was no place for an alternative home to Osborne. He also shared Sir James' interest in climatology. Where precisely, he asked, was his son convalescing beside the river Dee?

'He is with Sir Robert Gordon, Sir; a good friend of many years' standing. The house is called Balmoral.'

Prince Albert was thorough and systematic. It was imperative to find a second home and he would spare no trouble or expense. He arranged for sketches to be made of the scenery on Deeside, and, at the same time, for a report on the climatic conditions. He was impressed by both. So was Victoria. They decided to spend the next holiday on Deeside and there look out for an estate. Meanwhile Sir Robert Gordon was asked to be their confidential agent in case he should hear of anything at all suitable between Braemar and Aberdeen. Apart from being Sir James Clark's friend, he was brother to Lord Aberdeen, Victoria's Foreign Secretary in Peel's ministry, and until recently had been her Ambassador in Vienna. Albert considered it was proper to ask such a man for his discreet help in finding an estate somewhere on Deeside.

But Sir Robert had no opportunity. On the twenty-first day after the royal family left Scotland that autumn he went down as usual to breakfast, helped himself to a boiled egg, topped the shell, and collapsed. Within minutes he was dead.

Within weeks Lord Aberdeen had suggested that the Queen and the Prince take over the lease from the Fife trustees who owned the estate. It still had twenty-seven years to run. They hardly hesitated. They really wanted to buy an estate as it seemed improper to lease one from a subject, and under ordinary circumstances they would have insisted on making a personal inspection of the house and grounds. But the sketches hurriedly made and sent up to London confirmed what they had already decided. They accepted the offer, and the second family home was established.

But long before they could stay there, even before the legal formalities were concluded and Prince Albert became the lessee of Balmoral, the old ordered world began to be convulsed and threatened with extinction. Europe, as they knew it, was doomed.

Part Three

I

The explosion which altered the structure of so many European states, was first detonated in France.

On February 22nd, 1848, King Louis-Philippe paced a gallery in the Tuileries. To keep out the cold he wore a tall hat and a greatcoat. As he walked he frowned and sometimes he sighed. Occasionally he checked his pacing to cup an ear and listen. He heard nothing but he knew perfectly well what was happening in Paris. His people were stirring in a fashion he recognized only too well. Political agitators – communists, socialists, freemasons, free thinkers – had moved them to demand a change of ministry. Advised by his son Montpensier, Louis-Philippe had agreed. If he were to remain the elected King of the French he had to be conciliatory. The Jacobins were out. Republicans had said openly they would raise the tricolour above the Tuileries.

There were royal guards at each doorway in the gallery. They were watchful and silent. A chamberlain stood beside a charcoal brazier. All their eyes watched the King pace up and down. His heavy tread was the only close sound.

Then, abruptly, he stopped.

He and the guards and the chamberlain had all heard a new sound simultaneously. It was distant but distinct, and the King immediately identified it. He had first heard it as a boy of sixteen when the Revolution burst out all over France. He had heard it as a young man of twenty when Jacobins had guillotined Louis XVI and his own father in the Terror. The guards, even the chamberlain, were too young to know that it was a Paris revolutionary mob, but they stiffened in expectation of trouble.

The King commanded more lights, and the chamberlain ran to obey. Frightened officials came in one after the other. Louis-Philippe merely signed to them to be quiet and stand back. He sent for the royal family. Montpensier arrived with his frightened Spanish wife. Then the little Comte de Paris and his mother the Duchess of Chartres. Finally came the Queen. She stood beside her husband, wearing a proud defiant face. As a daughter of the King of Naples and Sicily she had had experience of mobs and knew how to confront them.

More and more candles were brought. By the time the leaders of the mob streamed into the gallery, it was ablaze with light.

There were National Guardsmen among the citizens and they were led by an officer.

The Duc de Montpensier leant forward and whispered in his father's ear. 'It is Girardin, a newspaper editor. He will ask for your abdication.'

With a barely perceptible nod Louis-Philippe signified that he had understood. Though the son of Philippe Égalité, and an elected King, and though not endowed with a commanding presence, he nevertheless showed his royal origin in the way he touched the rim of his tall hat.

'Messieurs!' he said quietly.

One by one the citizens removed their caps and hats until the King and the military were the only covered people there.

At that moment he might perhaps have bent the mob to his will. He might have persuaded them to see reason, to accept the new ministry they had asked for, to go home quietly. But by unhappy chance the tocsin began to ring out, the alarm bell for all Parisians. It stiffened their resolve and gave Girardin the opportunity to step forward and demand the King's abdication in the name of the people.

Louis-Philippe's instinct was to defy him, but Girardin was plausible. In this way French blood would not be shed. Montpensier added his voice. It was the only way to keep the throne for the Comte de Paris.

They prevailed and the King quickly signed an Act of Abdication which Girardin had with him. Then, taking his Queen's arm, and followed by the family, they walked out, through the gardens, to the royal coach houses. To everyone the King met he gave a small bow and said: 'I am abdicating. I am abdicating.'

When she heard the awful circumstances of the King of the French being driven from his capital Victoria had difficulty in controlling her agitation.

His escape from France was terrifying. Separated from his children, he and Queen Marie had made for the coast and begged for the help of the British consul at Le Havre. The consul himself described it as a hair-trigger affair, and when forwarding his official report to the Queen, Lord Palmerston said it was like one of Walter Scott's best tales.

Though the simile was accurate it did not endear him to his sovereign. Tales were tales. The bitter experience of the poor dear King and Queen of the French was another thing altogether: kept ashore and prevented from their first attempt to escape in a fishing boat by foul and dangerous weather in the Channel; driven to slip out of side doors and walk miles at night-time to avoid the mob; then forced to use a common ferry carrying passports as Mr and Mrs Smith; and again and again obliged to cower and make pretence and humiliate themselves before the *canaille* of their own kingdom. But the consul had done well. Victoria was proud that he had been able to serve the exiles with such cleverness and devotion. He had employed the minimum of agents, all of them trustworthy; had had a ship ready with a single mooring cable to the jetty, her jib half set and with steam up; had ensured that his charges were effectively disguised, and, as a clever diversion, had hired two pugilists to fight on the quayside and distract attention from the King and Queen at the moment of their embarkation.

Thinking of the last time Louis-Philippe had come to England, as an honoured guest on a state visit to Windsor, Victoria's heart went out to him when she heard of his landing at Newhaven with no money, luggage, nor any sort of personal possessions, his recognizable whiskers shaved off, a sort of casquette on his head, a coarse overcoat, and immense goggles over his eyes. It seemed worse that until he reached Newhaven he did not know that the Jacobins had refused to accept his grandson the Comte de Paris as King. France was again a republic and the House of Orleans doomed to permanent exile.

She did all that was possible. Funds were provided and Claremont was placed at the King's disposal for as long as he cared to use it. She did all that she could to help the other members of his family reach Claremont and she accepted his decision to remain in England in the strictest incognito as the Count of Neuilly.

She did not care for her Prime Minister's reminder that she should give no appearance of encouraging the royal exiles and that it would be undesirable for any of them to live in an English royal palace. No doubt he was right, she told herself, but she would not have the world think she was as cold as a Whig patrician. She asked Albert to go down to Claremont on her behalf and make sure that the exiles were as comfortable as possible. Comfortable. It did not bear thinking about that only a few weeks before she had been staying at Claremont herself, free for a time from the anxieties of being a queen, happy with her husband and the children, planning such small domestic matters as a glass dome for the gardenhouse so that the growing palms would not be stunted. Now the same house was filled with a shattered family, their honours gone, their estates and jewels and private fortunes sequestered by Jacobins.

She was angry with Lord John and his stony heart, and short to the point of rudeness when he wrote a condescending valediction to the French monarchy:

> *After the vicissitudes of a long life, it may be no irremediable calamity if a Prince of great powers of mind and warm domestic affections is permitted by Providence to end his days in peace and tranquillity.*

She strongly deprecated the Prime Minister's Olympian smugness and pomposity, and most of all his sarcasm. Nothing, she suspected, could heal the hurt that France had done to Louis-Philippe. No doubt in the past two years his government had made mistakes, but her own ministries had done no better. And she thought it base that the King's endeavours to maintain order and peace and mercantile wealth for sixteen long years should be so quickly forgotten.

At the very back of her mind she recognized something of which she was ashamed: great relief that this terrible thing had not happened to her and to Albert. The Paris uprising had sparked off revolution in many European states. Albert's suzerain, the King of Saxony, was driven from his capital through streets piled five feet high with corpses. Even the Austro-Hungarian Empire, so fossilized that Latin was still the official language, felt the shock of revolution. Mobs burnt and looted and murdered in Naples, Prussia, Bavaria, and in countless small principalities like Schleswig-Holstein, Charles' Leiningen, poor Feodore's Hohenlohe-Langenburg, Albert's own Coburg. Only three countries stood firm: Belgium because Uncle Leopold really was an excellent constitutional monarch and his government was good, and Russia and Hanover because the Tsar and Uncle Ernest were autocrats, the former too well protected and too ferocious to defy, the latter, oddly enough, too much respected by his people to provoke an uprising. And, cut off from Europe, there was England. So far the flame had not leapt over the Channel, but she knew it might not be long before it did.

179

II

England was in a pitiable state, ripe for rebellion.

For a variety of reasons people had tried to hide the facts from the Queen, but Albert made sure she knew the truth. Even whilst busy with the plans for Osborne and Balmoral neither of them was indifferent to the sufferings of the labouring classes. They had continued their daily round because Peel had taught them that steadying the country was their especial responsibility, but more than most they had a real pity for the poor. Cheaper bread ought to have been the panacea but it was made impossible by the lowering of wages. Albert did not mince matters. He made Victoria see that the remedy lay in the hands of the new capitalists. If they could be made to realize that the policy of profit at any price was unjustifiable, things would be altered. But this was out of the question. It infringed their rights. Each capitalist was an individual free to do what he willed with his own; and, according to modern thinking, the individual mattered more than the community.

Compassion quite as much as a dread of revolution after the French pattern made the Queen and the Prince acquaint the ministry with their views. But Lord John, whose brother, the Duke of Bedford, had six hundred servants at his country place, approved of individualism. He did not like it at all when the Prince announced his intention of accepting an offer to speak at a meeting of the Society for Improving the Conditions of the Labouring Classes. He liked it even less when in his speech Prince Albert said:

> To show how man can help man, notwithstanding the complicated state of civilized society, ought to be the aim of every philanthropic person; but it is more particularly the duty of those who, under the blessing of Divine Providence, enjoy station, wealth and education.

To show he meant what he said, he persuaded Victoria to show royal disapproval of the cost of bread. She ordered that only bread made from second-grade and cheaper corn be used in the royal establishments, and loyal to her example a number of large houses and institutions made the same ruling. But all their good intentions were frustrated by the millers and distributors who promptly raised the price of second-grade bread until it was as expensive as first-grade. The poor were in a worse state than before.

There was real famine in the kingdom. In Ireland it was indescribable, in England bad enough. The Prince was willing to lend his name to almost any enterprise which tried to solve the problem. But very little was done.

There were some who deliberately prevented it. In their passion for social justice there were belligerent radicals who would not raise a finger to help the starving. To them the thousands who died of famine were martyrs whose fate might force the rest of the poor to protest. For such a desirable end they would sacrifice anyone. Then there were those who preferred nature to take her course. They pointed to the Reverend Professor Malthus' essay on social economy in which he maintained that unless man and reason controlled population, it would increase faster than the means of subsistence. They claimed he was correct, and that as man had not used his reason, famine was the ultimate and proper check to the staggering increase in population. There were also those who desperately wished something to be done but who had more enthusiasm than knowledge. Of such was the Duke of Norfolk, husband to one of the most gentle of Victoria's ladies, himself humane and kindly. His solution was for the poor to stay their hunger by taking large draughts of curry powder mixed with water. And there were those who had the necessary knowledge and skills but who appeared to lack the ordinary common-sense to do anything practical. A large congress of scientists was called to discuss alternatives to corn for famine-stricken people, and after long deliberations suggested that a number of root-crops should be made into 'famine loaves', overlooking the fact that they would be far more expensive than real bread; and they also recommended that icelandic moss or hay should be dried, pounded and mixed with half-flour, not having taken the trouble to discover that neither was in any way palatable.

The Prince watched with growing anger. What little relief there was hardly touched the problem. But in his unique and difficult position in society he felt helpless to do anything about it. Anson's clerks were kept busy writing scores of encouraging letters to those private philanthropists who were particularly concerned. Then, to his delight, came an invitation to inspect some housing. He accepted.

Though he never saw the worst slums of London, those he was able to see, prinked out especially for the occasion, were squalid enough. He was horrified. The people knew he was concerned. The demonstration of loyalty when he made a detailed inspection of some houses in Bloomsbury, caused a Chartist agitator in the crowd to frown. He was heard to say: 'He'll upset our applecart.'

No one except the poor wanted the Prince – certainly not the agitators who valued famine and bad housing as the seedbeds of sedition. Nose-poker was added to his nicknames. Anson told him about it, guessing he would be proud of the name. He was.

The Queen was loyal to her husband, and no one would have known she had private reservations about the wisdom of what he was doing. Flying in the face of the Prime Minister and the vast majority of the millowners and industrialists in the country was admirable and brave, but it reaped no harvest save their bad opinion of an interfering foreigner. Wages remained low, costs high. And still at the back of her mind was that immense relief that so far they had escaped the horrible fate of so many crowned heads in Europe. She felt, all the time, as though they were on a tightrope and, though she wanted to be entirely loyal to Albert and support his brave stand, she dreaded that somehow he might contrive to topple them.

With these heavy anxieties pressing on her she began her confinement on a hot March day. She had a very bad time. Her labour was long and painful and exhausting. Afterwards she barely found the strength to open her eyes and examine the baby girl. Louise was her sixth child and still she wondered how anyone could describe such puce, wrinkled creatures as pretty. She kissed the baby, and lay back. Already the guns were booming out a royal salute for a new Princess of the Blood, but, with things as they were, Victoria doubted if that poor, purple scrap of a human being would ever take her proper place in the world. She might never even feature in the dynastic game of matchmaking which she and Albert loved to play. Events had made her future totally uncertain. Most probably it would be thistles rather than roses; clouds rather than sunshine . . .

She was reminded of something. 'Sir James,' she whispered.

The doctor bent over her and asked if she was comfortable.

'Not in the least,' she replied, and gave a faint smile. 'So much,' she added, 'for the pure, peaty air of Inverness.'

A rumour spread through the country. It caused the authorities to make inquiries. Eventually, on the very day Princess Louise was christened, it was considered important enough for the Queen to be informed. The Chartists were calling a meeting of all their followers. It would take place on April 10th, when thousands upon thousands would march into London carrying a petition demanding the six points of the People's Charter.

Victoria was emphatic. 'Inform the Prime Minister that the Duke must be sent for. He beat the French and a few rabble-rousers will be nothing to him.'

'My dear, it is not a few,' warned Albert quietly when the letter had been sent.

'Of course,' she said. 'But we have to pretend it is.'

On this sensible note of defiance she went into the christening. But there, sadly, at a ceremony and celebration which ought to have calmed her and helped to diminish her fears of public unrest, there were private family misfortunes.

Victoria had known that her Aunt Sophia was very ill,

and now immediately before the christening, Aunt Cambridge whispered to her that she was dying. She added that it was a disgrace she should be dying in isolation, cut off from everyone.

Vexed by the jeremiad Victoria retorted it was by Princess Sophia's own wish that she was left alone at Kensington. Still trying to hide the disgrace of having a bastard son, she refused to have resident Ladies-in-Waiting or allow anyone to interfere with her private life. Presumably, said Victoria, her son knew what was happening and had gone up to Kensington from Melton Mowbray to see her?

It appeared he had not. Nor had Aunt Cambridge been to see her.

'Perhaps you will be so good as to do so, aunt?' said Victoria through thin lips. 'On your word I am sure that my mother will wish to visit Kensington, and I should be prepared to do the same.'

The Duchess of Cambridge opened her snuff-box merely to clip it shut. It expressed her feelings well. Then she curtseyed, not with an impertinent bob which under the circumstances might have been acceptable, but with a far more insulting deep, slow and fulsome swing.

Victoria just managed to keep her temper, but it was difficult.

It was equally difficult to be patient with the new Archbishop who, presumably not recently practised in baptizing infants, and painfully nervous in close proximity to the Queen, muddled his pronouns in a hopeless fashion, referring to Princess Louise as 'him' and the Almighty as 'her'.

Then, the ceremony was hardly over and the baby being thoroughly kissed, when it became obvious that the Duchess of Gloucester had not the least idea where she was or what she was doing. Deciding it must be a grand affair she prostrated herself before Victoria. It was more of an oriental kotow than the way an English lady normally showed respect for her sovereign, and the Queen was distinctly embarrassed. Then, as she raised the old lady to her feet and saw the glazed uncertain look in her eyes, she knew that her favourite aunt was going out of her mind.

'Dear Aunt Gloucester,' she murmured, kissing her cheek, a tear stealing down her own. Gone was the imperious princess who had protected her foolish husband as fiercely as she had loved him, who had had the kindest heart and the sharpest wit of all the daughters of George the Third. Victoria held her closely for a moment and said again: 'Dear Aunt Gloucester.'

III

Not long after the christening Prince Albert found Victoria weeping and shivering uncontrollably. Her calmness, her defiance of all revolutionaries, had only been temporary. Still weak from her lying-in and even more depressed than usual, the threat of revolution made her despair. She shook with fear.

Albert tried to soothe her but she paid no attention to him. He took her by the shoulders. 'You are hysterical,' he shouted.

'I am no such thing.' The five words, loudly and clearly enunciated, showed the strength of her indignation. But she could not maintain it. Bursting into another passionate fit of sobbing, she spoke of the thrones toppling all over Europe. What would happen to her and the children when the English Jacobins took over the country?

He listened patiently, breaking in on occasions to try to reason with her, and he was hurt, deeply hurt, when she abruptly turned from attacking the Chartists and the feebleness of her ministers to recriminating with him.

'Oh, you are so heartless, so unfeeling! How can you be indifferent to the threats? And, seeing my terror, why have you done nothing?' She glared at him. 'What have you done while your wife and six children stand in peril of their lives?

185

What have you found the courage to do? Have you done anything?'

This time he slapped her face, very hard.

Her eyes opened wide and she stared at him. 'Oh,' she said. 'You have struck me. You have struck me.' She found it so difficult to believe that she repeated it again and again. Then she saw he was smiling at her.

He took her in his arms. 'Sweetheart,' he said gently. 'We are both worried. And something shall be done. That I promise.'

'You promise?'

He nodded. 'I promise.'

How he managed it, she never knew, but two days before the Chartist meeting the royal family left London for Osborne. The government had recommended it. The Duke himself had said that so large a prize must be kept safely away from the revolutionaries.

The Duke was at the centre of things. He was still vexed with the Whigs who had wanted to remove his equestrian statue from Hyde Park Corner. With little vanity, and being normally the last sort of person to object about such a matter, he was nevertheless determined that his work for England, and by inference the work of his soldiers, should not be insulted in the eyes of the world. Moreover, he told the Whigs, since he had been damnably inconvenienced by having had to sit for the sculpture, it could damned well stay where they had put it. It did. And now not far away the old field marshal worked in his headquarters on the defences of London.

Volunteers were rallying round to help. Amongst the extra police enrolled for the occasion was the late Emperor Napoleon's nephew, Prince Louis Napoleon. Whig and Tory statesmen had their retainers sent up from the country to fight the battles of London, and there was the unusual spectacle of seeing great houses guarded by gaitered keepers armed with shotguns.

The Duke accepted their help, but he did not take it very seriously. His plans were very simple and very clear. In addition to his staff of soldiers, politicians and police, he had a large number of runners. Gossips he called them. Men and boys, and a few women, who were given the straight facts about the disposition of artillery and cavalry and told to spread them. They did their work well. By the tenth hardly anyone in London was unfamiliar with the Duke's plans. Nor did anyone doubt his determination to fire on his countrymen if it turned out to be necessary. He was the coolest of customers, and knew what was what. And if, as he said, a lot of foreign revolutionaries were leading English Chartists by the nose to weaken the country, then they could whistle for support.

The Duke's reliance on the English working man's dislike of foreigners and the traditional reluctance of English women to let their men join lost causes, was fully justified. The agitators had whipped up some of the hungry poor, and the incendiary radicals and republicans had their customary following, but not a quarter of the expected people turned up on Kennington Common where the massive meeting had been called. Their chief, counting on half a million bold souls to march with him to the Houses of Parliament, found himself with a mere 23,000 most of whom knew the Duke's plans too well to risk bringing them into operation.

It was nothing like Paris at all. With the old Duke's menace hanging over everyone the leading Chartists were glad to accept the police ruling that there would be no march at all from Kennington. They were equally glad to take themselves and the monster petition in three cabs to Westminster. There the petition was formally presented, formally received, and no one heard of it again.

'Excellent, damn it!' the Duke of Wellington was heard to remark, and after his brief campaign, he went back to Stratfield Saye.

While the Chartist fiasco was being played out the Queen had curiously mixed feelings. She was uncommonly proud of the Duke and sent him a birthday present as well as a letter of congratulations. She was also enormously proud of English common-sense. With considerable lack of tact she assured Albert that it was this which had prevented her family from being driven into exile. 'Our revolution' as she called it, was of a very different character from that caused by excitable foreigners. Nevertheless she was profoundly thankful that the threat to her throne had been removed, and she did not like anyone making light of the danger. The Prince of Prussia, a temporary refugee in England, became her favourite when he told her the threat of revolution had been very real. He had gone incognito to Kennington to see the Chartists and assured her they wore the same beastly features as the rebellious peasants at Stolzenfels. Victoria was strangely gratified to hear it.

Albert could not keep pace with nor understand her changeability: frightened, proud, thankful, gratified, frightened again. She was also suffering badly from nightmares. They were jumbled, some being riots in the remote past when the rick burners had been out in England and the night sky near Kensington Palace glowed fierce red with fires; but most belonging to the present, her anxiety for the French royal family, for her cousins and uncles in revolutionary Europe, for Princess Sophia, dying alone by her own command, for Aunt Gloucester, her nervous fingers twining and intertwining, her poor mind gone.

Sir James Clark was consulted. Scotland would be her anodyne, he assured the Prince. Sleeping draughts for the moment, as little worry as possible, and Deeside as soon as she could go there and all would be well.

Lord Palmerston made her flight from London an excuse

for not sending down dispatches for her approval, but when she reproved him, and he sent them, they were so distressing as to cause her further nightmares. The flames of revolution continued to lick at European palaces.

Superstitious as well as depressed, the Queen was aghast to meet an army of toads swarming over the Osborne lawn towards the house. Her shrieks terrified the children. The Prince of Wales was physically sick.

She shrieked again when word was brought to her that a small army of Chartists had arrived at Cowes and was making for Osborne. The Prince calmed her, made himself generalissimo, summoned all the labourers working on the house and the constables on duty, armed them with sticks and guns, and waited. It was a small army indeed; merely forty members of a working men's brotherhood out for a Whitsun picnic. They had bottled beer, and pies, and cold cooked sausages, and were bent on enjoying themselves not overturning the dynasty; but Victoria was severely frightened.

Her fright turned to incredulity, and then to anger when almost immediately afterwards it was announced in *The Times* and other papers that a unique collection of one hundred etchings by the Queen and Prince Albert would shortly be exhibited to the public. The theft of her sketch book had been bad enough. This was intolerable.

Miss Skerrett was asked to go to the mainland to make discreet inquiries. Before she returned two copies of a catalogue of the engravings arrived at Osborne. They had been sent by Mr Judge of Windsor.

The Queen was very angry indeed. How dared this impertinent man admit his responsibility for the exhibition? How had he come by the engravings? Albert was equally angry, but he saw the wisdom of getting all the facts before doing anything. Impatiently they waited for Miss Skerrett's return.

That lady was surprised by the importance suddenly attached to her mission. She had gone from Ryde on the public ferry, but on her return she found a royal cutter waiting for her at Portsmouth Harbour. It had been there for more than twenty-four hours with orders to wait until she arrived. She hardly had time to transfer from the cutter to a pony carriage at Osborne pier, and go up to take her bonnet off, before she was summoned to the Queen's private drawing-room.

The Queen was seated at the grand piano but not playing. She was turning backwards and forwards on the old-fashioned screw music stool. Near to her, beside one of the brass-topped writing tables, stood the Prince. At a little distance, both looking grave, were Mr Anson and the Baron. She would have liked to have sat down and could have done had the Prince not been there. Victoria, seeing how tired she was, eyed Albert, hoping that perhaps this once he might relax the protocol, but he appeared to notice nothing. At once he asked Miss Skerrett if she would be so good as to report on her investigations.

As she did so his lips became more and more compressed. Every so often he glanced at the Baron or his Private Secretary. Towards the end of the recital he moved closer to the Queen and took her by the hand.

The facts were plain. Miss Skerrett herself had the superintendence of the plates and kept them securely locked up, but generally, because the press at Windsor was heavy to use, etchings were sent down to the printing offices of a Mr Brown in Windsor for impressions to be taken off. The first testing copy of each, made on common paper and therefore worthless, had been collected together by his copperplate pressman until he had a collection of about a hundred and thirty plates. To him they were valueless, being discards and even in some cases trampled underfoot, and simply for interest's sake he had pasted them, rather clumsily, into an album. He made no secret of the fact to Miss Skerrett that he had been surprised to receive an offer from Jasper Judge of fifty shillings for the album, and had laughed the matter off. It appeared, though, that Judge's offer had been serious. He returned later with a larger one of five pounds, which the printer took. These were the etchings to be exhibited in London and, no doubt, sold as separate lots.

'They shall not!' cried the Queen rising to her feet. 'He

has no right to our work and must be made to give it up.'

The Prince feared this might not be possible. If in good faith Judge had bought something useless in the trade for five pounds then, presumably, it was his property. And he had another fear, he said. He had been outspoken in his views on art critics, describing them as drones in the busy hive of painting. He was right for, at that time, they were noticeably corrupt. Almost without exception they allowed prejudice to blind them to merit, discouraged new painters, and were not above accepting bribes to puff an exhibition of meagre quality. They would gather at Judge's exhibition of royal engravings like ogres at a bloodfeast, and he and the Queen would be held up to contempt.

'Oh!' wailed the Queen and burst into tears. Miss Skerrett ran to comfort her.

'It is no use, my dear, deceiving ourselves,' said Albert loudly.

'That I know; oh, that I know,' she wailed. Sick with anxiety she listened to the men discussing how best to deal with Judge.

Anson's advice was to write to the printer of the catalogue and tell him the exhibition was prohibited. That ought to be enough for he knew well that defiance would involve him in an expensive lawsuit.

But this easy way of preventing the exhibition from taking place allowed the journalist to go scot free. And that Prince Albert would not have at any price. Judge's malice had increased. Besides his offensive newspaper articles and his deliberate misrepresentation of facts to attract a public, he had been publishing little books on the uselessness and the expense of the royal family. If it was at all possible the Prince was determined he should be crushed by the law. The Baron agreed. He hoped he was giving disinterested advice but he feared it might be coloured by the fact that his own position, as the unofficial Merlin to the Court, had been held up to blistering ridicule by Jasper Judge.

The ponderous processes of law were set in action. Affidavits were sworn and injunctions obtained to restrain the printer from publishing the catalogue and Judge from holding the exhibition, and there followed a long court case. The defence was able, but not thorough enough. Both printer and journalist lost with costs: the former, his business ruined, went abroad; the latter, unable to pay, went to prison.

Mr Judge, lawsuits, picnicking working men, the plague of toads, her royal aunts, and 'our revolution' were all put out of Victoria's mind when she embarked on the royal yacht and they sailed for the northern kingdom. Already she felt the excitement of going to their new home. It would have to be altered; pulled down and rebuilt perhaps, as at Osborne, in order to make room for everyone; and somehow or other Albert must persuade the Fife trustees to sell the property. She knew, positively and definitely, that this time Sir James Clark's cure would be effective. Scotland would be her anodyne.

As it turned out, getting there in this year of upheavals and anxiety, was not without its moment of adventure.

Councils and corporations along the east coast had arranged to show their loyalty with bands, flags, pyrotechnic displays, and the firing of maroons as the royal yacht passed by, but they had no chance. After waiting for hours – in some places in chilly, damp weather – they learnt the truth. It seemed quite incredible and caused great consternation. Somehow or other the royal yacht had been separated from her escorting steamers, and the Queen and the Prince were lost at sea.

In fact no such thing had happened. Lord Adolphus was simply showing what the new royal yacht was capable of. The official time schedule had vexed him. It appeared to suggest that he commanded a tarry scow or a Thames barge, not a streamlined, screw-driven steam yacht which was the pride of his old heart; and so once at sea he gave the order for full steam ahead, lost the naval escort and reached Aberdeen twelve hours early.

The authorities there were dismayed to be caught napping, but the Queen was not displeased. Her experiences of the North Sea had never been happy, and the less time she spent on it the better. Moreover she loved the way the old admiral gleefully rubbed his hands together and kept drawing everyone's attention to the time just in case they had missed the fact that his ship was as slippery and as beautiful and as capital as anything afloat.

Their reception in Scotland was indeed a royal and loyal one, but when they reached Balmoral they were left alone. There they continued to live as simple and ordinary Scotch gentlefolk. The house was small, the rooms small, the Household small. The sovereign's guard was limited to a single policeman who patrolled the grounds to warn off trespassers.

To Victoria it was perfection. The life so suited them that almost at once she was back on her old terms with Albert: no weeping, no frightened hysterics, no recriminations. She devoted herself to him afresh and was with him as often as she could; out with him when he shot ptarmigan, eating a picnic luncheon with him at the summit of the mountain Loch-na-Gar, walking with him in the Dee valley – which at first sight had reminded him of Thüringerwald, accompanying him to a fir and heather hide from which he shot a royal stag; watching him play billiards with Mr Anson; getting his help in arranging her collection of cairngorms; sharing his interest in the estate and assisting, when she could, with his plans for alterations and improvements. Her calmness and her composure returned as her nerves and her tired body relaxed. All the things which, earlier in the year, had so distressed her, fell into proper perspective. She could now see them in proportion.

But one vexation clung like a barley cockle. Lord Palmerston, charming as he was – and few could be more charming – was still continuing his wilful way at the Foreign Office. He sent out dispatches which she had never seen, fierce provocative demands to foreign chancelleries which they naturally resented; and when he did send her dispatches, he often ignored her comments and suggestions and calmly sent out the original unaltered.

A fortnight of Deeside air gave her the determination to deal with Pilgerstein. Lord John was the Minister in Attendance and she sent for him. She told him candidly that she wished Lord Palmerston to be moved from the Foreign Office. Could he not be given the Lieutenancy of Ireland instead? Lord John thought not. He had been warned, he told her, that if Palmerston was put aside by the Whigs, he would turn against them. What of it? said the Queen. Lord John confessed he was not anxious to cause internal trouble in his own party.

For the moment Victoria was satisfied. She had made her point and made it strongly. Moreover she knew she had no right herself to get rid of a Foreign Secretary. In theory she could dismiss the whole ministry, but she doubted if anyone would be persuaded to form an administration in Lord John's place if she behaved so drastically. Nevertheless she left the flavour of the idea in the Prime Minister's mouth.

'Very well, Lord John; I must accept your advice, much as I regret it. I ought to tell you, though, that sometimes my health has been impaired by Lord Palmerston's violence and eccentricity. Sir James Clark will inform you that if I am obliged to read a foreign office dispatch before dinner it invariably makes me bilious; and I am afraid that some day I might have to tell you, frankly and without any sort of prevarication, that I am unable to put up with Lord Palmerston any longer. That,' she finished, eyeing the little man, 'would be very disagreeable and awkward.'

'Indeed, Ma'am, it would,' he replied.

V

Not even her holiday at Balmoral gave the Queen sufficient fortitude to face the news which came from Brocket that November.

> Lord Palmerston [he wrote] *is here engaged in the mel-*
> *ancholy occupation of watching the gradual extinction of*
> *the lamp of life of one who was not more distinguished by*

his brilliant talents, his warm affections, and his first-rate
understanding, than by those sentiments of attachment to
your Majesty which rendered him the most devoted sub-
ject who ever had the honour to serve a sovereign.

'Sentiments of attachment.' The phrase now hurt her for
she felt she had let down poor Lord M. She knew how
deeply attached to her he was, but she had allowed herself to
forget it in the past year or two. Since his breakdown she
had tried to write regularly and she had been patient when
he rebuked her, as forgetful old men do rebuke those they
love, for not writing more often. She had invited him to
Windsor whenever it had been possible but he had made it
clear the Castle was no longer the same now that the suite of
rooms numbered 343 was denied to him. And only on rare
occasions had she seen him at private houses where he had
contrived to beg an invitation for himself.

She put away the letter and sat quietly beside the tall
windows which overlooked the terrace and the Great Park.
How often in the old days had Lord M. ridden beside her
out there, thundering along in their mad gallops, his curling
silver whiskers peeping out from the grey tall hat, his knees
high in an old-fashioned jockey stirrup, with his smiling face
and his great whoop of a laugh. The thought of all he had
done for her, his patient instruction in statecraft, his deftness
in preventing her from making a spectacle of herself; most
of all the memory of his kindness, his gentle understanding
kindness, made her heart ache. She longed to go to his
deathbed. But she was his Queen as well as his friend and
protocol forbade it.

So far as Lord M. was concerned Victoria was actually
there at Brocket. His sister was at one side of the bed, his
brother at the other. At the foot was that scamp Pam, looking more cherubic than ever. And there was the girl who had
caught his heart as a young queen of eighteen, and who had
kept it ever since; the only person who had been able to lift
him from his two crosses of a mad, adulterous wife and a
mentally deficient son. He saw her dancing beneath a thousand wax candles at Windsor. He saw her bathing her

spaniel Dash, panting because he struggled, and with an escaped curl plastered by splashed water to her forehead. He saw her studying state papers, pouting because they bored her, and smiling at him when she skipped the more complicated parts, begging him not to scold her as she was sure it did not matter in the least. He saw her on the throne of St Edward in the Abbey, a tiny crowned figure, with a sceptre and orb, and with a sweet smile on her face as he knelt before her to do homage.

'Pam,' he whispered.

Palmerston moved. He put his ear close to the hot, dried lips and listened.

Melbourne wanted to remind him of something he himself had said a long time before when a lost vote in Parliament had threatened to separate him from Victoria. Then he had made a prophecy to his brother-in-law that when everything mutable had changed, when Victoria had married and borne children and altered in a score of ways, and he himself lay under a stone at Brocket, his love for her would still continue circling the world – like light and warmth.

But Palmerston heard nothing.

Quite quietly, Lord Melbourne had died.

George Anson was not at all happy that Jasper Judge was in prison. He had been cruelly vindictive to the Prince and the Queen, and a continual pest from the time he settled in Windsor, but Anson thought he had been punished enough. He went to Prince Albert and said so.

The Prince was of a different opinion. It was not in his nature to be vengeful, but having caught the wasp which had so often stung him, he thought it an error of judgement to let it go. But, pleading for Mrs Judge and her children, and asking it as a personal favour, Anson persuaded him to agree. A cheque for the legal costs of Judge's case was sent to his wife so that she could get him out of prison. Once out, Judge promptly sat down and wrote one of his little books, a long account of his persecution by the royal family and the judiciary.

'Well, Anson?' said the Prince with a wry smile. 'Did I not warn you?'

Anson promised to buy up all the copies as soon as the book was published. 'I thought it right, Sir. And I still think so,' he added.

'In Germany he would have been checked right at the beginning of his unworthy career.'

'But in Germany, Sir, throne after throne has toppled, but the Queen of England's is as a rock.'

The Prince smiled. 'Perhaps you are right.'

He permitted Anson such liberties; in fact, after nine years, he no longer considered them as liberties. His Germanness had been Anglicized more by Anson than by anyone else, and he had implicit faith in his instinct for knowing what was right and prudent and what was wrong and foolish. It was this trait which had liberated Judge.

Their first, slow friendship had developed into a trusting, intimate relationship. Stockmar was ageing, his crabbiness increasing in almost exact proportion to the greying of his hair, and he was still more of a mentor to Albert than a close companion. Though Löhlein his valet was naturally in Albert's confidence, his small German Household was not as important to him now as it once had been. Coburg relations came over less than at the beginning of his marriage, and there were no more visits from fellow students. His nostalgia for the camaraderie of beer and radishes and bawled choruses had evaporated with the years. His separation from Ernest had been like losing a limb, but he discovered after a year or two that, once amputated, a man lacks interest in looking for his severed arm or leg.

Maturity had brought him to realize that four stars were enough for his firmament: his wife, his children, the savants who so vastly interested him with their knowledge and their speculations, and George Anson.

With his friend he relaxed. After much practice Anson found how to relax as well. Each showed his own mind, each learnt to appreciate the other's qualities, and each contributed something to the development of the other's personality, the growth of his character. With time they discovered they depended on, and needed, each other.

When Anson mourned his old master Lord Melbourne, the Prince succeeded in comforting him – but, to his surprise, he felt a stab of jealousy. Possessive love, of the intensity Victoria had for him, was something he had never experienced. Now he felt a trace of it because George had been so utterly cast down by Melbourne's unhappy end. Characteristically he mentioned it. In their relationship hardly anything was kept back. Then, equally characteristically, they reasoned it away between them.

For such a man the Prince would have done much, but one cause, because each was so determined to have his way, came between them.

Not long after Judge's release Albert began a methodical piece of surgery on the Book of Common Prayer. Having strongly anti-papist views, as much based on prejudice as on theology, he was anxious to expurgate the Prayer Book of the Church of England of any trace of popery. Words like 'priest' and 'absolution' were horrid to him and had to be altered. So did all the directions for the congregation to kneel. No one knelt to pray in Germany or in Scotland, and it was an English piety which he disliked. Indeed he had a running battle with Lady Lyttelton for some years about his own children being taught to kneel, a battle which, to his mortification, he lost. In his new Prayer Book there should be no mention of kneeling. By the time he had made these excisions and others of the same nature, the book, though hacked about, was still recognizable; but he felt obliged to alter and amend and add to the Church Services themselves. No matter what the Thirty-nine Articles of Religion stated – and they were invariably tucked away at the back – the Prayer Book was liberally sprinkled with Catholicism: in the Ordinal the doctrine that priests can forgive sins on behalf of the Almighty; in the Catechism a declaration of a Real Presence in the Lord's Supper, and in the Lord's Supper itself, as well as in the Visitation of the Sick, clear invitations to auricular confession which he regarded as a beastly, degrading practice. Greatest enormity of all, nowhere between the covers of the Prayer Book did the blessed word

'Protestant' ever appear. Not once. The Prince put it in, several times.

As an intellectual exercise, or as the present expression of one particular point of view in churchmanship, Prince Albert's emasculated book was harmless. But when he announced his intention of publishing it, Anson was quick to advise against it. In one sense he was in a bad position to do so because he preferred the other Janus-face of the Established Church, the quaint ceremonies and pious practices of the High Church suiting his temperament. Nevertheless the Prince listened, and, as he thought, agreed to abandon the idea.

Believing it done and finished with, Anson was surprised to hear the Prince tell the Queen he was having copies printed of his selective work on the Prayer Book. It was after dinner at Osborne, and he and Miss Skerrett were playing a rubber of whist with the Duchess of Kent and Madame Späth. What he had heard, and knowing what a printing might lead to, made him play very badly. His partner, the Duchess, grew more and more irritable. When he actually revoked she declared he was unwell. He must be to do such a thing.

In fact he had been feeling less well than usual. Perhaps his face was showing it. Hoping so, he excused himself from finishing the game.

'Go and lie down, Mr Anson,' said the Duchess in her heavy German accent, and with the asperity of someone dismissing a child. After the way he had played it was no wonder.

He did not lie down. Instead he waited for the Prince.

His advice this time was worded more strongly. The publication of such a book would cause great offence especially as Prince Albert was a foreigner brought up in an alien Church.

The Prince shrugged. 'Lutheran, Church of England, Church of Scotland, they are all the same.'

'You will pardon me, Sir, if I beg to contradict,' said Anson warmly. 'They are no such thing.'

They wrangled theologically for half an hour or more

when the Prince said he would think the matter over. He had ordered a small printing but undertook that the copies should not be distributed until he had taken other advice. In any case, he said, there was barely time to come to a conclusion for the present. In three days they were to make a State Visit to Ireland on their way to Balmoral.

Without exactly badgering his master, Anson kept the subject alive from time to time during the visit to Ireland and the holiday at Balmoral. But the Prince had other things on his mind. When he was not shooting or deer-stalking or driving out or learning to dance reels with the Queen, he was exceptionally busy planning new plantations, stables, cottages and workshops, and visiting two large neighbouring estates which he hoped to buy and add to Balmoral. Then, though Balmoral was sufficiently cut off, the Prince and the Queen had made an even more isolated retreat; a double bothy in Glen Muich, twenty minutes' walk from a dark loch, still on the estate, but a long pony ride from the house, and they went there for three days' solitude with a minimum of attendants, and left George Anson behind. It was his duty to deal with incoming dispatches.

While they were away a parcel arrived, forwarded from Windsor. It contained twenty-four copies of Prince Albert's Prayer Book. Anson had, of course, seen the original mutilated Book of Common Prayer, and his clerks had made a fair copy of the amended text, but he had never studied it thoroughly as a whole. Now that he had the leisure he did so. At the end of a reading he wanted to order a pony and go straight to Glen Muich. It was a deplorable book, a distilled essence of bigotry. But it was impossible to break in on the Queen's privacy. He needed someone to talk to, but the Minister in Attendance would jump out of his skin if he saw a copy of the book, and the only other person there of sufficient standing was Mr Greville, Clerk to the Privy Council, and he was too much of a gossip. There was nothing for it but to wait the remaining five or six hours until the Prince returned. He filled the time by giving the book a second, even more thorough reading. He made marginal notes, and added a detailed memorandum on his own reception of the book, which was not important, and what he believed would be the public's reception, which was. He left these papers in a prominent position on the Prince's desk, and told the clerk to make sure he looked at them first of all. By now his feelings were so strong that he could not trust himself to speak on the matter.

When the party returned from Glen Muich for the first and only time in his life Anson sought an ally in the Queen. Asking for a private audience he poured out the whole story. What she herself believed was always a mystery to her courtiers, but it was generally known that she shared the Prince's antipathy of ritualism. Then her love for everything Scotch caused her to enjoy Kirk services with an eagerness that embarrassed the leaders of her Church in the southern kingdom. Nevertheless, she was not rigid – regarding Sabbatarians, for instance, with a candid scorn; and she was a woman of common-sense. She agreed that, if the occasion arose, she would do her very best to support Anson.

By dinner time the Prince had read the notes in the memorandum. He was unimpressed and not at all pleased with his friend's persistence.

'You will drive me to publish, Anson,' he warned.

'That, Sir, I cannot believe. And I am sure that with time you will come to see the lack of wisdom in considering such a thing.'

'Here,' said the Prince, tapping the paper, 'you call it rashness . . .' He adjusted the reading eye-glasses he had recently taken to wearing. 'And inopportune. That perhaps is the kindest word your memorandum contains. You rap my knuckles with such words as "bias", "dogmatic" and "quirk".'

'I should not be doing my duty,' replied Anson gruffly, 'if I praised the book and advised you to publish.'

The Prince raised an eyebrow. 'You dislike it so much?'

'Yes.' Anson took a deep breath. He felt a little faint. 'Yes,' he repeated. 'It is an emasculation, and publication can only cause harm.'

'There,' said the Prince, 'we shall have to disagree. For the moment let us leave it. We have a few days of holiday left, and it would be a pity to spoil them.' He was adamant. Even when the Queen found an opportunity to ask if he was well advised to publish his amended Prayer Book, he refused to discuss it. With her, too, he said the matter could be left until they returned to Osborne.

George Anson accepted his decision. He could do no else, but the thought that it was ten to one the Prince would publish, was very distressing. Yet, as long as there was a ten per cent chance of making him change his mind the Secretary was willing to persevere.

They were hardly settled back at Osborne than he looked out for an occasion to bring up the painful subject once again.

But he never did have an opportunity.

One day, when a late September wind was blowing hard from the Solent and making the hall chimney smoke, Anson was standing beside the fire and talking quite ordinarily when, momentarily, he faltered. His jaw fell. He gaped, his eyes took on an abnormal brilliance, and he crumpled to the floor. He did not speak again. By October he was dead.

Lady Lyttelton suddenly found herself to all intents and purposes head of the Household. The Prince was inconsolable. The Queen, mourning on her own account the loss of a faithful servant, felt it with double keenness because Albert was so distraught. The reckless way in which he had collected and burnt all the printed copies of his Prayer Book showed his state of mind. He whipped himself with regrets and, which was quite unlike him, he stopped work. His carefully planned daily schedule was put aside. His engagements were cancelled and he refused to read letters and see government boxes. Day after day he sailed on the Solent, his valet Löhlein crewing for him; and the darker and the angrier the sea, the better it suited him. In the house he did little save grieve silently for his friend. Listlessly he accepted Victoria's nervous suggestion that the Privy Purse, Colonel Sir Charles Phipps, take Anson's place. The Colonel was an obvious choice as he knew already what work was involved and the Prince liked him. But a fortnight passed before the new Private Secretary could get the Prince to reorganize his life again. This he did by shrewdly suggesting that they work together on the Prince's nebulous plans for an exhibition of arts and sciences in London. It had been one of Anson's particular interests and therefore the Prince threw himself into the work. It was his own private tribute to the memory of his friend.

As superstitious as ever, the Queen swore there would have to be a third death. First poor Lord M., now Mr Anson. A third, the death of someone close to them was inevitable.

Seeing how the idea cast her down, Miss Skerrett and the Queen's ladies tried their best to make light of it. But Victoria's dismalness increased. After a blessed gap of more than eighteen months she was once more carrying a child. It would be her seventh, that is if the poor thing were born alive, if she herself could survive the awful labour pains of her last confinement.

The gloom about her was darkened by a frightening accident in November.

The Prince of Wales was taken on a pheasant shoot. Colonel Grey, an equerry, was there to look after him, and his father, of course, was in charge of the shoot. He had his own apartments now, and a governor and a tutor and a Household of his own, but to the Queen he was still a small boy and so she went to the shoot to see for herself how her son carried his gun.

She was gratified to see that he did well – but then, suddenly, she was alarmed because the Prince told Grey to take the boy forward out of the firing line to look for a runaway bird. She called out to Albert, and he was in the act of assuring her that no one would shoot in their direction, when one of the guns did take a shot and hit Grey in the head.

The Queen shrieked.

Colonel Grey, his head in his hands, turned gallantly to reassure her. He was not seriously hurt. Lord Canning, the gun who had peppered him, realizing how close he had come to shooting the heir to the throne, promptly fainted away. Victoria had every reason to do the same but she was far too angry. When Canning came round she gave him a piece of her mind. Then she rated Albert publicly for his ill-disciplined shoot. Finally she commanded the Prince of Wales and Colonel Grey to be put in her carriage and she drove them home.

The full realization of what might have happened made her more maternal than ever before. For a day or two afterwards whenever her feelings got the better of her, and this happened at the oddest times – just after breakfast, in school time, or even at night – she would rush to Bertie's apartments to seize him in her arms and cry over him. Only fate, she thought, had saved him from being the third great sorrow. Perhaps, after all, it was reserved to her and to the baby she was carrying.

Feeling unhappy and insecure in a way she had not before experienced she was almost relieved when after a long illness which caused neither discomfort nor pain her aunt Queen Adelaide died at her country home. It was the third death she had waited for.

Queen Adelaide's was an affecting funeral. By her own wish her body was carried by English sailors to its resting place beside her husband. Victoria sincerely mourned her aunt who had ever shown kindness to her as a girl. Neither she nor King William had had any trace of that resentment and dislike which most monarchs, and certainly all Hanoverians, felt for the heirs to their throne. On the contrary, they had done their best to brighten her dark childhood, sending her costly presents and giving balls and concerts for her; and they would have done much more had it not been for the implacable hostility between Kensington and the Court. Now even that hostility had vanished, smoothed away by Aunt Adelaide's tact and charm, and no tribute to her sweetness of disposition showed more clearly than the Duchess of Kent's grief at her death. This had the excellent effect of binding Victoria even more closely to her mother. Indeed she suggested that her mother take the lease of Abergeldie Castle next to Balmoral so that on the annual visit to

Scotland they would continue to see a good deal of each other.

Lord Melbourne, George Anson, Queen Adelaide. For the present death's pattern was complete.

VI

Prince Albert had many accomplishments, but seldom was his enthusiasm and efficiency geared more successfully to a great enterprise than his conception of the Exhibition of 1851.

It was never an easy task. Again and again he met with obstacles. Some existed because he was a royal prince and this did not endear him to certain sections of the community. Others existed because he was a foreigner and a number of the more short-sighted English were still reluctant to accept his leadership. And yet others were caused by circumstances which did not really relate to him at all.

Going out into the country, and sending agents to those parts where he could not go himself, to persuade artists and mine owners and iron masters and manufacturers and farmers to exhibit their wares, Albert found Britain was as regional as his native Germany. The railways had not yet brought a feeling of unity between the regions and consequently near neighbours like Staffordshire potters and Yorkshire woolmen had little in common. Traders in remoter regions were almost ignorant of each other's existence, and to a Cornish miner, a Merioneth slater was as foreign as a rice farmer in China. It said a great deal for the Prince's powers of persuasion and organization that he was able to draw the regions together.

The preparations were bedevilled by a series of international crises and even a threat of war with Greece, and Albert quickly learnt that, no matter how warm the invitations to his festival of work, peace and brotherhood, foreigners were not going to accept them while Lord Palmerston remained so cocksure and bellicose, sending out gunboats and abusive dispatches, and bullying the little nations.

Finance was a perpetual anxiety. The government showed an unwillingness to underwrite the Exhibition and the Prince was obliged to collect a number of rich supporters and persuade them by his own zeal and detailed arguments that the project must turn out a success.

Worse was a public commotion about the site. He and his commissioners chose Hyde Park. At once there was an outcry from those who rode in Rotten Row. Let the Prince's trade fair take place at Smithfield, they sneered, or in the city. He did not reply because his own dear friend Sir Robert Peel had just been thrown in the Row, and, a rib piercing his lung, he had died after three days' agony. Peel like Anson had been another forward-looking man who had had the vision to see what benefits the Exhibition could bring to the country. Now he and his support were gone as well. As a tribute to both the Prince put his private grief on one side and carried on. Whatever anyone said his trade fair should be held in the Park.

How to house such a vast Exhibition was a problem which he left to be solved by competition. Of the designs submitted, that of the Duke of Devonshire's gardener, Joseph Paxton, showed the greatest originality. It would be of metal and glass and one thousand feet long. The Prince remembered Paxton. He remembered being shown at Chatsworth the great conservatory designed by him and the lily house where Annie Paxton had stood on a lily leaf. All Paxton had learnt about stress and strain from the structure of that leaf was incorporated in his plan. Iron girders would support hundreds and thousands of panes of glass. But the choice of Paxton's Exhibition palace raised a storm from the Prince's opponents. A member of the Commons predicted it would be smashed to atoms by hail. Someone else said it would crash to the ground under the weight of bird droppings. A third Jeremiah pointed out that the conservatory at Buckingham Palace had just collapsed for no known reason, and had made such a devastation that the military had been called in to clear it up. Was there any reason to suppose, he asked, that a larger structure, more open to wind and other pressures, would be any safer? The Prince knew it was, because Paxton was an engineering genius, but he said nothing. Some people could not be reasoned with. His best answer was to ask Victoria to make Paxton a knight for his services to arts and science. She promised that she would do so on the closing day of the Exhibition.

Throughout the months of preparation the Queen was unquestioningly in support of everything he did. She could not follow all his plans. They were too many, and too complex. But she knew in her bones that he was doing an excellent thing for her country and her people, and she looked out for ways in which to help him.

One she discovered quite by accident.

The birth of her seventh child, a son, took place with less discomfort than she had feared on May Day. As it also happened to be Wellington's birthday and she was increasingly fond of the old man, she asked him to be godfather to her little boy and to give him his name. It was no easy task, shrieking her request into his ear. But it got through at last, and the victor of Waterloo was delighted. So were quite a number of his supporters who up to that date had looked with suspicion on the royal family's promotion of an Exhibition which seemed to glorify free trade. Seeing the way of it, the Queen took the trouble to be especially pleasant to Mr Disraeli, who had become leader of the Tories in the Commons. She thought him reckless and unsafe, far too flashy with his oiled ringlets and yellow waistcoat and ruby rings to be considered trustworthy; but for Albert and Albert's Exhibition she would have tried to charm even Lord Palmerston. Disraeli was the cleverest man in his party as well as its leader. He saw what his sovereign was up to, and admired her for it. He knew quite well that for ten years or so protectionism would be the deadest of political ducks, and that nothing was being sacrificed in supporting an

Exhibition which would do the country good. From that time the Tories were with Albert, except for a few eccentrics on the extreme edge of the party.

Realizing that Albert ought not to be distracted by domestic and nursery worries she tried her hardest to deal with them herself. When Kennaird, her page for many years, disgraced himself by appearing drunk in her presence, it was she who spoke to him afterwards and discovered he was becoming an alcoholic; and it was she who sent him privately to Sir James Clark. When Bertie's tutor, the Reverend Mr Birch, told her frankly that the child was very backward and learnt so slowly he could never reach the high academic standard his father required, she kept it from Albert. And when Colonel Phipps came to tell her that a newly-built arch had collapsed at Osborne, killing a workman and injuring two others, she begged him to be careful how he told the Prince. He must choose the best possible time and let him know the bad news in dribs and drabs, rather than all at once, or he would be terribly shocked and upset.

Ordinarily they discussed problems together. Now, for his benefit, she did without the relief of unburdening herself. On the occasions when her young ladies were vexing she suffered it patiently saying nothing to Albert. When the rapid growing-up of her children seemed a threat to her rather than a comfort, and made her feel older and plainer, she talked to Skerrett about it, not her husband. Even when people died – the poor *ci-devant* King of the French down at Claremont, and King Leopold's wife, Aunt Louise – she wept and she mourned them as unobtrusively as possible so that her distress should not increase his. And when Sir John Conroy, the devil of her childhood, also died, and thoughts so crowded back that she felt a great need to talk to someone about him, she remained silent. She would not distract Albert from his work.

The worst burden of all was laid on her a bare few months before the Exhibition was due to open. Lady Lyttelton came to her and admitted that she was not well. She had grown old in the royal service and now felt her years. The superintendence of the royal nurseries was too much for her and she begged to be allowed to retire. Victoria was very upset. Lady Lyttelton had been close to her since her accession and she loved her dearly. She knew, too, how the children loved her, and she could not bear to think how they would manage without her. But at the forefront of her mind was Albert. He would be more than distressed to hear Lady Lyttelton was leaving. For his sake, could she not be persuaded to change her mind? Lady Lyttelton shook her head. She really was not well enough. She would have to leave soon. But she quite appreciated that the Prince should be upset as little as possible. It was arranged that between them they should find a suitable replacement, before he was told anything.

Finally Victoria was enabled to give Albert the greatest help of all quite involuntarily and unwittingly. Her uncle, the Duke of Cambridge, was dying and, as often happens at such times, regretting the fact that they had not been on good terms for a long time, Victoria went to visit him. Afterwards, with the Prince of Wales and Alice and Alfred beside her in the carriage, they were held up for a moment by a press of people at the narrow gates of Cambridge House, and a man leapt from the crowd, climbed up beside her and with his cane he hit her as hard as he could on the head. Had it not been for the stiff rim of her bonnet she might have been dangerously wounded. As it was she had severe bruises, a black eye, and a headache which plagued her for weeks.

Besides having to suffer the pain, two aspects of the attack particularly annoyed her; first that three of her children had seen it all, and had been terribly frightened; second that the attacker had not been a labourer or a political agitator but a respectable retired officer of the Tenth Hussars, with no apparent motive for his vicious attack. On this occasion she allowed herself to feel vindictive satisfaction that the crowd had manhandled him and set about him with his own cane, and that later he was sentenced to transportation for seven years. She was also delighted because quite inadvertently the attack helped Albert's cause. As her own popularity soared up after details of the attack were known, so did his, and diehard opponents were more disposed to be sympathetic with his schemes.

But, in the end, it was not her own people who most offended Albert and put the most awkward obstacles in the way of the Exhibition. Foreign monarchs made it difficult if not impossible for their subjects to attend. Two were particularly objectionable. Passports were withheld by the Tsar and the King of Naples, on the grounds that in such a 'liberal' country their people would be contaminated. Even the King of Prussia, with whom Albert and Victoria thought they were in rapport, offended them by asking Albert if it was really safe for the Crown Prince and his family to be under Paxton's glass domes. He replied that there was not the least fear in England, however panic-stricken people might be on the continent, but as he could guarantee no man's life anywhere at any time, he would withdraw his invitation to the Crown Prince and his family.

Up to the last moment there were alarms. Medical cranks said that such a gathering of all races could only result in a colossal outbreak of the Black Death; economists prophesied that so many people could not be fed and London would have a famine; reactionaries were sure that subversive masses of socialists and other undesirables would descend on Hyde Park like foreign birds of prey; Low Churchmen warned that amongst the trade exhibits were crucifixes and altar plate from Belgium and the Pope could not be far behind; moralists declared that simple country people up from the provinces would be debauched by the vice of the metropolis. There stood Paxton's masterpiece, the girders and frame painted a royal blue, the glass shading from turquoise to white; so large that it enclosed large elm trees, and the Jeremiahs still prophesied disaster. If it rained, they said, the weight of water would break the glass planes; if the sun shone, exhibitors and visitors alike would be roasted to death. The Prime Minister joined them. He was sure, he said, that the royal salute of guns, scheduled to be fired at the moment the Queen opened the Exhibition, would bring the whole thing down in a tinkling ruin. Then the exhibitors complained. The hundreds of sparrows which had been built into the structure and had not the sense to escape, were twittering up in the elm branches, and fouling the carefully prepared exhibits below. This last unforeseen difficulty was one of the smallest Albert had had to face, but after months of opposition and obstacles it was too much for him. He put his head in his hands and said he could do no more. That evening the Duke of Wellington was at the Palace visiting his godson. Greatly agitated the Queen asked for his advice.

He was by no means tall but she was tiny and had to stand on tiptoe to shout into his cupped ear.

Eventually he understood, and thought for a moment.

'Try sparrow-hawks, Ma'am,' he bellowed.

The Duke was gratified to note his advice had been taken and there was not a sparrow in sight when he went to the grand opening of the Exhibition. It took place on May Day, his eighty-second birthday, and with him he had his old cavalry commander at Waterloo, the one-legged Lord Anglesey. Because of their age and infirmity they were offered stools, but this only made them stand straighter than ever.

Both were greatly impressed by the vast throng of people. It was estimated that over thirty thousand were packed into Paxton's Exhibition hall, and outside at least 700,000 lined the procession route from the Palace.

'The young man's done very well,' shouted the Duke.

Lord Anglesey did not like the Prince, but in such circumstances he could not grudge him a nod of approval.

It was, indeed, the Prince's day. His philosophy that labour, invention, science, industry, art and the free exchange of ideas and goods would bring a universal harmony, was about to be tested in a practical sphere. He was pale as he took his place at the head of the commissioners to welcome the Queen.

'Looks tired,' commented the Duke loudly. 'Washed-out. But, bless us, look at the Queen, Anglesey. Just look at her!'

Victoria was certainly worth looking at. Miss Skerrett had

tactfully controlled her exuberance and helped her choose a becoming dress of light pink watered silk. Across it she wore the Garter ribbon. She also wore a small crown, two feathers and the Koh-i-Noor diamond. But it was her radiancy which made her so especially attractive that day. She was supremely happy, and showed it, because this great Exhibition in its awe-inspiring palace of crystal was Albert's creation, and she was enormously proud of him. 'Pretty,' bellowed the Duke. 'No, beautiful, by God!'

'Wellington,' warned his friend at the top of his voice. 'You're shouting too much.'

'Yes, I know,' shouted the Duke imperturbably. 'Who wouldn't on such an occasion? It's splendid. Glorious.'

The Queen was in tears when Albert as head of the commissioners read out a report. Then the Archbishop blessed the Exhibition, and one of the largest organs in England, plus an orchestra of two hundred instruments and a choir of six hundred, burst out in the *Hallelujah Chorus*. It was a stirring scene, and so moved one Chinese gentleman that he came forward and made a profound obeisance to the Queen. She gave him a gracious bow because she could understand his expression of his feelings. Her own moved her to further tears. Nevertheless she was glad that when the procession was formed the Chinaman was put in his proper place amongst the diplomatic body. Oriental ecstasies might otherwise have proved embarrassing.

The great organ, orchestra and voices died. Then trumpets pealed. Other organs, hidden in the aisles of the great hall, began to play. The Queen's procession moved off to view some of the exhibits.

'Now, Anglesey,' bellowed the Duke. 'Step it out, man. Don't drag that wooden leg of yours. We've a good deal to do, and I want to see some gadgets.'

The two old warriors set out arm in arm, and the Duke's liking for anything curious and intriguing was quickly gratified. On that first visit to the Prince's Exhibition – and later he paid many others – he and Lord Anglesey inspected a carriage drawn not by horses nor by a railway locomotive but by kites, a clasp knife with three hundred blades, a group of stuffed frogs, a zinc statue of the Queen, a physician's walking stick with a convenient enema apparatus stuffed in its handle, and a pulpit connected by gutta-percha tubes to the pews of the deaf.

Late in the afternoon the Duke went to the Palace. The Queen and the Prince had been persuaded to show themselves to a huge, enthusiastic crowd from a balcony on the new front, a practice which from that time they carried out whenever it was necessary. The Duke thought it an excellent idea. Royalty, he told the Queen, should be seen sometimes but not too often. Then he told her about the pulpit with gutta-percha tubes. Had she seen it? he asked. Apparently she had not, but because he was so deaf she said she thought that perhaps such a device might be useful.

'Invention of the devil, Ma'am,' he shouted. 'There aren't many advantages in losing one's hearing, but avoiding the weekly exhortations of my chaplain is one. He's a capital fellow, but I hope he don't see that pulpit. And now, Ma'am, with your permission, I'd like to see my godson. It's his birthday as well as mine.'

The Queen took him to the nursery herself. He didn't, he said, want the child to be brought to him; better to see him as he really was. As it turned out Prince Arthur was in excellent spirits and delighted to pull his noisy godfather's silver whiskers. He accepted a gold cup which the Duke took from a pocket, and gave him a posy of flowers in return. They bubbled at each other and kissed.

It was hardly believable, thought Victoria, that there were eighty-one years between them.

That evening, in the large confines of the royal bed, Victoria and Albert talked of the day's events.

What a triumph it had been for him, what a reward for all his patience and months of hard work. And how appreciative everyone had been, even those once hostile to the Exhibition. The alarmists and pessimists who had come to see their jeremiads fulfilled and cast scorn on Paxton's crystal palace had been moved to tears by the magnificence of the opening ceremony ...

Albert still said little. He simply nodded and agreed with her. For the first time he felt warm in all England's praises.

How well the choirs had sung, she said; and how touching it was to see those old veterans, the Duke and Lord Anglesey, tottering along together in the procession. And didn't Albert agree that the orientals had a superb sense of occasion. The spontaneous obeisance of the plenipotentiary of the Dragon Throne of China had deeply moved her ...

She stopped. It almost seemed as if her husband had chuckled. Surely, she asked, he must agree that the envoy's unrehearsed act of respect was extraordinarily appropriate?

'It was,' he said; and this time there was no mistaking it. He was chuckling.

'Albert! It was a most wonderful *thrilling* thing to happen. And he looked so grave and dramatic in his blue tunic and black and scarlet cap.'

'Of course, my dear. Of course. In every respect it was a perfect performance. But ...' Laughter stopped him.

Victoria sat up in bed.

'For the newspaper reporters,' he continued when he had controlled himself, 'the Exhibition Secretary had to find out his name and rank. And it seems he is not an official representative of the Celestial Empire.'

'Oh!' Victoria was disappointed. And she was still puzzled by Albert's amusement.

'He is a junk skipper, my dear, who shows off his craft at a shilling a head.'

'A *junk skipper*!' repeated the Queen.

'Yes. A Chinaman called He Sing, from Clapham.'

'Oh,' said Victoria again. Then suddenly she hugged Albert. The room was noisy with their laughter for a long time.

VII

Albert's popularity made Victoria very happy. Fortune, she felt, was being very good to them, and as she was superstitious she did all that she could to ensure its continuance.

The Balmoral custom of the Queen being given a posy of white heather at the breakfast table was transferred over the border. Common-sense told her this could hardly be as efficacious as being given fresh heather, but it could do no harm and a touch of luck, however weak, was always welcome. For the same reason she was fascinated by what the Duke, a great reader of newspaper advertisements because of his fondness for gadgets, told her about Cornish pixies. It was tea-time talk to him, a light subject to raise a smile, but the Queen took it seriously. She was interested to hear how they were transported and delivered, and appeared disappointed to discover they were not living creatures, but metal images which were said to carry good luck. Only Miss Skerrett knew that within a fortnight one of the Queen's most private trinket boxes contained a Cornish pixie. Superstition even affected her choice of dogs. Since Dash's death she had never been without a spaniel, and she liked to have Skye terriers because they had such character, but quite her favourite dogs for a long time were turnspits from Germany – because turnspits out there, and especially tan-coloured ones, were believed to bring good fortune. She had loved gypsies since her childhood and had had charms presented to her many years before in a smoky encampment by Claremont House. She would have given a good deal for the freedom to consult a gypsy fortune teller, but for the Queen of England it was out of the question. Instead she obtained, through Skerrett, a book on predictions – the telling of fortune by cards, by ashes, by tea leaves, by dots made at random on a paper, and by dropping melted wax into water.

She confessed she thought most of these methods of divination suspect and she excluded all save the first.

Albert teased her unmercifully about her superstitions. She was the sort of person, he said, who would have ladders arranged in her way for the sheer pleasure of walking round them, and he had her worried for hours by pretending that while the possession of one turnspit brought good luck, owning two was disastrous, and as for three – the number she owned – no one in Germany had ever dared to try the experiment. He was hard put to it afterwards to persuade her he had been joking. And whenever the cards told her anything, he was instantly ready with an alternative and very mundane interpretation.

When she was told she would have trouble with a neighbour, he told her to be on the lookout for Mr Judge. She, on the other hand, saw it as a warning to watch out for Louis Napoleon of France. This impertinent nephew of the great Emperor had turned up at the right time and got himself elected as President for life. Then by a *coup d'état*, he proclaimed himself Emperor as Napoleon the Third. Very slippery when the poor princes of Orleans were still in exile. *He* was the neighbour to watch.

In the domestic sphere the cards were disappointing until one day they predicted the solving of a knotty family problem and the Queen was sure it had been fulfilled by the timely appointment of a new tutor for the Prince of Wales. Of all family problems Bertie was the knottiest. He was incorrigible, and neither whipping nor deprivations made a great deal of difference to his sloth and truculence. Baron Stockmar had suggested it might be the tutor's fault. Tutors were frequently difficult. Very recently a tutor to the Spanish princes had gone off his head. One known personally to the Duke of Norfolk had stuffed his charge's head full of egalitarianism. It might be that Mr Birch was insufficiently strict with Bertie and that was why the boy adored him. And so a Mr Gibbs was appointed, a clergyman whom Bertie detested, and he undertook to be severe. Victoria hoped so, and that he would improve Bertie. Poor Albert was so easily upset.

Albert made the lightest of suggestions about the prognostication on knotty family problems. He was equally frivolous when the cards foretold the downfall of an opponent. Victoria herself wondered if it could be that self-same serpent Louis Napoleon, and anxiously watched the dispatches from France; but when the downfall came, and to the cards' credit it did, it was of someone even more vexatious.

With regular persistence the Court had continued its campaign against Palmerston, sending complaints to the Prime Minister about the Foreign Secretary's improper professional conduct and about his notorious lecheries. Albert convinced Victoria it was the Court's duty to give moral tone to the nation and it could hardly be said to have succeeded as long as Palmerston remained in office. She had been scandalized to hear from Albert an old story about her Foreign Secretary's satyric ramblings at Windsor, when, mistaking the place of a nocturnal assignation, he had crept stealthily into her poor, dear Mrs Brand's bedroom and given her the shock of her life. Public opinion was at last hardening against eighteenth-century roystering, and Lord John had listened with shocked attention to this account of Lord Palmerston's concupiscence. Yet still he had protected him, and he had continued to do so until one day Palmerston over-reached himself. He offended the Whig oligarchs and, quite unexpectedly, deliciously, marvellously, Lord John dismissed him for undertaking affairs without consulting his fellow ministers. Pilgerstein was ruined at last. The Prime Minister read out to the House of Commons an old letter from the Queen in which she accused her Foreign Secretary of being discourteous to his sovereign. It seemed a dubious piece of political chicanery but it was successful. The Commons made it clear they no longer regarded Lord Palmerston as the people's idol. The times were tempestuous. Lady Palmerston whose salon was the most consequential in London described Lord John in public as 'that little blackguard'. Palmerston said the Whig ministry had doomed itself. He could bring it down. And he did, dividing the Whigs on an unimportant matter, and letting the Tories in. Lord Derby became First Minister and flash little Mr Disraeli Leader of the Commons, but they called themselves Conservatives now, no longer Tories. The cards had predicted well. The thought of overseeing the foreign policy of the country without Pilgerstein in the way was intoxicating. Surely, said the happy Queen, it was really too good to be true? She was right to have misgivings. After exactly 300 days the Conservatives fell, and back popped Pilgerstein; this time as Home Secretary where it was hoped he could do less harm. His threat to the Whigs had not been an idle one. They were never able to form another administration. Lord Aberdeen was at Downing Street as head of a group of Free Traders. They called themselves a Coalition Liberal government. It was something, said the Queen, that Pilgerstein was not at the Foreign Office, but she was cross with her cards. Having predicted the downfall of so great a nuisance, they might at least have announced his political resurrection.

Her faith in the cards was restored when they announced she had bright financial prospects. Albert declared it was not feasible because her interpreting book specified she would be enriched in one of three ways; through an increase in investment percentage, through a substantial raise of salary, or through a bequest. None, he said, were possible to the sovereign of Great Britain.

He was wrong. An eccentric old miser died and left Victoria half a million pounds. He had no relatives and advisers made it clear that if the Queen refused the bequest the half million would go to the government. Not that on any account, she said, and she accepted the money which became the foundation of her private fortune.

Albert had to reason hard with himself that in fact the fall of cards placed against the printed interpretation in Victoria's book on prediction made it possible for almost any prophecy about any event in anyone's life to come true. But he joked less and less about her fondness for reading the cards, and he was positively angry when, as was bound to happen, one day they foretold the death of a loved one. It was a prophecy which upset her so much that had it done any good, Albert would have seized and destroyed the book and the cards. Sensibly he saw that her present obsession was only temporary and that it might be made permanent if he did anything foolish or precipitous. He made light of the prophecy as best he could: inevitably, he told her, if one waited long enough some loved one or other was bound to die.

She paid little attention, and waiting began to fray her nerves so badly that Albert was heartily thankful when quite unexpectedly the King of Hanover died. He died regretted by almost everyone in his kingdom and by almost no one in England. Victoria felt a sentimental moment of remorse because she had never liked him, and she regretted that the commission called to settle the disputed ownership of the family diamonds had come to no decision before his death. She also regretted the deplorable taste of *The Times* which appeared without the customary black edge to the paper and insolently wrote of her uncle *'The good to be said of the Royal Dead is little or none.'* Nevertheless she insisted that as she had not loved King Ernest, this could not be the death prophesied by the cards.

Albert was nettled. It was wrong of her, he said, to accept such nonsense and wait ghoulishly for someone close to her to die. She would not argue, but he knew she was unpersuaded. She was convinced it was not nonsense, and in the following September a death occurred which so upset her that instantly she detested the cards which had predicted it.

The old Duke of Wellington, never having been really ill in the whole of his long life, fell unwell one morning and by three in the afternoon he was dead. This was indeed the death of a loved one. On the day she had the news she wrote in her journal:

> *In him centred almost every earthly honour a subject could possess. His position was the highest a subject ever had ... The Crown never possessed – and I fear never will – so devoted, loyal, and faithful a subject, so staunch*

a supporter! To us (who alas! have lost, now, so many of our valued and experienced friends), his loss is irreparable ...

Her resentment against the cards and the book of predictions made her abandon both. To Albert's great relief she said she would have nothing more to do with prophecy. Whatever the future held, she preferred neither to guess at it nor have it anticipated in any way. She would face events in her own strength, and, thank God, she had never felt stronger in her life: Queen of a rich and expanding kingdom, mother of seven healthy children, and married to the cleverest and most beloved of men.

She could not know what waited for her, nor how close it was.

VIII

A fire in March 1853 upset Victoria.

At ten at night smoke poured from a dining-room in the Prince of Wales' tower, and, by the time the alarm had been given, flames were leaping out of the windows. Because of a stiff breeze blowing from the wrong direction there was a fear the fire might spread to all parts of the Castle but in the Prince's domestic crusade the antique fire engines had been replaced and a trained gang of grooms and footmen were soon fighting the blaze.

Her first sight of the flames made Victoria catch her breath. She had been frightened of fire all her life, and now, with her eighth confinement only three weeks away, when her size and weight made her sluggish, panic welled up inside her.

Instinctively she looked round for Albert – but he was not there. She had seen him bend a moment before to put on his galoshes. Surely he had not gone himself to douse the fire? His place was beside her, especially now.

'Where is the Prince?' she asked.

No one there knew.

She did her best to remain composed; but Albert's unexplained absence upset her almost as much as the fire which burnt not far away. She decided it would be wise to go to the Green Drawing-Room. There she and her ladies would be safe and they would be in touch with what was going on.

In the Green Drawing-Room they huddled together. The Duchess of Norfolk took it upon herself to calm the two Maids of Honour on duty, but it was quite unnecessary. They chattered together and gave every appearance of enjoying the excitement. Skerrett, emulating a noble Roman matron, stood between the Queen and the fire, her eyes reflecting the flames. Through the open doorway of the Red Drawing-Room they could see the fire fighters at work and servants moving furniture and pictures under the direction of the Sergeant Footman. But still there was no sign of the Prince.

Then, abruptly, he was at her side.

'Oh, Albert,' she cried. 'I have so missed you. I felt deserted.'

He soothed her. There was no need for anyone to worry. The fire would be under control directly. And he had not deserted her. No such thing. But he had been dragging out a small chest from his room with the aid of a servant.

'A chest?' she asked.

He nodded. 'I thought it wiser to remove it in case the fire spread.' He patted her head. 'Now, my dear. You should remain here until my men have things under control. You will be safe enough.'

'And you?' she said, and because she could not help it she added, 'Are you going to save another chest?'

She said it petulantly. He should have realized she was aggrieved because he had left her to look after his own valuables. To clear the situation he could have explained that never for one moment had he considered her to be in any danger. And he could have told her what was in the chest to correct her impression that his first thought had been for himself. But her petulance made him petulant. He resented

221

her insinuation, and so, proudly, he would not defend himself to explain anything at all.

'Very probably,' he replied shortly, and left her.

It was not until four the next morning that the fire was brought fully under control. The Queen sat in her chair for six hours; no longer in the least frightened of the fire, in fact, quite uninterested in it. Her ladies gave her warmed wine and toast fingers. They wrapped her in quilts. But she was not physically cold. She felt cold inside, frozen by Albert's own coldness, his indifference, his heartlessness.

This was the tiny beginning of a period of strain in Victoria's family life.

Three weeks later she was delivered of a boy, Leopold, named for his godfather the King of the Belgians, and never before had she enjoyed such an easy birth.

Sir James Clark was a doughty warrior against those clicky-clackers as he called them who averred that women must suffer pain in childbirth. It was scriptural, they said, woman's divinely appointed destiny, and it intensified a mother's love for her child. Such views incensed him and he scorned all clicky-clackers. Anaesthesia was equally scriptural, he told the Queen. Why else had the Lord caused a deep sleep to fall upon Adam? And in his experience unnecessary pain did no patient any good. The Queen was easily persuaded. A famous anaesthetist was invited to give her chloroform during her labour; not much, never enough to make her insensible, but sufficient to reduce the pain and make her call it 'that blessed chloroform'. The clicky-clackers were largely silenced. The head of society had set her seal of approval on the use of anaesthetics in childbirth. More, she was able to say that never had she recovered so quickly and so well from having a child.

But though well physically she suffered a crisis of nerves. It was something far worse than her usual post-natal lowness, with which Albert was familiar and which he knew how to treat. Her emotions surged and heaved like a river in flood, and she lacked the will or the power to control her explosive bouts of ill temper. They distressed Albert unbearably. The ground between them crackled with pointless arguments and hurtful quarrels. The smallest accident or a misunderstanding could spark off an hysterical outburst which was followed by twenty-four hours' misery for them both.

Desperate with worry Albert tried to return to their old relationship, to return to normal. He tried all the ways he knew to help her, and to escape himself from her tantrums. He tried to reassure her but in her present mental state it served no purpose. He tried to reason with her and point out how wrong she was and, with great firmness, he told her she was too wrapped up in herself; but Victoria had no liking for being preached at and his reasoning simply made her angrier. Then he affected not to hear or fully understand when she deliberately aggravated him, but the pretence only doubled Victoria's hysteria. She told him he was insulting; she demanded that he answer her questions.

Neither sought the advice of their friends: Albert because he had not wholly recovered from the loss of George Anson and consequently found it difficult to confide in his new secretary; Victoria because she was in that state of lowness which made her think no one could understand her, no one could help. It was a pity because certainly Colonel Phipps and even Albert's old chess opponent, now Bishop Wilberforce of Oxford, might have warned him not to take the Queen's explosions too seriously. The very best thing was to wait for her hysterics to die, then let her sob, kiss her, and make it up. And Skerrett, though a single woman, might have found the courage to warn her mistress that too much bludgeoning of a man's love can't be good for him or it.

Nothing went right for them. The baby Leopold was puny, and that despite the fact that Victoria insisted on his having a wet nurse from the Highlands. Scotch children seemed so healthy, she told Sir James. He agreed. He could have added that those who survived the bleak climate had no cause to ail, but loyalty to his native land made him hold his tongue. A Mrs Macintosh was sent to London; a fine, brawny woman in cottage clothes. She was a romantic figure, though difficult to entertain as she had no English and Mackay the Queen's Piper had to be employed as an interpreter. But it turned out that her milk was unsatisfactory. Prince Leopold remained puny. After a month she was sent off again, and a replacement found in that regular depot for royal wet nurses, Cowes. Nourished by her, the baby grew. For a time he thrived, and during that time Victoria was less bellicose with Albert. At the back of her mind had been the awful suspicion that giving way to Sir James' persuasions, and having her baby in the fumes of blessed chloroform, had somehow affected the child. Now, clearly, that was not the reason. It was a question of diet.

Then came the day when Sir James begged for a private audience with the royal parents and told them bluntly that Prince Leopold had the bleeding disease, haemophilia.

The Prince turned deadly white as though he would faint.

The Queen's instinctive reaction was to deny the possibility, to tell Sir James he was wrong, that he must, had to be wrong.

On his own initiative Sir James went to the tantalus and poured two glasses of brandy.

'It is indisputable,' he said when they were calm again.

'My father and my brother were sufferers,' said Albert. 'And, though both had to take care, they lived ordinary lives.'

As gently as he could the doctor explained why Prince Leopold's state was graver than theirs, and he thought it prudent to warn them that without the greatest possible care, he would not live to make old bones.

'Then he shall be cared for,' said the Queen decisively. 'With the greatest possible attention.'

'Is it wise,' said the Prince, 'to condemn him to an unnatural life simply in order to make that unnatural life longer?' He looked from Victoria to Sir James and back again, and took her hand. 'It would be kinder, I think, to be reasonably careful and warn the other children not to be rough with him.'

Dumb with misery she merely nodded. Over her shoulder the Prince made a small sign to the doctor who slipped out of the room. He adored his children, and the news had shattered him, but he saw one good thing come from it. Here was a God-sent opportunity for a reconciliation. He took Victoria in his arms. 'Sweetheart,' he murmured. 'We have been so lucky with the other boys. Leopold is our fourth son . . .'

Abruptly she pushed him away. 'I do not intend to have any more children,' she said. Seeing the shock and pain in his eyes, she salted it. 'No more children,' she repeated. 'No more.'

Now there were no more quarrels. Instead there was a silence between them.

Albert busied himself with planning for the establishment of new galleries and museums. The Exhibition had been such a financial success that, with the profits, he had been able to buy a large site in South Kensington. His schemes were elaborate and time consuming.

The Queen continued to function as a sovereign, but with increasing lack of interest. Signing state papers became a perfunctory, unthinking task. Meeting her subjects at levées and drawing-rooms became a burden. Because she was bored and exasperated she insisted on the strictest application of Court protocol. Woe betide the chamberlain who allowed anyone to slip past him who was not correctly dressed in all particulars. And though once famous for her charm to debutantes she was now better known for her lack of interest and her uncertain temper. Sometimes the presenters of eligible matrons and young ladies found her positively objectionable.

Everyone, from the lowest to the highest, suffered from her fractiousness. The upper servants often felt the edge of her tongue, but so did her Maids of Honour. They were in waiting in pairs for a month at a time, and generally enjoyed their time at Court. Now they keenly looked forward to going home again when their duty was finished.

When the Queen's cousin George, the new King of Hanover, came over on a visit she had a military review arranged for him, and complained crossly to the Commander-in-Chief, because the manoeuvres were not up to standard. He was dumbfounded. She had never complained in such a fashion before, and it seemed particularly unjust on this occasion when the principal visitor was blind and could not himself see the manoeuvres.

It was at another military review that the Queen rebuked her eldest daughter, the Princess Royal. It was deserved, but given publicly it caused great embarrassment. Vicky was sitting in the front seat of the royal carriage and was disposed to be overfamiliar with some of the junior officers in the escort. Her mother frowned and gave her several reproving looks, but it made no difference. Vicky continued to be coquettish, and went so far as to drop her handkerchief over the side of the carriage. Instantly three young officers leapt from their saddles.

This was too much altogether for the Queen. 'Stop,' she cried.

The carriage stopped, the officers stopped stock-still.

'You need not trouble, gentlemen. Have the goodness to remount.'

They did. The Queen nodded to a footman who stood by the steps. He at once let them down and opened the carriage door.

'And now, Victoria,' said the Queen in an awful voice. 'You will get down from the carriage and retrieve the handkerchief which you dropped deliberately.'

Red-faced, the Princess Royal did as she was told.

Victoria wondered if there came a time in every mother's life when she was frightened of her own children. Her own had certainly begun to threaten her peace of mind. It was not because they were sometimes disobedient to their tutors and governess, nor because on occasions they could be wilful and discourteous, but because the older ones seemed to have grown up too quickly. She recalled Lady Lyttelton rebuking her for treating them as toys, and she wished she had paid more attention. Now they had matured into distinct individuals, pretty and sweet and well-mannered and well-cared for, yes; but some of them temperamental and almost all with strong carnal appetites. She did not like it. And because she conspicuously lacked understanding them herself, she rather resented Albert's patient and loving way with them. He understood them well, and they knew. She felt out of things. It sharpened the knife-edge of her misery.

There was some relief for her at Balmoral, where it seemed impossible to be dejected and especially now that Albert had been able to buy the estate and a new house was being designed. But even there she was not herself.

Lord Aberdeen was in attendance, dancing reels with the Queen and going out of his way to charm her. And now that his political teeth had been drawn, Lord Palmerston was also a guest. The destroyer of the Whigs played billiards with the Prince and talked with him privately – though not about home affairs and his own department, but very solemnly about the troubles that were fermenting between St Petersburg and Constantinople. The Prince seriously doubted if Palmerston was as toothless as they had thought.

Out of temper with politics the Queen gave cursory attention to threats of war. She was now interested in arranging the ceremony of laying a foundation stone. Her mother came over from Abergeldie with her house party and the foundation of the new castle was well and truly laid with the burying of parchment and coins in a bottle, prayers from the village minister, the pouring of oil and wine from a cornucopia, pipe music, a banquet, a ball, and a great deal of whisky. Yet even on that happy family occasion the Queen was uneasy and by the end of the holiday, when Lord Aberdeen begged her to return to London because of the Turks and Russians, she was being waspish with the upper servants.

François d'Albertançon, the steward, and Grant the head keeper, both of whom had been taken over with the old castle, agreed for the very first time that things had been far better in good Sir Robert Gordon's day. And the old Frenchman's eyes bulged when a youngster named Brown who led the Queen's pony had the insolence to contradict.

Unlike most women, said Brown, their royal mistress was not a nagger. He was told to hold his saucy tongue and leave the steward's room to his betters. His place was in the tack-house with the other lads.

IX

The strongest public feelings in England are invariably hatched from one of two eggs, that of high moral righteousness, or that of irrational xenophobia, and circumstances combined soon after the royal family's return from Scotland to hatch a huge egg of the latter.

Turkey declared war on Russia, and almost immediately the ministry and the country were divided. Palmerston wanted England to ally herself with France and go to the Sultan's aid, and he resigned office because his colleagues in the Cabinet would not agree. But it was only a temporary resignation. The government, quite literally, could not manage without him, and Palmerston returned to fight the anti-war party in the Cabinet. He had with him the majority of the people who were spoiling for a fight with Russia. The Prime Minister and his colleagues were wholeheartedly supported by Prince Albert. He had such a loathing of unjustifiable war that he did all he could for peace and made no secret of it.

For this the Prince was execrated. England's good opinion of him as the genius behind the Great Exhibition dissolved overnight. Newspaper men combined to dismember his reputation in the public prints. He was accused of interfering improperly in state affairs, of being a diabolical *eminence grise* who took upon himself the duties of Foreign Secretary, Commander-in-Chief, and Prime Minister, of causing the popular Lord Palmerston's resignation, and of being in secret alliance with the Tsar through his German relations. And so successful was the campaign against him that people began to think he might actually be arraigned for high treason and imprisoned in the Tower of London.

Victoria's relationship with her husband was of two kinds. Almost always she thought of herself as his dutiful child wife; his paternalism expressing itself in letters which told her how to behave and which were directed 'Dear Child'. It was this relationship which had suffered since the fire at Windsor and the birth of Prince Leopold. Victoria the rebelling child wife had cut herself off from him and had made herself miserable. But the other relationship, when she felt maternal towards her husband, was no less strong and devoted. Rarely was it invoked. When it was, she was fiercely protective.

Her people's xenophobia disgusted the Queen, the malevolence of their attacks on the Prince enraged her. Instantly she forgot all differences with Albert. She declared herself personally affronted by the insults levelled at him. And he, breathless with surprise as well as with joy because the shadow over their marriage had so abruptly disappeared, declared that having her at his side gave him the fortitude to put up with anything. But, as he soon discovered, she was not really at his side. She was well out to the front, in command, and championing her Prince in the teeth of the war party, the press, and all his detractors. She was ferocious in his defence, and at length demanded that as soon as Parliament was opened he should be exonerated publicly by Lords and by Commons from the calumnies which had been spread about him.

There was a suggestion that, in view of the uncertain temper of the people, she would be advised not to open Parliament in person. She rejected it. For Albert's sake she stifled her terror of mobs and drove through the streets facing the shouted abuse with calmness and with dignity; and, as often as not, by the sheer force of her reproving looks, she made those who threw things at her carriage feel rather ashamed of themselves.

Impressed with her courage and her persistence, both Lords and Commons did as she asked and refuted the charge of illegitimate interference in state affairs, which had been levelled at the Prince. It was also made clear in society, by Palmerston as well as by the Prime Minister and by many others in positions of influence, that, though the Prince had worked for peace as a matter of principle, he was not intransigently opposed to the idea of a just war. Should the country be thrust into war with Russia, no one would be more wholehearted and loyal in his support of the fighting forces. It was as well that this should be known because public opinion, however wrong-headed, was leading England to war.

Sadly the Prince looked on. Not so the Queen. Battling against Albert's traducers gave her a taste for battling against the Tsar. She felt it keenly that as a female sovereign she could not lead her fighting men into battle. She watched her soldiers leaving for Turkey; getting up at seven o'clock in the morning to wave to men of the Scots Fusiliers as they marched past the Palace. When the day came, and the Crimean War began, she was full of pride for her forces and convinced that England's cause was just. A question asked in the Lords about holding a national day of humiliation to atone for the sinfulness of the nation, made her shrill with indignation. She had no time for such things, she wrote to the Prime Minister; people always dragged in menacing and inappropriate passages from the Old Testament and the Psalms, and not for one moment did she think the sinfulness of the nation had caused the war. It was the Tsar's fault, she said, and no Englishman need humiliate himself for the Tsar.

Her maternalism, forced into robust growth by the need to protect her husband, now embraced all her people. For the first time in her reign a considerable war was being fought. It made her feel like a mother to the nation.

Off Osborne she stood on the deck of the small royal yacht *Fairy* to say goodbye to her Navy. Lord Adolphus was in command and it was the proudest moment of his life when *Fairy* took her station in the van and led the fleet for several miles out to sea. There she came to and the squadron filed past, each ship saluting as she passed. The

Admiral's flagship, the *Duke of Wellington* brought up the rear.

Moved to tears the Queen stood on tiptoe and waved her handkerchief. The sailors raised their straw hats and cheered, guns saluted. Bosun's whistles trilled. Flags and pennants dipped. The ship's officers stood to attention and saluted.

For a long time after the squadron had passed the Queen stayed where she was, waving again and again and again. The Prince would have replaced his hat because the breeze was ruffling his thinning hair and the March day was cold, but as long as Victoria waved he did not like to. She was lost in the majesty of it all; her loyal sailors sailing off to fight in far-off waters.

The *Duke of Wellington* was barely recognizable on the horizon when the Queen turned away. Would it be proper, she asked Albert, to send a message to the fleet that she desired the sailors to be given extra rum? Lord Adolphus was consulted. 'It's termed splicing the mainbrace, Ma'am, when all hands have an extra tot. But wait till they're victorious. Much better to send the signal then. That's my advice, Ma'am. Wait till they've beaten the French.'

'We are fighting Russia, Lord Adolphus,' the Prince pointed out. 'And France is our ally.'

The Admiral nodded respectfully but he had not really taken it in. He had grown up in the Napoleonic Wars, and to him there was only one enemy.

X

The Crimean War had begun with flag waving and the flourish of trumpets, but the people's enthusiasm was rapidly subdued by the government's mismanagement of affairs. Ghastly tales leaked out and found their way into the newspapers, of the setbacks suffered by the Army, of the blunders made by high-ranking officers, of chaos in the commissariat.

Victoria also heard these stories and knew far more of the actual circumstances at the Crimea: that her soldiers were often struck down with dysentery and fever, that they were frozen, soaked through, famished and without much hope of regular rations, bivouacs or blankets; and that the troopers' charges were so starved that, as they stood in the lines, they sometimes chewed each other's tails to bloody stumps. She also heard from Miss Nightingale of the shocking state of affairs in hospitals at the front. Grieved by the suffering, she was fierce in her private protests to the Horse Guards and those ministers who were responsible for the conduct of the war, but she was consistently loyal to them in public. There was no point, she remarked, in advertising England's miseries and failures. They were simply feathers in the Tsar's cap. Therefore she refused to be a defeatist or show her feelings in public. She personally encouraged Lord Raglan, the Commander-in-Chief at the Crimea, visited the wounded who could be sent home to hospitals in England, and decorated the brave at ceremonies which moved everyone. And no voice was louder than the Queen's in praise of victories and gallantry.

She was ashen-faced when she read the dispatches about the charge of the Light Brigade and took in the terrible facts. It had all been a mistake. For no gain seven hundred men had charged the Russian guns and only 195 had returned. More than five hundred horses had been killed. One regiment, the Thirteenth Light Dragoons, had been virtually annihilated. At roll-call only two officers and eight troopers had mustered. The rest were all dead.

It was a disaster; but the Queen came to see it as England's Thermopylae. To her it was a glorious achievement because seven hundred soldiers had had the courage to face awful odds and she would not allow their glory to be tarnished by those politicians, military rivals, and armchair tacticians who were busy laying blame. Someone had blundered, but Victoria paid no attention. She wrote to Lord Raglan to congratulate him, and she was warm in her wel-

232

come to the commander of the Light Brigade, the Leonidas who had led his Spartans right up to the guns and was first in at a battery, her old favourite Lord Cardigan.

Cardigan's role at Balaclava had been sensational. Before the battle, by special permission of the commander-in-chief, he had lived aboard his own private yacht in Balaclava harbour; an elegant vessel sent out especially from Cowes, complete with Lord Cardigan's French cook. There, comforted by exquisite dinners and a feather bed, he had earned the sobriquet 'Noble Yachtsman', and had commanded his brigade of cavalry through the brigade major. But the brigadier was there in his place on the field of battle when the extraordinary order came to advance down a valley with an enemy battery to the front and batteries and riflemen on both sides. Cardigan checked that the order was correct, then put his brigade into two lines and took his place quite alone two lengths ahead of his staff and five lengths in advance of his own front line. A single trumpet sounded. He ordered the advance and, resplendent in the cherry red and blue of the Eleventh Hussars and wearing his gold-laced pelisse, he led the Light Brigade steadily down the valley. Walk, march, trot, gallop; never once looking back, he led them all the way there and all the way back. After the battle he rode down to his yacht for a hot bath and a bottle of champagne.

The hated Lord Cardigan of so many scandals was now a national hero. He was mobbed at Dover where he disembarked on returning to England. His picture was on sale everywhere. The sort of woollen jacket he had worn on cold evenings during the campaign was named after him a cardigan and sold in thousands. The Queen immediately invited him to Windsor for two nights. After dinner he stood at ease in the drawing-room, a resplendent figure in the pink, gold and blue of the uniform which had so suited Albert, and told her exactly what had happened at the charge. Though a first-hand account it lacked, she thought privately, the fire of the new Poet Laureate's description in his hour of the charge. As a compliment to Lord Cardigan she repeated four of Mr Tennyson's verses:

Theirs not to reason why,
Theirs but to do and die:
Into the valley of Death
Rode the six hundred.

But he hardly accepted it as such. 'A lot of gammon, Ma'am, and spinach. Cuts a hundred troopers from my brigade to satisfy his metre. I had seven hundred, Ma'am, not six. Maddening fellow.'

Victoria left it at that. War, she considered, had made Lord Cardigan rather alarming, and she was not sorry when he left the Castle. But what a wonderful example he was to the nation – the one golden light in what she realized was a very dark and dirty war.

Though her patience was tried, the Queen never let down her Army. When Lord Raglan died at the front, and people said, probably with some justification, that his heart had been broken by the waste and filth and disease and misery and slaughter suffered by his men, she would only accept the official reason, that he had died of fever. And it was typical of her that she disapproved of people who thought war was simply a military business and would have nothing to do with it. It was, of course, important to carry on with a normal life, because on this the economy and ultimate health of the nation depended, but she let it be known as the Queen's view that her soldiers deserved the interest, the goodwill, and the encouragement of their fellow countrymen at home. She wished herself that she could be personally involved and was envious of Miss Nightingale and her nurses who were there on the spot. No sacrifice, she thought, was too great to offer for England.

She was even prepared to offer her most beloved possession.

When Albert came to her and said he wished to join his regiment and in a fighting capacity, not as a royal highness on the staff, she instantly consented. His own high sense of duty made him wish to go. Her passionate maternal feelings for him wished to keep him safe, and yet she wanted him to win honour because, in her view, no man could do more. It occurred to neither of them that a wholly untrained and inexperienced field-marshal, whose rank as the Queen's husband made him an obvious target for enemy action, would be an embarrassment at the front; but it did occur to the ministers, and Victoria was not required to make this sacrifice. Nevertheless she was content to make others for the country's good.

She had to sacrifice her principles and her friendship with the House of Orleans when her ministers told her it was essential to invite the Emperor Louis Napoleon and his Empress for a State Visit. The *entente cordiale* rested on it. Smothering her own personal dislike, she did what was required for her country's sake, and she was surprised to find Louis Napoleon quite charming. He reminded her that he had once helped to protect her throne by enrolling as a special constable when the Chartists had threatened London, and he went out of his way to amuse her and interest her in French policies. As for the Empress Eugenie, Victoria so fell under her spell that she was glad to accept her gentle overtures of friendship. She accepted, too, an invitation for a return State Visit to France to see the Paris Exhibition, though she was uneasy at the thought of entering Paris, nerve centre of the Terror where kings and emperors and presidents were raised up and cast down at the caprice of mobs. But when she went there it was summertime, and Paris wore her brightest colours, played her sweetest music, and set out to charm the first English sovereign to visit the capital since 1431.

There were, of course, some Anglophobes at the French Court who mocked her Englishness. Miss Skerrett had tried her best to retrain the Queen's love of colour on this occasion but she had been unsuccessful. In the royal wardrobe there was a dress patterned with a hundred bright red geraniums, a parasol of lettuce-green, bonnets as big as coal scuttles, and a handbag embroidered with a white poodle. These extravaganzas were the butt of a number of Parisians who were as patronizing as only Parisians can be. But had she been aware of their condescension Victoria would not have taken the slightest notice. She was too busy inspecting Paris.

It gave her some satisfaction that the Exhibition was not in the same class as Albert's and, greatly daring, she teased the Emperor on the small number of exhibits. He declared, quite truthfully, that he did not mind in the least, and astonished her by giving her an orange flower to press and keep, insisting that she take the finest delicacies at all meals, and generally flirting with her. Victoria thought it shocking, not that this political adventurer should flirt with her, but that she enjoyed it. She decided it was all part of the topsy-turvyness of Paris, and no country was more full of illusions and surprises.

The most bizarre of her experiences in Paris was when her hosts took her to the Hôtel des Invalides to see Napoleon's tomb. She enjoyed the baroqueness of the setting, the still guards, the wall torches, the fanfare of trumpets, the organ music. But the great tomb under the dome was not yet finished and the empty vault looked more like a plunging bath than a receptacle for the remains of the little Corsican. She asked to see his coffin and was taken into an adjoining chapel. At that moment the organist began to play 'God save the Queen' on the massive organ, and a flash of lightning preluded a storm. Organist and nature contrived to make it a melodramatic occasion. There she stood before the coffin of her country's most bitter foe, in the light of flashing torches and zipps of lightning and to the sound of rumbling thunder and the English National Anthem.

Victoria's disciplined acceptance of France as an ally happily turned into a real willingness to be friendly with the Emperor and Empress. But another demand made by the exigencies of war, she received with horrified dismay.

Parliamentary dissatisfaction with the condition of the Army in the Crimea drove Lord Aberdeen from Office, and popular opinion thrust Lord Palmerston into his place. It seemed unbelievable, but there he was, Pilgerstein in Downing Street, and with his old chief, Lord John, under him as Colonial Secretary.

Victoria made the best of it. If her soldiers could stand up to the ankles in mud, and freeze, and go hungry, and be cut or blown to bits by Russians, she could steel herself to meet the mockery which would be in Pilgerstein's eye when he took over suite number 343 at Windsor. Because the loads of white heather sent regularly from Scotland ought to have brought her some degree of luck, perhaps his mockery would be gentle, but after all she and Albert had said and done to make their dislike plain, her new First Minister was entitled to some retaliation.

To their astonishment he showed no signs of wanting any revenge. At his first audience he was charmingly courteous, referred with obvious sincerity to the honour of being in the post once held for so long by his brother-in-law and greatest friend, Lord Melbourne, and undertook to prosecute the war with all the vigour he had at his disposal.

He was as good as his word. Within a month of his appointment affairs at the front looked far more promising, and, with so pugnacious a Prime Minister, England was given greater respect by the Powers.

Victoria was impressed. She wondered if at seventy-one, Lord Palmerston had mellowed. Because of his dyed hair and whiskers he still looked much the same and from all reports he behaved as scandalously as ever, yet he was much easier to get on with and she found herself trusting him just as she had trusted Lord M. and Peel because, like them, he was more devoted to England than to any political party. To her delight he invited Albert to use his undoubted administrative skill and help to untangle the chaos in the military commissariat. This recognition of her husband's talents sealed her new opinion of Lord Palmerston. He was Pilgerstein no longer. She went out of her way to be pleasant to Lady Palmerston, not a difficult thing to do as she was dear Lord M.'s sister and from her she learnt the most intriguing facts concerning political salons, and she forced herself to be patient with the Prime Minister's idiosyncrasies. She put up with his lackadaisical way of going about business and said nothing when he forgot to tell her of battles lost or won and she had to learn the facts at second-hand. She even managed to make her mind a blank when word circulated that he was enjoying the pleasures of the alcove with yet another lady. Albert was more censorious of the Prime Minister's dalliance, but he said nothing. To begin with, he knew that on so pucklsh and jocular a statesman it would have made no impression at all; and, to go on with, he was aware that Palmerston was the only man in England who could bring the war to a satisfactory conclusion. So he held his tongue and helped brilliantly with the complicated but boring process of sorting out the commissariat and making recommendations. Thorough to the last particular, and sensing how much the Prime Minister depended on comfort, he consulted Lady Palmerston on the furnishings at their country house Broadlands, and had suite 343 modified to suit his requirements. He also took the trouble to remind the royal kitchens of Lord Palmerston's known appetite for all kinds of meat. Eight meat courses at a meal was not too much for him.

Palmerston was touched by these attentions and he surprised himself by coming to admire both Victoria and Albert. Their poking about in peacetime policies had enraged him but the Prince's systematic and thorough way of going about things was now invaluable to the country and he considered England very fortunate to have such a wartime monarch as Victoria. Her maternal care for her people and her belligerent attitude to their enemies were worth an extra battalion in the field. He much approved of her stubborn refusal to be defeatist, of her dislike of those who would end the war by an unsatisfactory negotiated settlement before it was properly won. And he respected her Spartan refusal to show her feelings when things went wrong.

Victoria was convinced that people at home had to be courageous as well as the soldiers at the front, and she put on a brave face to meet personal sorrows and troubles. When her youngest child almost bled to death three times during the war hardly anyone knew of it. When her great favourite the piper Mackay went out of his mind, she hid her feelings, and she even managed to do the same when the most shocking news came from Cowes that Mary Ann

Brough, once wet nurse to the Prince of Wales, had butchered her six children with a carving knife. She recalled that Brough had disgusted Albert because, when the nursery was warm, there were always traces of dried saliva at the corners of her mouth. The thought that the woman had been mad all along was quite terrifying; but the Queen wore a mask of imperturbability. When her dearly loved half-cousin, Lord Adolphus FitzClarence, fell ill and died, her face was lined and red with weeping, but she refused to accept any sympathy and carried on as best she could, as though nothing had happened. It was important, she thought, in time of war for people to have self-discipline and self-control.

Some blessings came out of the war years. Very high amongst them was the appointment of a new Lady of the Bedchamber. Jane, Lady Churchill, had two advantages over her seven colleagues. They were all older than the Queen, and she was a few years younger; and whereas they waited in turns and afterwards were glad to get home to their husbands, children and grandchildren, she professed a readiness to be in constant attendance should the Queen desire it. A few months of Jane Churchill's company persuaded the Queen that she did desire it. She was granddaughter of the Lady Conyngham who had been George the Fourth's last mistress and whom Victoria remembered as a plump, managing woman, pinning a jewelled miniature of her uncle to her left shoulder. The old Marquess Conyngham was Lord Chamberlain for the first two years of her reign, but after his death there had been little connection between the family and the Court.

'People said the most dreadful things about your grandmamma,' she said to Lady Churchill, 'but I may say that as a child I was struck by her kindness.'

'She would be glad to hear you say so, Ma'am.'

Victoria raised her eyebrows. 'She is still alive?'

'Indeed, yes; an ancient, and, I may add, a highly respectable widow who lives near Tunbridge Wells. She goes out little in society, preferring it to come to her.'

'And,' said the Queen, 'if I know anything of Lady Conyngham, it does.'

'It does indeed,' replied Lady Churchill.

Victoria was enchanted to hear that this relic of the colourful past still kept a small court in Kent.

'I heard nothing, but I presumed, of course, that your grandmamma had died,' she said, and she added reflectively: 'Would it be proper, do you think, to invite her to Court?'

Lady Churchill smiled and indicated that while it would be quite proper for her to be invited, it would be very unwise. 'For she would accept, Ma'am, and come here, you may be certain of that. And she would arrive thickly painted and bejewelled, and with a mountain of luggage including her pet cockatoos, a bad-tempered monkey, her own sponge bath and a medicine chest the size of a pianoforte to keep herself going. Her insides, she tells everyone, are not what they were; and I beg to warn you, Ma'am, she is absolutely right.'

'An intriguing lady,' murmured the Queen wistfully. 'But, then of course she is a Paget.'

Lady Churchill's smile broadened. 'As a quarter Paget myself you will allow me to claim that full blooded members of the family invariably run to extremes; they are either outstandingly ugly or very handsome, unnervingly exciting and adventurous or as dull as Dutchmen.' The mock-serious way in which she selected the plainest contemporary Paget from a substantial number of possibilities was so droll that the Queen laughed until tears came to her eyes. Then, to balance the scales, Lady Churchill chose, as the best-looking Paget of the day, Lord George who had ridden with his troop at the charge of the Light Brigade. This debonair and mettlesome officer had fortified himself with boiled eggs, biscuits and watered rum before the battle, and had shown his high spirits by refusing to abandon an excellent cigar when the brigade was commanded to charge. In fact he had smoked it all the way down the valley and still had it in his mouth as he plunged into the Russian battery in the wake of the Earl of Cardigan.

The new Lady of the Bedchamber had a large store of such anecdotes, and they delighted the Queen. If they concerned her family she allowed her mordant wit full licence, but with other people she was always charitably disposed. Victoria came to the conclusion that never in her life had she come across such a clever and kindly woman; and, just as she admired her skill as a raconteur and her lack of malice, so she appreciated her more spontaneous gifts, her shrewdness in giving advice, her sympathy when there was trouble, her enormous capacity for enjoying herself. Lady Churchill shared the Queen's romantic bent. Certain music and poetry, sunsets, sublime scenery, shrieking storms, and tales of heroism, all affected her as they affected her royal mistress; and she could people a tumbledown ruin with an imaginary family, complete with pedigree and personal biographies, or see sprites in a peat-hag, Herne and his minions at Windsor, or pictures in the fire, as clearly as Victoria ever did.

Shared interests and feelings quickly made them into friends and it was not long before Victoria regarded Jane Churchill as her most confidential Lady-in-Waiting. Wisely, Lady Churchill pleaded with the Queen not to make too much of her in public. If the Household thought of her as a resurrected Mrs Freeman, or even as another Baroness Lehzen, there would be endless tittle-tattle and nothing but trouble for everyone.

How *sensible*, thought the Queen. She was very impressed, and she did as she was asked. Only when they were alone or within the small and exclusive circle of the family and their most intimate friends did she show any special regard for her new Lady of the Bedchamber. But privately she made wide use of her cleverness and when, that summer at Balmoral, things began to get on top of her and weigh her down, she went for help to sensible Jane Churchill.

A betrothal, which ought ordinarily to have been a happy family event, was the cause of the trouble.

Despite Albert's icy refusal to guarantee anyone's safety at the Great Exhibition, the King of Prussia had sent over his family and they had greatly enjoyed it. Prince Fritz, who would one day inherit the Prussian throne had taken a great liking to the Princess Royal, and since then an understanding had grown up between the Royal House of Prussia and the Royal House of England. Now the boy prince who had walked round the Exhibition with a girl princess had proposed himself for a visit to Balmoral. Victoria wanted to refuse. She said the new castle had only just been completed and the family needed time to settle in. Besides, though France was a loyal ally in the war, Prussia had stood on one side. But Albert insisted that as an understanding had been initiated they would need better reasons for refusing the request. And so Prince Frederick William of Prussia arrived for a visit on September 14th. He begged that there should be no formality, and that he should be called Fritz as he was at home. Within six days he had asked the Queen and the Prince if he might pay his addresses to the Princess Royal. Victoria said yes. There was no possible reason to refuse. But at once she regretted it. She was thrilled and panic-stricken in turn as the courtship was played out. Fritz was assiduous. He gave Vicky white heather for luck and a bracelet as a gift, and he took whisky to give himself Dutch courage. In less than a fortnight he had proposed, been accepted by an hysterically happy Princess Royal, and had gone. The Queen smiled in public, but inside she felt as hysterical as her daughter.

After Fritz's departure the Queen, the Prince and the Princess Royal dined together. Vicky as an engaged lady had now to be treated as grown-up. It was her privilege to dine. The meals were a great strain on Victoria. She was driven to beg Albert to intervene in the engagement. Vicky was too young, she pleaded; no fourteen-year-old girl could know her own mind.

Albert, aware of Victoria's strict rule about trying to control her feelings in wartime, was conscious of her deep distress, but for everyone's sake he gently said that nothing could be done. It was too late to retract without causing terrible offence. They would have to go through with it, but the wedding would not take place for some time. Before then Vicky had to be confirmed and everything prepared for her marriage.

Utterly wretched the Queen turned to Lady Churchill. She could not explain it, she said. She ought to be happy. Her daughter was in love, or claimed to be. There was no question of a forced marriage. Prince Fritz was an excellent young man; good-looking, well-behaved and considerate, and ultimately he would come to the throne of Prussia. It was the perfect romantic situation, and yet she was miserable.

Jane Churchill hazarded a guess at what was the matter. Jealousy of young mothers for young daughters was not uncommon. But she held her tongue. Even if it was true, the Queen could not be objective enough to see it. The only way to help her out of her present misery was to divert her.

To begin with Victoria was not easily persuaded to think of anything except her daughter's betrothal, but in time the plan turned out a success. Never had the Queen had such a fully-occupied holiday on Deeside as she did that summer, and then, in London and at Windsor, whenever there was a rest from routine affairs, Jane Churchill seemed determined not to allow her a moment's peace. But she supposed she really ought to be grateful. Being kept busy at least kept her from brooding on that dreaded wedding which she was inclined to do on the rare occasions when she found herself alone ... Shrewdly she became aware of the pattern, and thanked Lady Churchill for what she had done. Undoubtedly her arrival at Court was one of the great blessings she had been given during the war years.

Deep down inside her Victoria knew that the greatest blessing of all was Albert's patience. He could not speak too highly of her industry in writing letters to the widows of fallen officers, but she sensed his disapproval of her martial attitude, that he thought her visits to Army hospitals lacking in true modesty, and her atavistic longing to wear uniform and fight the enemy in person, unpleasantly unfeminine. Yet he said nothing. This she appreciated. She valued, too, his marvellous patience with her fixed resolve to have no more children. With delicacy and gentleness he tried to persuade her that the course they had chosen was rather unnatural, and that this was why, maybe, small differences between

243

them were exaggerated: but when she remained adamant he respected her wishes. He said nothing but he hoped and believed that her decision was only temporary. As time passed she felt the tragedy of Leopold's disease far less keenly, and he was satisfied that when her preoccupation with military affairs was done, and she became entirely feminine again, everything would alter.

In this he was right.

The war ground to an inglorious end. The Peace of Paris was signed: a peace said Palmerston which, like all other Peaces of Paris in history, resembled the peace of God in that it passed understanding. Victoria rewarded him for all he had done with a Garter, and turned her energies to welcoming home her soldiers from the Crimea. Her consciousness of the bond between Army and monarch grew even more acute. She had touched the rough hands of private soldiers and felt as if they were her own children. The men filed past her and she called them England's heroes. She invited herself to a field day at Aldershot, and attended a series of great military occasions there wearing for the first time a specially designed uniform: a round hat decorated with a white and crimson plume, a deep blue skirt piped with white, and a scarlet, gold-braided tunic.

The apogee of it all came when there was a great review of the troops lately returned from the war. Or it should have been the apogee. But the weather tarnished what was intended to be a brilliant occasion. Wet to the skin, the men were disgruntled. Their officers were eager to have the day over and done with. No one paid much attention to the Queen's short speech of one hundred words which she had learnt so carefully by heart. As she spoke it with her beautifully clear voice she wondered if even the Tilbury speech of her illustrious forbear could have enjoyed more than a half-hearted hearing in such a downpour. Her uniform was ruined. Then, to cap it all, the Commander-in-Chief, Lord Hardinge, through age and overwork, toppled from his horse and fell prostrate in a paralytic seizure at her feet. She was horrified, and sat, pale and trembling, until he had been removed. On his resignation her cousin George of Cambridge was appointed Commander-in-Chief. But she treated it like any other appointment. After that review things were never quite the same again. The military mystique had dissolved. Ichabod.

Victoria's maternal attitude to the people changed. And her love for her husband imperceptibly shifted to another plane. She looked up to him again for, in his strong security, he had no need of her protection. In a short time after that soaking review she found that she was once more carrying a child.

XI

Victoria would have looked forward more to her ninth confinement had she not been so unwell. She felt querulous and physically she was enfeebled and found it a great effort to take any exercise at all. Sir James spoke sharply to her. Being already the mother of eight children had surely taught her the necessity for keeping healthy while she carried a child. Sloth, he told her, was a very awful thing in any woman. In a monarch and an expectant mother it was worse. And because he still had faint traces of an Aberdeen accent and he pronounced 'sloth' to rhyme with 'moth', it sounded worse still. She was to walk as much as she could, drive out, take a lot of fresh air, and not greet.

It was excellent advice. Victoria knew that. But she did not follow it.

As the winter drew on there was nothing she liked better than to sit close to a large beechwood fire and listen to a Maid of Honour reading aloud. Lazily she refused to hear the parliamentary reports or selections from the daily newspapers which, during the war, she had considered a sacred duty; nor would she hear the books which Albert carefully recommended to her and which lay on a special table in her sitting-room. Instead she had novels read to her one after the other. There were her old favourites like *The Talisman* and *Peveril of the Peak*, and dazzling new discoveries such as *Coningsby*, *Sybil*, and *Tancred* all written by that surprising young man Mr Disraeli who, in his books if not in Parliament, appeared to have a gratifying appreciation of the crown, the church and the aristocracy. Then there were disturbing, frightening stories by those quaint girls from a Yorkshire parsonage, one of which, *Wuthering Heights*, so affected the Queen that the reader had to pause again and again, and getting through it was as slow and as painful as an elaborate torture. In sharp contrast, she heard a dozen or more light, insignificant novels with singular names like *Destiny*, *The Adventures of Susan Hopley*, *The Widow Barnaby*, and *Peg Woffington*. And some of the works of Charles Dickens actually qualified for a second reading. By no means all, of course. She found characters like Micawber, the Kenwigses, and Mr Jingle inexplicable, but she doted on Oliver, Cousin Feenix, Tim Cratchit and Little Dorrit, and the deaths of Nell Trent and Paul Dombey made her howl in a most unregal fashion. They were read over frequently, and in honour of the author a puppy kept from one of her Skye terriers was named Boz.

The name might have given Albert a hint as to how Victoria spent most of her time that winter, but he was so busy at his desk that he failed to notice or think of it. Far from slackening off in peacetime, he appeared to have more to do than ever and his work was increased because, after sixteen years of self-exile in his apartments at Windsor, the Baron had decided it was time to go home and some of his day-to-day routine work devolved on his pupil. But the Prince made no great effort to make him change his mind. He did not fear the extra work. He had trained himself to be industrious and, indeed, seated at his desk, assembling facts, organizing them and analysing them gave him the greatest satisfaction. And he saw that neither he nor Victoria could usefully learn any more from their tutor. He merely thanked Stockmar, assured him that he would always be welcome in England should he ever wish to return, and saw him off for Coburg. There the old man surprised his wife and children who, by now, were almost total strangers, and settled down to write regular letters and memoranda for dispatch to the royal courts of Europe. To Victoria it was all one whether she received his letters from a tower in Windsor or a tower in Coburg. In her lethargy and lassitude she did not read them very carefully anyway. But she rather resented Albert's easy acceptance of extra work. He already had enough, she thought; too much in fact. And she was feeling neglected. Sir James' adjuration not to greet was disobeyed. She told Albert to his face that she felt lonely, and that she was unnecessarily deprived of his presence.

The Prince still had not learnt by previous mistakes, still did not know that in her depressed state she needed spoiling however much it was undeserved. Instead of fussing over her, he told her she could not possibly be lonely. Did she not have Ladies and Women of the Bedchamber and Maids of Honour in constant attendance to obey her slightest whim, and eight children to love and to enjoy?

The Queen would not hear of this. Only in exceptional circumstances were her ladies good company, she said; and as for the children, they were not companions at all.

Well-meaning but tactless Albert told her this was her fault. She was too busy with the little children, and scolded the older ones too much. What then could she expect? And, having made her burst into tears of anger, and regret and sheer hopelessness, he made the hurt worse by writing her a letter, tepid in love and understanding, in which he told his 'Dear Child' not to be so self-centred, and to be better controlled.

Victoria cried first in Skerrett's arms and then in Jane Churchill's. They did their best to lift her out of her depression. Skerrett went so far as to withdraw her veto on the Queen's choice of a custard-coloured dress of silk flounced with orange lappets; and Lady Churchill was assiduous in searching for sentimental or horrific novels to carry discreetly into her apartments when the Prince was not about. But the Queen went on moping and her wretchedness was doubled when news came that her half-brother Charles had died suddenly and unexpectedly. She had not known him well but she grieved for her mother who had been particularly devoted to him. Then she grieved for dear Aunt Gloucester. The old lady had been in such a state of idiocy that death had been a real release, but Victoria hated to hear the cruel and humiliating circumstances which had robbed her aunt of every shred of dignity. The third death she expected came fast enough. She found fresh tears for Madame Späth when that faithful old servant caught the grippe and died even before she could bestow her few and valueless possessions. Her pathetic end and all she had meant in the past, her connection with Kensington and the banished Lehzen, smarted Victoria's sorrow. Dolefully she complained to Lady Churchill that, though not yet forty, she had reached the dreadful stage when the anniversaries of her friends' deaths were beginning to outnumber the birthdays of her living friends. She noticed this she said, because her birthday book, a stiff-covered volume with marbled edges, showed more erasures than new entries.

At this point Jane Churchill risked their friendship by reminding her of Sir James' instructions. She was to walk, drive out, take fresh air, and not greet. Victoria was so astonished that words failed her. She found herself being led from the baking beechwood fire to the private entrance and there dressed in cloaks, caps, muffs and furs. Outside was a carriage. Its hood was down although the wind was keen and there were heavy snow clouds over Staines.

That drive did Victoria the greatest good. It put life into her, and blew the cobwebs away. She began to realize exactly why she was avoiding her elder children. The understanding came suddenly as they were going through the Great Park at a spanking pace, the keen air making her gasp. She sheltered her face from the cold, and told Lady Churchill that in her present state she felt degraded, physically swollen and sluggish and repulsive to her own children. Vicky was to be married herself very soon. Bertie was an adolescent who turned his eyes away, because he could not help it, whenever he saw his mother carrying her heavy load. Alice was the same, though she did not look away but stared in interest.

'Jane, it is terrible, this affliction of shocking my own children. They consider me horrid, disgusting, beastly.'

Lady Churchill made no attempt to argue or to reason her into an acceptance of things. She simply stated the facts as she saw them, and then made a great fuss of the Queen. It was surprising, she thought, how everyone believed a born queen must be the most spoilt and happiest woman on earth merely because she had a crown and riches and power. Her own poor queen had been less spoilt by her mother and her husband and by fortune than almost any woman she knew. Helping her, and making her see she was not grotesque, took time and love and patience. Happily for Victoria, Jane Churchill had all three.

Princess Beatrice, Victoria's ninth child, was born on an April day, and she was perfect in every way.

The Queen, under that blessed chloroform, experienced little pain and recovered with extraordinary rapidity, and the lowness which invariably followed her confinements was neither as deep nor as sustained as usual. But it multiplied her resentment against Vicky being present at her private dining-table. She chafed at the loss of those rare and precious evenings when she and Albert had been able to dine privately. Nowadays she did not have him to herself until after ten when the intrusive Vicky went to bed.

One night Albert warned her that she was making her pique too obvious, and it was not kind to show how relieved she would be when Vicky had been packed off to Prussia. He spoke with some warmth for he had a special attachment to his eldest daughter. It would be pain enough to lose her without her mother crowing over the event.

Victoria burst into tears.

When he tried to comfort her she pushed him away. Standing by the mantelshelf, leaning abjectly against the wall, she sobbed and sobbed.

Albert apologized. It did not come easily to him, nor, under the circumstances, did he think it was justified; but Sir James had alarmed him a few weeks before. Reporting on Victoria's state of health just before her confinement the physician had said gravely that he had no fear at all for her body, but her mind was another matter. Until the Queen was fully herself again, she ought not to be thwarted. For this reason Albert apologized, to help Victoria; and, to his surprise, she at once slipped into his arms. She had responded more quickly than she would ever have done to a reasoned argument.

'I see so little of you,' she wept. 'And I do so long to have you with me more often.'

He kissed her forehead. 'You shall, my dear,' he reassured her. 'But first we have to prepare for Fritz the prettiest, best-dressed, happiest bride in England.' He pressed her hand. 'After that you and I will return to the old days again – when we were younger.'

She looked up at him through tear-filled eyes. 'Oh, yes,' she said. 'Oh, yes.'

A maelstrom of blood five thousand miles away from Osborne abruptly banished the Queen's self-pity. Far off in India the sudden uprising of native sepoys against their European officers started the Mutiny.

Victoria sat with an expressionless face and silent as she read the reports which came in from province after province. There was nothing in them to invoke the martial ardour she had experienced in the Crimean War. There was no gallantry or glory; little even of noble suffering and sacrifice. The flame which burnt over India produced nothing but squalor and ferocity.

Victoria was haunted by the terrible things done by sepoys to white women and children, and then haunted by the terrible revenge wreaked on the sepoys. Blowing them from the guns and committing atrocities on their families seemed a bludgeoning way to make the natives loyal.

It was a relief when her ministers advised her that as the Company had been rejected by India, it had forfeited the right to rule. Lord Palmerston elaborated the scheme. India would have to belong to her. The natives who hated the Company nabobs and entrepreneurs would eagerly accept Victoria as their great white Queen. Being at such a distance from India she would rule them, as in Ireland, through a Viceroy.

Victoria consented without delay. She had not forgotten her mortification when the Court of Company Directors had once summarily dismissed her governor-general because they disliked the haughty tone of his dispatches. She and the Prime Minister had immediately shown their disapproval by making the dismissed man an earl and a Grand Cross of the Bath, but they had been powerless to do anything else. That sort of humiliating experience would be impossible if she was Queen of India, and she would be in a far stronger position to make her wishes known. Besides this, adding so vast a territory and so many million subjects to her kingdom would make her one of the greatest sovereigns in Europe. The very thought braced her and dispelled whatever lingering traces there remained of her lethargy and her lowness.

XII

A proposal from Prussia that the wedding should take place in Berlin made Victoria shrill with indignation. Recovering herself, she wrote to Lord Clarendon, the Foreign Secretary:

> *The assumption of its being* too much *for a Prince Royal of Prussia to come over to marry* the Princess Royal of Great Britain *IN England is too absurd, to say the least ... Whatever may be the usual practice of Prussian Princes, it is not every day that one marries the elder daughter of the Queen of England.*

Having fired this salvo for England's honour she then set about managing her family with great zeal and energy.

Vexed by Parliament's continued reluctance to give

Albert any sort of royal title, she took Lord Palmerston's advice and created him Prince Consort by letters patent. There was scarcely a ripple of comment from the country, but Victoria was satisfied that Albert was henceforth safe from the possible indignity of being given precedence below his eldest son.

That settled, she concentrated her energies on Bertie. He was sent abroad with a tutor – to sip at wisdom in Bonn – while she and Albert considered his future. Neither parent was very sanguine for him. For some time he had been in a sullen state of rebellion against his father, and ruffling his mother's conscience because, although she felt for him and worried about him, she found him very hard to love. Something would have to be done to improve this state of affairs. They had sheaves of Stockmar memoranda to guide them, and were conscious that his presence brooded over their discussions.

First they decided that Bertie should leave their roof for the first time and have his own establishment at the White Lodge in Richmond Park. There he would live with tutors and equerries and fit himself as far as possible for his inheritance. In view of his increasing years certain concessions would be made. He was to be allowed to choose his own clothes, though he was warned against extravagance in dress and told the cautionary tale of his great-uncle, the last Prince of Wales, taking his seat in the House of Lords in a black velvet coat covered with pink spangles. That sort of thing would not do. Nor would extravagances at the table. His mother had a healthy appetite though she was not very adventurous and ate quantities of potatoes, butcher's meat, poultry, and tarts, and his father, despite a growing corpulence, was fairly abstemious; but Bertie, so it was understood, was a gobbler and spent a great deal of his time dreaming up fabulous meals. His ambition, he said, was to eat a roasted swan stuffed with a peacock, stuffed with a goose, stuffed with a guinea fowl, stuffed with a pheasant, stuffed with a partridge, stuffed with a woodcock, stuffed with a snipe, stuffed with a quail. Under no circumstances was this Lucullan ambition to be gratified. He must not gormandize.

Meat, vegetables, pudding, and claret with seltzer would be sufficient at the White Lodge.

Unknown to everyone the royal parents also began to play the dynastic game on Bertie's behalf. They first discussed the matter in the privacy of the royal barge when making a pleasure cruise on the Thames. Between them they drew up a list of eligible princesses. Uncle Leopold, who had proved his expertise by marrying them to each other, had sent a helpful list of seven names from Laeken. But five of the seven were German, and Victoria with shattering candour said this did not predispose them in her favour. She did not want anyone, she told Albert, to suffer as he had done. The English did not like Germans, as they had made abundantly clear when Vicky's engagement was announced. Most of them had been contemptuous. *The Times* had called the Prussian Royal Family 'a paltry German dynasty'. Seeing the hurt in Albert's gentle eyes she said: 'Because ours was a love match, and we hope that Vicky's is the same, we can bear these difficulties. But Bertie will have to marry the most suitable Protestant princess available and she would be happier if she were not German.'

Albert thought for a moment. 'I am sure you are right,' he teased her, 'because you are so English by temperament.'

She laughed and was grateful that he had accepted the hurtful fact so readily and graciously. Even after all these years, it could not be easy.

'That, then,' she said, in her most practical manner, 'reduces our list to two. We must find out more about them.'

Their conversation was cut short by the rise of a horrible smell from the river. At the point they had reached, open ditches drained into the Thames and the stench was unbearable. The Prince Consort clapped a handkerchief across his nose and mouth and waved urgently to the bargemaster to turn about and head for the shore.

It was appalling, complained the Queen, that fifteen minutes on their lovely Thames should be ruined in such a fashion; and she set about seeing that the matter was investigated.

Victoria's greatest amount of bustling was done in preparing for her daughter's marriage. Still nettled by the pretensions of the Prussian royal family, she determined that they should be dazzled by England's riches and hospitality. The chefs and master cooks were invited to attend a conference, and arrived with their blue pocket books of royal menus to discuss the wedding banquet. Victoria thought their final recommendations were entirely suitable. She also approved the arrangements made by the senior gardeners who had control of the royal conservatories and forcing houses. And she made a point of sending her personal command to the Master of the Household that accommodation should be allocated in accordance with continental protocol. This was very necessary as the Lord Chamberlain's people were arrogantly insular, and regarded a Somerset squire as of more account than a Pomeranian baron. Without being reminded, they would not trouble themselves if a graf had a view and a margrave had not, or if a serene highness found herself without a dressing-room.

The Queen looked into everything so that no royal or semi-royal wedding guest should have the slightest cause to condescend. She also oversaw her daughter's trousseau and resolved that the Prussians should be made to gape at the splendid way such things were done in England. At the back of it all might have been the memory of her own mother's parsimony, and the wretchedness and dullness, and slenderness of her wardrobe as a girl. Vicky's *toilettes* should be very different. Rooms were given over to the royal sewing-women and milliners. There were great bolts of tweeds, velvets, serge, plush and crêpe de Chine; electric heaps of silks – glacé, Benares and marocaine, silk gauze, tussore and sarsenet; with bombazine and grenadine. India muslin and tarlatan, Carrickmacross lace and blonde, and lace of Honiton. The Queen was a frequent visitor to this factory of finery; quick to admire a piece of *passementerie* here or a worked fascinator there; equally quick to slap Boz when he tried to make a bed in a heap of sashes and flounces and floral cornucopias; laughing when she told the seamstresses not to apply to her for an opinion on colour blending but to consult the inimitable Miss Skerrett; and quicker than anyone there when it came to remembering mundane articles like galoshes and sponges. Twenty pairs of the former would hardly be adequate she said, and she made sure that two large drawers full of the latter were included in the bridal baggage. Besides linen and under and outer clothes, clothes for all seasons and all occasions, for day and for night, the Princess Royal was also heavily adorned with jewels. Victoria and the royal lapidary selected gems and settings. There were pearls and emeralds, sapphires, rubies, topaz and turquoise, and Vicky's favourite precious stones, heliotropes and hyacinths. There were to be no diamonds yet; not until it was seen what the Prussians provided.

The Prince kept apart from all this bustling activity. He showed interest when it was expected of him; but every aspect of the preparations reminded him that only too soon his dearest Vicky would be gone, and he preferred if possible to put it out of his mind. Fortunately he had a new equerry that year, a Lieutenant-Colonel Henry Ponsonby of the Grenadier Guards, and found his company very congenial. He picked his brains about conditions in the Army and both agreed that some sort of reform was necessary. They shot and rode together with rather more regularity than was customary with the Prince and his equerries, and Ponsonby, being unmarried, did not mind keeping his master company out of hours, which the Prince appreciated. Not since Anson died had he felt so inclined to give someone his friendship. Ponsonby's arrival helped a good deal to smother the dejection which threatened to engulf him whenever he thought of the approaching wedding. And keeping himself busy also helped. Two projects held him to his desk for many hours a week: the gradual laying out of the Balmoral and Abergeldie estates, and a sanitation scheme for the Castle and barracks at Windsor. Then there were guests to entertain. It was a duty which devolved more and more on him as Victoria absorbed herself in marriage preparations, though she did do her duty and temporarily abandoned her work when the Emperor and the Empress of the French proposed themselves for an informal visit to Osborne. As it turned out, neither of them required much entertaining as Empress Eugenie did little but smile sweetly and Louis Napoleon did little but make side glances at Victoria, smooth his considerable moustaches, and talk endlessly about the occult. Albert wished, heartily, that their guests had talked about almost anything else for immediately Victoria was entranced. She had rejected her book of predictions and, fortunately, after one try at table-turning 'as a game', she had given it up, but her interest in anything from talismans to magnetism was vigorously stirred by the Emperor's descriptions of experiments in contacting the spirits of the dead and amazing successes of a Scotch magician named Daniel Dunglass Home. She wanted to know everything. The Emperor, to Albert's great vexation, was delighted to oblige her. But happily it did her no harm. Her overheated imagination soon cooled down again when the Emperor left and she was able to concentrate all her energies on Vicky's trousseau.

Receiving the Hohenzollern relations was a hateful business to the Prince Consort. Obliged to smile and remain composed, when all he wished to do was to hide himself and weep, was an intolerable strain on his nerves. He accepted Ponsonby's advice and, to steady himself, took a great deal of brandy, more, in fact, than at any other time in his life. But though it lessened the offensiveness of those guests who patronized him and those who bored him, it did not dull the pain in his heart.

Vicky knew what was wrong with him and why. With uncommon good sense for so young a girl she was distant with him on public occasions and she refused to respond when he took opportunities to squeeze her hand. Her coldness hurt him, but it enabled him to control his feelings and this was what she wanted.

Sitting miserably at a state dinner for the English and Prussian royal families, their Households and their friends, and with the spectre of the wedding ceremony still before him, Albert happened to catch his daughter's eye – and, with a single look and no words at all she managed to tell him

that her indifference was pretended and all put on for his
dear sake.

His eyes glistening with tears, he looked hastily away.
He wiped them dry, and forced himself to think of other
things; of the excellence of Prince Fritz who truly was a fine
young man, and how extraordinary it was that he should
have so many odious relations.

Then moodily he looked at a reflection of Victoria in the
polished gold surface of a dish before him. She was smo-
thered in diamonds – glittering like rime in January, wearing
for the last time the family jewels. The Commission which
had sat for years and years and years had at last hatched a
decision, and it was substantially in favour of the King of
Hanover. So, as soon as the wedding was done, the majority
of her diamonds would be taken to her blind cousin George.
Albert thought it was probably a good thing. Tall stately
women could wear cataracts of diamonds and look capital.
His dear little Victoria could not. He smiled at the
reflection, noticing for the first time that the be-diamonded
Queen of England had chosen to set off the glitter of her
jewels by wearing artificial grass and flowers in her hair.

XIII

The Prince had once said in a frank moment to his friend
George Anson that behaving out of character was behaving
in character to the Queen. And he wished Anson could have
been there to see how true this was after the marriage of the
Princess Royal.

With her daughter out of the way, Victoria had Albert all
to herself again and she clung to him like a vine. Simultaneously she began a correspondence with the exiled Vicky
which brought them closer together than they had ever been
before. She wrote endlessly to Königsburg. Mostly the
letters were full of advice. She wrote about trifles such as

curing head colds, repairing furs, and how to quell young
Prussians who teased her with coarse jokes; and she wrote
on weightier affairs such as dealing with Fritz's uncle the
King, who had gone off his head, and the need to pay special
attention to the Prussian statesman Bismarck who, as huge
as a giant from Teutonic mythology and with the look of a
man who eats an innocent child or two for breakfast, was
quite the coming man in Germany. She also wrote at length
about what she termed the darker side of marriage, urging
her child to be dutiful and loving and yet to restrain Fritz's
ardour if it was possible. A whole year without having to
carry a child would be a great benefit to them both; and,
after her own experiences, she said she doubted if it was wise
to have a baby too soon.

> *For it is* [she wrote] *such a complete violence to all one's
> feelings of propriety* (*which God knows receive a shock
> enough in marriage alone*).

Vicky's replies were not quite as long, nor as well written,
but they arrived regularly. She painted clear pictures of her
new life and country and while most of them pleased Victoria a great deal, not all did. She urged her child to remain
faithful to her English upbringing even though she lived in
an entirely German Court, and to stand up for herself if
people were at all critical. She bridled when the Prussians
told Vicky she was very tiny.

> *After all you are taller than I am, and I am NOT a
> Dwarf.*

Both took great satisfaction in the correspondence. To the
mother it was a safety valve, a means by which she could
express herself at enormous length and mostly with complete candour about anything at all; to the lonely daughter
in Königsburg, it was quite as good as being with her
mother. In fact, she decided, it was better.

Despite warnings from England, Vicky found herself
carrying a child within two months of her marriage. If the

Prussians were pleased, Queen Victoria was not. Nor was she pleased that rumour said she herself was in the same condition. She was not, she wrote indignantly to Vicky. Nor, she said, could she fathom her daughter's sense of pride in giving life to an immortal soul.

I think much more of our being like a cow or a dog at such moments; when our poor nature becomes so very animal and unecstatic . . .

Let the theologians say what they would, the Almighty's plan which doomed their unhappy sex to so much humiliation was inexplicable to the Queen of England.

As Vicky was facing her first confinement and in a strange land, she wanted to go and see her, but, although Albert had already been to Prussia for a short private visit, she felt that so soon after the marriage it was hardly proper for her to propose herself for a formal visit. The Foreign Office came to her aid and arranged things diplomatically. King George of Hanover was very happy for his cousin Queen Victoria and the Prince Consort to make a family visit; and from there, of course, it would be only natural for them to go on and see their daughter. This would be quite understood by the Prussians. And so the visit was made possible.

Nevertheless none of them really enjoyed it.

The young Prussian princes flicked up the ends of their military moustaches and condescended to the Prince Consort. He pretended not to notice, but Victoria flew to his defence and she froze them with her disdain. She told herself that in their blindness they could only see a portly, balding, short-necked man with a severe expression who struck attitudes because he was nervous, and they knew nothing of his astonishing beauty as a young man. In their arrogance they did not pause to consider his nobility of mind, his high intellect, his kindness. The Queen was so unremittingly glacial that some of the young men excused themselves from Court and did not return until she had gone. This was not all. Vicky herself was on the defensive. A mother who wrote sharp letters could be tolerated. One who found fault with everything she saw, and wanted it altered, could not. Then, inevitably, Albert's great joy at being with his adored Vicky awoke Victoria's slumbering jealousy. She decided it was better for them to go home.

Lehzen had written to say she hoped to see her old pupil, no matter for how short a time, at Bückeburg station on the way, but, thoroughly put out by the failure of their visit and made peevish by the August dirt and heat, Victoria did not order the royal train to be stopped. As they rattled through the station she saw a tiny bent figure holding a parasol against the scorching sun and waving a handkerchief, waving and waving. And then the figure was gone. Victoria immediately regretted they had not stopped. She felt ashamed of herself. Lehzen had been a faithful friend once and by now she was seventy-five or more. The heat and the dust of the August day must have tried her severely. It had been cruel to leave her standing there and make no sign. But it could not be remedied now.

The Queen had a remarkable capacity for recovering herself. Quite soon after her return she had forgotten about the unpleasantness of her visit and her shabby treatment of Lehzen. She took up her pen and once more inundated Königsburg with long and affectionate letters.

Then came an infuriating piece of interference – or rather, several – from a number of sources.

Albert was the first to complain, saying he did not have his fair share of letters from their eldest daughter. Vicky had claimed it was impossible to write frequently to both her parents, and her mother was so demanding, so urgent in her questions, so incapable of accepting any sort of denial, that writing to her came first. There was also a plea from Germany, but not from Königsburg. Baron Stockmar took upon himself to write from Coburg that he understood the Queen was writing too often to her married daughter; and this, he wrote, was a fault which could only hold back her full acceptance by the Prussians. Would the Queen desist for her daughter's sake? Victoria's high opinions of Stockmar fell considerably. She took exception to his sermon, and she said so. Last of all, her own Secretary of State for Foreign Affairs came to Court with a semi-official complaint from Prussia that so intense a political correspondence was influencing Princess Victoria against the interests of her new country.

Victoria was offended and highly exasperated, but she felt obliged all the same to bend her will to so powerful an alliance of opinion. She told the Foreign Secretary that her correspondence with Königsburg would in future be curtailed, except, of course, when her daughter was carrying a child and was obviously in need of a mother's advice. He appeared to be satisfied. And so to some extent was she. She thought it likely that Vicky would quite frequently be in that condition and she was prepared to defy the Prussians to read any political significance into motherly chats on obstetrics.

Right up to the time of Vicky's confinement her advice was sound and eminently practical; and when, after a hideously difficult labour her first grandchild was born with a dislocated left arm, her sympathy was touching in its sincerity.

My precious darling you suffered much more than I ever did, and how I wish I could have lightened them for you!

XIV

Victoria had hoped that as she grew towards middle-age, her passions would be less inflaming, but, as time passed, she found herself disappointed.

She kept two journals; the diary of daily events which she had been writing since the age of thirteen, and another more private volume entitled *REMARKS – CONVERSATIONS – REFLECTIONS*. It was in the latter that she recorded her conviction that over-sensitiveness and irritability were to be millstones round her neck for life. They made her sullen or they made her flare up. In either case she quarrelled as often and as pointlessly with Albert despite many resolutions about better self-control.

But, though her passions were no less inflammatory, she did notice one unlooked for benefit as she grew older; she took a far keener pleasure in life. Once before she had felt the same high sense of satisfaction in being alive. That was in the leisurely days when Lord M. had looked after things, and in the first months of her marriage. Something must have happened to dull her zest in life, perhaps the humdrum side of being a sovereign, a wife and a mother. But now she believed that her approaching middle-age was going to be the *crème de la crème* of existence.

Never before had she been so interested in her children. Even Bertie held a horrid fascination for his mother. He was still too like a caricature of the house of Hanover, with almost all the deplorable habits of her uncles though little of their native intelligence and raffish good looks, but his father, thank God, had him in hand. Tutor Gibbs was leaving and Bertie was being given a governor and chosen companions and ultimately sent to Oxford and then to Cambridge. It was also thought proper that he should visit overseas possessions on her behalf, and serve perfunctorily as a subaltern in Albert's regiment, the Grenadier Guards. She hoped he would succeed and be a credit to his father, and leave his puppy ugliness behind – for there never was a more unprepossessing prince with his knock knees, small head, large nose, receding chin, and spots. It was an abiding consolation that in Königsburg there was Vicky to be sent warnings, advice, news and gossip, and to be scolded because she had barely finished her lying-in before the golden-bearded Fritz had inconsiderately given her another child. And all Victoria's other children meant far more to her. Alice was now a very pretty pawn in the dynasty game and discreet feelers were being put out in the Courts of Holland and Hesse-Darmstadt. Alfred was enduring service as a midshipman in her Navy. Helena and Louise were schoolroom misses; both sweet and neither causing her parents a moment's anxiety. Little Arthur appeared to have caught something of his illustrious godfather's manner of speech because, when prohibited from singing at meals as company was present, he asked: 'What's company, hey? Tell me. What's company?' And Leopold, allowed to lead as ordinary a life as was possible, managed to survive haemorrhage after haemorrhage and fall in love with his grandmother Kent's Lady-in-Waiting. He showed the most desperate jealousy when she was accompanied on a walk by her own brother. What darlings they were, even the young Beatrice. Victoria had no real fondness for tiny children, but Beatrice was precocious and amusing. One day at luncheon she had occasion to rebuke the child for so loudly demanding a certain dish.

'Baby mustn't have that,' she said sharply as Beatrice caught hold of the dish. 'It's not good for baby.'

To her astonishment the child replied: 'But baby likes it, my dear!' and helped herself.

With such spirited children Victoria was certain they would prove a blessing and consolation as they grew up.

Then there were her friends. Victoria took a fresh delight in sharing pleasure with her friends, in making up folios and albums, sketching views and engraving, in water colouring flower-pieces – Albert's favourite convolvulus and her own favourite posies of striped tulips and pocotee carnations, in needlework and beadwork, singing and playing duets and enjoying new operas, a new book, new paintings, new fashions; in making meals out of doors, picnicking in wild places and boiling the tea kettle in the open; in drinking Athole brose when they followed the guns on ponies; in bathing in the Solent under the watchful eye of Mary Rush. With certain friends she enjoyed certain pleasures. There was view-quartering with Miss Skerrett when they studied a view as though it were framed, examining the details of each quarter, and enjoying them slowly as though they were tasting rich cakes. With Jane Churchill the pleasures were more *outré*; a pony race across bad ground, rowing in a loch by moonlight, experimenting with cigarettes, practising archery, trying to frighten each other with tales of mystery and horror.

And, quite unexpectedly, Victoria and her mother had become more intimate.

The Duchess was feeling her age. Her sight was beginning to fail and she was ailing with a disease that had begun in her left arm and gave her great pain. She found it difficult to play her beloved pianoforte, and she suffered badly from *nostalgie du passé*. But it seemed as if all these severe handicaps had sweetened her disposition. Mother and daughter had their own establishments and routines, and they could not see each other very often; but Clarence House was not far from the Palace, Frogmore House close to the Castle, and Abergeldie only a short drive from Balmoral; and on occasion they dined and drove out together. The Duchess liked the way her daughter was mellowing, and Victoria was delighted, if a little surprised, by her mother's amiability. She was excellent company and very popular in the schoolroom when she told the children stories, composed marches for them, and made clever pencil drawings of them in a variety of poses. It could serve no purpose to talk about the old days at Kensington and so they avoided the subject; but they both loved discussing family trivia – romances, betrothals, weddings, confinements, lyings-in, illness and death.

The royal round, strung in a changing pattern between the four points, London, Windsor, Osborne and Balmoral was immensely satisfying to Victoria. It was something to hold on to as the background altered, when events chased each other and history was made.

Victoria became the great white Queen of India, an event which she received with cool and typical detachment. Just as after her solemn Coronation in the Abbey she had gone home and bathed her dog, so now, while Skerrett and Jane Churchill gasped at the grandeur of being sovereign to a hundred million eastern peoples, Victoria seized a large umbrella and went for an hour's walk in the rain.

There were rumbles of trouble far away. The Celestial

Empire made war on all Europeans, and in America the southern planters, who had England's undeclared support, were being subjected to stronger and stronger pressures from the north. There were the same rumbles closer at hand. Austria's war with France made the Queen grieve, and in the matter of taking sides there was a temporary rift between her and Albert. He had so many cousins in the Austrian Court and Army that he supported the Hapsburgs. Her own sympathies were for the French, and especially after Austria had basely attacked Sardinia. When the King of Sardinia had visited Windsor he had captivated the Court by his disturbingly attractive appearance and manner. He had worn the brightest of tunics at the Garter ceremony, shot stags by moonlight, gone to bed at three and got up at five to smoke strong cigars with his aides, and amused Victoria by proudly describing the fine physical appearance of his horde of illegitimate children. She could not bear to think of him as the victim of Austrian aggression, and was delighted when he and the French turned the tables and won a resounding victory at Solferino.

At home Lord Palmerston lost office to the Conservatives, but he gained it again a year later much to Victoria's relief. Having at last got used to Palmerston the idea of any change was disagreeable. There had to be one change, though, which she found difficult to bear. Sir James Clark, after years in the royal service, begged leave to resign as Queen's physician. How, she asked him, were they to manage without him? And for a long time she simply refused her permission. Then, because the old gentleman persisted, she affected a compromise. He was to continue living in the grace-and-favour houses at Bagshot near Windsor, and at Birk Hall near Balmoral, and he would kindly move north and south at the same time as the Court. In this way, though another would be appointed to his place in the Household, he would always be at hand to watch and advise. Sir James found himself obliged to consent. Wryly he told himself this was the oddest form of professional retirement he had ever heard of, but he had observed the Queen's small rounded chin set in the familiar position of implacable and absolute determination to have her own way – and what could a man do in face of that?

Setbacks checked her, some events thwarted her, and a few hurt and saddened her, but on the whole Victoria consumed life just as she consumed potatoes – regularly, with a good appetite and digestion, and as gratefully. She was especially grateful for her husband. Though she often disagreed with him and there were dreadful scenes between them, she very rarely failed to look to him as the pivot on which everything depended. He was her critic and could be severe at times, but he was also her mentor and helper, her lover, and the inventor of wonderful happenings. If the pleasures she shared with her friends and with her mother were increased in enjoyment during this leaf-fall of her youth, the pleasures she shared with Albert were almost unbearably happy. She was blessed in that at the very moment some things took place she knew she would remember them all her life: their private expedition, travelling incognito as Lord and Lady Churchill, staying at great houses or making do in Scotch inns; their boating trips on lochs and sailing together from the pier at Osborne; those very rare and therefore doubly precious times when alone in her sitting-room he would play and they sang duets together; their walks out into the country unattended, picking ferns and flowers or collecting shells for the children; looking through folios together, sometimes drawings and etchings from the Royal Collections, at others their own family engravings, or prints made to their order in Scotland, or views with memories – for her of Kensington, Folkestone, Ramsgate and Tunbridge Wells, for him of Thüringen, Rosenau and Ketschendorf, and long views of the Jungfrau and the Fischbacherthal.

Victoria became increasingly dependent on her husband; so absorbed in her devotion that despite the friction which occasionally burned between them he was everything in the world to her.

XV

The Prince Consort planned a family holiday in Coburg for the autumn of 1860. Vicky was to join them there with her elder child, Prince William, and after a long interval there would be an opportunity to see poor Stockmar. The Baron was growing old; not frail, his frame was too rugged for that, nor was the machinery of his mind in the least affected by advancing years, but he had been unwell recently, more and more a victim of bronchitis and ordinary mortality. The Prince judged this might be their last chance to see him.

They would have been received and fêted formally as before but for the sudden death of the Dowager Duchess of Saxe-Coburg which put the Court into mourning. Victoria did not pretend to hide her satisfaction that their visit could be quiet and private. It was so much more comfortable, and so much more suitable for a family holiday. Moreover, it would help when they saw their grandchild for the first time.

Twelve months before Vicky had gone alone to Osborne to tell her parents that little William's dislocated arm was wasting. Neither had shown the least horror as she had feared. Victoria, being a mother herself, had felt most for her daughter. She was sure, she said, the child would be all right. Maimed children were often blessed with compensations. Albert hid his feelings by showing a scientific interest in atrophy and promising to consult Sir James and the best medical men in Britain on the subject.

On their first day in Coburg, they saw William, a sturdy little boy led in by his English nurse. Neither missed, but neither examined the cold, blue arm which he tried to hide behind his back, and neither made the least attempt to fuss him. Albert quite naturally picked him up and took him to the window. He wore the look Victoria knew so well and she made no doubt he was already telling William one of his quaint tales, or reciting one of the extraordinary nonsense rhymes of her drawing-master, Mr Edward Lear. Yes, the child came back from the window convinced that his grandpapa's moustache was really a sable sea anemone which had settled on his upper lip while swimming in the Solent. She made no demonstration of affection herself because children know all about humbug, but she put out a forefinger for him to pull and then had to slap him because he tried to wrench off her ring. Albert talked with the English nurse about German nursing, and Vicky, who had dreaded this meeting, suddenly realized it was not an ordeal at all and began to relax. It marked the beginning of a very happy family holiday when they saw a good deal of Ernest and his wife and children, and the Stockmars.

Then, one day, it was entirely spoilt for Victoria. She was alone outside the windows of the Rosenau drawing-room, sketching a view and drinking tea, when Lady Churchill begged leave to interrupt her with a message. The Prince Consort had met with an accident. Would her majesty come at once?

Victoria jumped to her feet.

'They have taken him to his dressing-room,' said Lady Churchill.

The Queen hurried through the open windows and across the drawing-room until she could restrain herself no longer and she broke into a stumbling run. Jane Churchill did her best to keep up and, at the same time, tell her what had occurred. The Prince was being driven alone in a four-in-hand, she said, and the horses had bolted.

The Queen stopped abruptly. Her hands flew to her face. 'Oh, Jane, he is dead?'

'No, Ma'am. The horses bolted towards a railway crossing where there was a waiting waggon and his royal highness leapt out of the carriage.'

Victoria wailed.

'He is not badly hurt.' Lady Churchill took her by the arm. 'Ma'am. He is not badly hurt.'

Victoria found him lying on his dressing-room bed with the shutters drawn. His equerry, Colonel Ponsonby, stood at the bed's head. He made way for the Queen who, barely looking at her husband's chalk-white face, laid her head upon his chest and burst into a storm of tears. Through it Albert tried to calm her, to reassure her, and gradually the paroxysm passed. When she was collected she demanded to see a doctor. Why was there not one in attendance?

A tall, young man stepped out of the shadows. He had examined the Prince he said, and there was no great injury.

'You are the physician?' she asked brusquely. 'A Court physician?'

He bowed. 'His royal highness is shocked, and has a few minor cuts and bruises. Nothing else.'

'You are too young,' said the Queen. 'Colonel, Jane, for the love of God get a physician.'

'Ma'am,' urged Ponsonby, 'this gentleman is one of Duke Ernest's doctors.'

It took a great deal of time and patience to persuade her that the Prince Consort was not in danger of his life. Then she insisted on sitting beside him, which did him no good at all. Her constant questions and tears upset him, and prevented him from sleeping.

Eventually Ponsonby risked a great deal for his master's sake and told the Queen frankly that it would be better for the Prince if she was to leave. She was surprised into doing what he suggested. Outside the room he bowed. 'Ma'am, with all respect, it would be wiser for Lady Churchill to accompany you to your room. His royal highness needs rest.'

So did Victoria. She was sick with anxiety, sick with relief, sick with the horror of what might have happened to her beloved Albert, and as soon as she reached her room she collapsed on her bed with exhaustion.

It was some time before they dared tell her how fortunate Albert had been. The coachman had been hurled against the waiting waggon and his ribs crushed so badly that he almost died, and one of the horses had had to be put down by the royal farrier.

*   *   *

'I ask your advice, Stockmar; therefore you must know the truth of it all. One half of the Queen has been radiantly happy in these past months, but the other half, which I recall and she forgets, has been a shadow over my life. Disagreement makes her violent and when I try to finish a quarrel she will persist in begging my forgiveness. Sometimes, I have left her simply to get away, and she has followed me from room to room, beseeching me, in front of her ladies and before my own gentlemen, to agree with her or to pardon her.'

He paused, and shook his head slowly from side to side as though trying to rid himself of the painful memory.

Candles had been brought in but, preferring to talk by firelight, he had put them out. Even in the small flickering light Stockmar could see the lines of anxiety on his face. To comfort him he said quite truthfully that in all his experience of the Queen she had never fundamentally altered. Though when the occasion demanded it she could be magnificently regal she lacked serenity. She had always been excitable, sometimes impulsive.

The Prince said nothing for a moment.

'Tell me,' urged Stockmar, breaking the silence. 'Tell me about that half of her character which has thrown a shadow over you.'

'Her frenzies seem the worst,' said the Prince slowly, 'and yet sometimes I think her morbid fancies are as bad. For months she has been fascinated by the King of Prussia's lunacy. She has studied it, Stockmar, brooding on it, writing to the Princess Royal and to our ambassador for the fullest details, and consulted Clark and other physicians at home—' The Prince broke off, and shook his head again. 'Equally painful is her vindictive attitude to the Prince of Wales. I find him objectionable enough, God knows, but I keep it to myself that he vexes me past bearing; and I can see his few good points. Victoria is wilfully blind to them, and she does not like it if I try to open her eyes. Even worse, she allows people to see her dislike. Though iron-strong in so many ways, she has weaknesses of temperament which she does not trouble to conceal from the Household, and this makes her prejudice alarming. When Austria came close to winning the recent war she was clamorous and threatened to leave Europe altogether.'

'Mere talk?' suggested Stockmar.

'The talk of queens is never mere talk, Baron. I am surprised you did not hear of her threats here. She spoke of taking the children to Australia. All the Court heard it, and, within hours, all the embassies.'

Stockmar held his tongue, although, in fact, he had heard the rumour and had paid no more attention to it than he believed the Prince ought to have done.

'The Queen, naturally, has many worries,' he pointed out.

'And if she lacks them,' said the Prince, 'she dreams them up. All this summer her nerves have been upset by young Louis of Hesse-Darmstadt. Not that he has offended her, on the contrary. She thinks he is ideal for our daughter Alice and when he came over for Ascot Week she hoped for an engagement: but, wisely as I see it, the young people are taking their time, and the waiting is driving Victoria ma . . . mad.' He tripped over the last word, and looked wretchedly at Stockmar. Then he looked at the fire again, wishing he had not jibbed at the word.

The Baron kicked a log. Sparks spattered over the fire dogs and into the hearth. In the increased light he saw the Prince was leaning forwards with his head in his hands.

'Come,' he said. 'This won't do at all. A little brandy and water, perhaps, and hot?'

The Prince made no reply.

'Let it be hot, then,' said the Baron. He mixed the drink, gave it to the Prince and then, without asking permission he took a chair and toasted his hands.

He was worried, but not about the Queen. It seemed to him that the Prince himself was ailing and that it had little or nothing to do with the carriage incident. He had aged perceptibly and not in an ordinary healthy manner. He had no gloss about him, simply dullness. His thinning hair was scurfy, his features sallow, the weight he had put on was flabby not firm. Consciously or unconsciously he had let

271

himself slip, which accounted, perhaps, for the strange letter which Stockmar had received from him some months before and which at the time he had found inexplicable. In it the Prince had complained of great lassitude and of the constant troubles and worries which had fallen to his lot.

Stockmar made another attempt to reassure him about the Queen. She was so passionate, he said, that to a stranger the violence of her outbursts might seem to indicate she was unbalanced. But had she not always been the same?

The Prince looked up from his glass. 'Could she not be deteriorating as she grows older?' he asked.

'Maybe,' said the Baron, 'though I do not have that opinion myself.' He put his hand on the Prince's shoulder. 'You are not yourself very well. It is evident. And that prevents you from being properly objective about your wife. Therefore you will have to rely on me, and trust me as you have all your life. You must believe that the Queen is robust enough mentally to withstand the violence of a good many more outbursts before she stands in any danger. If you will be calm, she will be calm, and when great matters frustrate or grieve her let her have her own way and time will be her medicine. As for yourself' – and here Stockmar looked steadily at his old pupil – 'it seems to me that you stand in need of rest. You can, you know, be the architect of your own health; and if you drive yourself too hard and fail to take the regular exercise you once did, you will jade your own spirits and harm your sense of judgement. Do I make myself clear?'

The Prince said yes, he understood.

XVI

The Duchess of Kent was very ill.

Sir James Clark had been called from his provisional retirement and had told her frankly she had cancer. It had spread malevolently from her left arm, and the surgeons had tried a temporary remedy by operating on her wrist and side. But there was no hope of recovery. All this was very clear to her Household, and to the Prince who was taken into Sir James' confidence, but the Duchess was so strict in the face of the pain, the discomfort and the humiliations to which her corrupting body was subjected, that Victoria remained optimistic. Seeing her mother neat in cap and shawl and crinoline, and knowing nothing of the pain she endured to appear fully dressed, Victoria supposed her mother was better than she was. Therefore when the news came that her mother was dying, she found it difficult to believe.

That afternoon she had gone with Albert to visit the new gardens of the Horticultural Society. She had gone for Albert's sake. For her own, she would have preferred to avoid the windswept site in South Kensington and remain at the Palace on such a blustering March day, and she had been relieved to go home early at his suggestion while he remained on the site for a committee meeting. Since then she had sat before a beechwood fire, eaten her tea, and gone through the boxes brought in that afternoon. And then, quite unexpectedly, there was Albert, obviously upset and trying to hide it, telling her Sir James had just come from Frogmore and her mother was very ill indeed. They had to go to her at once. A train had been ordered and would be waiting for them now.

She said little on the journey until the train was drawing into Windsor station.

'It is certain she is dying?' she asked.

'I believe so,' said Albert.

Frogmore House was in a state of upheaval when they arrived: not because the Duchess of Kent was dying, but because the Queen and her family were unexpected guests and hurried arrangements were being made.

Victoria went at once to her mother. Her ladies had removed her crinoline and she was in a silk dressing-gown and a nightcap, but still sitting upright on a sofa and trembling. Her daughter knelt beside her, took her hand and kissed it. But the Duchess, though she looked at her with open eyes, brushed Victoria's hand away.

The gesture meant nothing. A dying woman had failed to recognize her daughter, but Victoria felt it keenly. Albert did not notice her distress. His own great affection for his aunt blinded him to anything but her suffering. He saw that she was in a particularly uncomfortable position, and though it made her bite her lip with the pain, he eased her into a better one.

Victoria did not like to take her hand again. She sat in a low chair watching her mother's face. Her features were far less rounded. Either the dim light was playing tricks or her face really was growing longer and sharper. Victoria closed her eyes. She did not want to look at death.

Death had claimed so many in the past nine weeks. It had brought release for the mad King of Prussia, though not to old Lady Conyngham who had relished life to the last and had died at the age of ninety-one. The Duke of Sutherland, one of their most particular Scotch friends had also died, and the Duke of Buckingham, who had once entertained them lavishly at Stowe and yet died in a hotel bedroom, miserable, bankrupt and divorced. Then the Duchess' Comptroller, a kindly man and so much more suitable than Conroy had ever been, had died only two weeks before; and Doctor Daly the new royal physician, a man chosen with particular care by Sir James Clark as his successor. His death in a railway accident at Wimbledon had been a tragic loss; though Doctor Jenner, his successor, was also excellent, thank God . . .

Victoria opened her eyes and looked about the room. Jenner ought to have been there. She beckoned to Sir James and asked in a whisper where he was. Apparently Jenner had already been, as had the Duchess' own private physician from Windsor, but because neither could do anything they had gone home. The Queen frowned. She thought they ought to have stayed.

'They could do nothing,' repeated Sir James. He took the opportunity to suggest that the Queen go and lie down for a time. 'Be sure I shall send for you if it is necessary.'

274

Victoria took another close look at her mother and quietly left the room. A bed had been made up for her in what was known as the Scarlet Fever Room, but she did not get in between the sheets. Fully dressed she lay on a sofa at the foot of the bed, sipped hot milk brought to her by her tiring-maid, and looked at the many shadows cast by the firelight on the ceiling. Eventually she dozed off, but slept fitfully, and woke feeling guilty because she was not keeping watch below.

Three times she took a lamp and went downstairs.

On the first occasion all was well. Momentarily she knelt by the bed and kissed her mother's hand. On the second occasion her mother's wounds had just been redressed and, though both windows and the door were open, there was a cloying smell in the room. This drove her away again and she lay upstairs listening to cocks crowing and dogs barking in the distance, thinking not of the present but of the past, not of Frogmore House but of Kensington Palace. When she could bear it no longer she seized her lamp and went downstairs. Her mother was still oblivious of everything. Lady Augusta Bruce, her Lady-in-Waiting, gave her sips of wine and water from a spoon, but she was finding it increasingly difficult to swallow. Victoria sat by the bed, and this time she took her mother's hand. She sat there listening to her slow and faint breathing and the striking of her father's repeater watch at every quarter. It hung from the bedhead and she had not heard it tick or strike for twenty-three years.

As time passed she realized there were many others there besides Albert and Lady Augusta and Sir James. And she realized that, though none of them stood as close as she did to her mother, none of them had been separated from her in the midst of such bitterness for so long. Her tears when her mother died at half-past nine in the morning were for that estrangement.

No one could help the Queen. She even refused to look for consolation. When she wrote her feelings to Uncle Leopold it was not for comfort, but because he had known the situation at Kensington and could understand her regret at the wasted years. In fact he was appalled to read such explosions of emotion. The tear-blotched paper, the hysterical underlinings, the excesses of grief, her constant self-reproaches, her accusations against Conroy and Lehzen whom in her mourning she blamed for everything, her moping and her morbid dwelling on death, keenly shocked him. He tried to give her a sense of proportion and told her not to shake her precious health too much. She must not give way, he told her, and, to strengthen the point, he added: '*Your dear Mamma, who watched your looks so affectionately, would not approve.*' His adjuration made little difference. She declared she was so beaten down by sorrow that she was unable to bear noise. Loud conversations, too many people talking at once was forbidden. She whipped herself with regrets. If only she and her mother could have been friends – as they had been in the past months. If only she could have realized, as she realized now in going through her mother's papers, how much her mother cared for her. Then, worst of all, remorse caught hold of her. She tormented herself by remembering clearly all the bitter things she had said and written about her mother, all the dreadful things she had done to her.

Albert did all he could for her. He managed to keep her away from the funeral. He fell in with her wish to make a splendid mausoleum at Frogmore where the Duchess' remains could be placed in a granite sarcophagus, and where she could go to weep away her grief. He asked Lady Augusta Bruce to look after the Queen; a temporary arrangement which pleased them both because Victoria found great relief in being close to her mother's faithful Lady-in-Waiting, and Lady Augusta, deprived of her beloved mistress, and with no one now to care for and love, found comfort in being able to look after her daughter. It was so successful an arrangement that it became permanent. Lady Augusta was appointed Victoria's Resident Bedchamber Woman, and another loyal friend was added to the Household. Meanwhile Albert had agreed that Frogmore House should always be kept as it had been, and that the servants should be transferred into the royal service. And, as his aunt's sole executor, he gave a great deal of time and attention to her complicated affairs and kept anything to himself which he thought might upset Victoria.

But for a time Victoria was really beyond his comfort or help. It seemed that for long periods she hardly knew what was happening. She was suffering from a breakdown which had the courts of Europe whispering that at last grief had driven her demented, and she was as mad as her grandfather.

Albert who had feared it all along now stoutly refused to give the idea any countenance. Vicky wrote agitated letters from Königsburg, Ernest wrote them from Coburg, Uncle Leopold from Laeken, his cousin Ferdinand from Portugal. Albert recalled Stockmar's considered opinion that Victoria had a certain mental robustness which could withstand almost anything, and he was determined she would soon get over her grief and her illusory remorse and be herself again.

To take her mind off things he decided they must return to London. She went tearfully. He tried to interest her in affairs. The Bourbon kings had been driven from Naples, the Pope driven from Rome, and Italy was unified under the King of Sardinia. Meanwhile Civil War had broken out in America. Victoria was not indifferent, but her reactions were more those of an automaton than of a real person. To make her be herself Albert arranged a family reunion, first in London and afterwards at Osborne. Uncle Leopold, Vicky and her husband and their children stayed for long periods; and there was a series of visitors at Osborne from Baden, Austria, Sweden and Hesse.

Gradually Victoria pulled herself together. Albert's patience, his studied awareness of her need, and his readiness to let her have her own way unless it was clearly against her interests, was her greatest solace. His loving attention and the care of Miss Skerrett and Jane Churchill and Lady Augusta gave her the will to conquer her depression, and once the Frogmore mausoleum had been built and her mother's remains transferred there from the royal vault at Windsor, and once she and Albert and Alice had taken wreaths there on a first visit she seemed much more herself. She calmly discussed with Albert what sort of statue should be carved for placing on the sarcophagus and said she wished to remember her mother as she had been in the latter part of her life: an erect little figure, with a lace cap on her head, a dainty lace shawl, pearls, and ribboned bows on her dress. This was in strong contrast with the stout but strikingly handsome figure with raven hair of Victoria's childhood, and which she now preferred to forget.

Miss Skerrett spoke privately with the Prince Consort about something which had been worrying her since the Duchess' death. She had been intending at that very time to ask for permission to leave the royal service, but, in view of the Queen's great distress she had postponed it again and again. Did his royal highness think that, as the Queen appeared to be much stronger, she could now mention the subject? Albert considered. Victoria was attached to Skerrett and would dislike her leaving the Household. A compromise suggested itself. If Miss Skerrett would be so kind as to postpone her retirement for twelve months but give the Queen warning now, she would have ample time to accustom herself to the idea. Poor Skerrett, who was feeling her years, was rather dismayed but for the Queen's sake she agreed. And it seemed to answer. Victoria was immediately cast down when the subject was broached but when she realized the worst would not happen for at least twelve months, she brightened up again. Skerrett was not to torment her, she said; and, to take her mind off the subject, she swept that lady into the wardrobe where they spent two full hours sorting through drawers and hanging cupboards and enjoying gossip.

The longed-for engagement between Princess Alice and Prince Louis of Hesse-Darmstadt had come about and there was a good deal of romantic talk in the fluff and dust of the cupboards, though the Queen confessed how badly the young man's parents were behaving in the matter of a German palace. An even more delectable piece of news to confide in Skerrett was the Princess Royal's plan for her brother the Prince of Wales. The list of potential princesses

for his hand had at last been reduced to one: Princess Alexandra of Denmark who had the special advantage of being
beautiful and non-German as well as Protestant. But said the
Queen – lowering her voice although they were in the wardrobe – he was not to be pushed into marriage. Having had
the inestimable advantage of a love marriage herself, she
would not force her son to accept her choice unless it happened to coincide with his own. But she was confident that it
would. Princess Alexandra was so beautiful she said and – in
a still lower voice – the Princess Royal was inviting her back
to Germany in September where she would arrange an 'acci-
dental' meeting between the two. Both would be taken sightseeing simultaneously in Speyer Cathedral . . .

Skerrett was delighted. The Queen's relish in this little
conspiracy showed how far she had recovered. Within a few
days more noticeable improvements had taken place, and
very soon she was beginning to look forward to their annual
holiday at Balmoral.

Albert breathed freely again. His loyal defiance had not
been able to silence the malicious rumours that Victoria was
mad. But now her sanity was so obvious that they were
killed outright. He was very thankful, and on his own account, he was relieved her breakdown was past. He felt
exhausted in every way. There were as many demands on his
time and energy as ever, and he now carried to platforms
and committee rooms, to consultations with ministers and
scientists and artists, a body which was regularly racked
with the pains of rheumatism, gastritis, swollen glands and
toothache. Moreover, the reserves of mental energy he had
used in looking after Victoria were almost exhausted. For
her sake, to guarantee the continued improvement in her
health, he never let her see the deterioration of his own, nor
the extent of his weakness.

His valet Löhlein saw it, and worried silently. So did
Colonel Phipps and Colonel Ponsonby. As Englishmen will,
they joked about what troubled them, saying that the Queen
and their master were like Lady Macbeth and her husband!
for as the spirits of one rose, so the spirits of the other went
down; but each on several occasions begged the Prince not

to spend himself too freely, to rest a little, and recuperate.

It was wise advice, but Albert could not take it. He was no longer a tightly-coiled spring, working tirelessly and able to make swift and shrewd decisions; but the spring still had some force in it. While there was any work to be done he would do it.

On the royal visit to Ireland which they made on the way to Scotland he went out of his way to meet the Irish and have long and serious talks with Lord Carlisle the Viceroy. The Prince of Wales was there learning to be a subaltern at the Curragh Camp. They took luncheon with him in his hut, a less ascetic apartment than its name suggested as it had a sitting-room and a drawing-room as well as a bedroom and a dressing-room; and, between showers of rain, they watched a review. The Queen, satisfied that her heir was in good hands and that soon he would be off to Germany to meet the Princess of Denmark, merely noted in a letter to her uncle that *'Bertie marched past with his company, and did not look at all so very small'*, and she cried because the band in an excess of loyalty, played one of her mother's compositions. The careworn Prince Consort worried himself because neither the Prince of Wales nor his brother officers were serious enough about the profession of arms for, instead of discussing military tactics, they frivolously spoke of little but shooting, fishing and dancing. At Holyhead where they were to go by rail to Scotland, he left the Queen resting and paid formal visits to Caernarvon and Beddgellert, receiving addresses, making speeches, asking endless questions and storing facts in his tired head.

At Balmoral it was the same. The farm buildings and estate offices had all been modernized according to his instructions and had been completed just before his arrival. These had to be inspected. After that he settled to designing a new dairy: octagonal in shape to let in the maximum light, with under-floor ventilation pipes, marble shelving and flooring, constant supplies of hot and cold water, and a scalding boiler for sterilizing churns and cream pans. He also went carefully through the shrubberies and gardens with his gardeners and through the plantations with his foresters.

There was deer stalking to arrange, and shooting parties; and, for the children, geological and botanical excursions and moth hunts at night time with the aid of lanterns. Then there were his treats especially for Victoria which this autumn did so much to help her forget the loss of her mother.

He organized three expeditions. To Victoria and Alice and her fiancé Louis they were delightful because everything seemed spontaneous, but, in fact, when a great chief met them on the marches of his land and the meeting seemed so casual because he was alone and dressed quite informally it was the result of careful planning. Transport was arranged with equal care, so that sociables, luggage carts, and fresh ponies met them in the right places and mostly at the right time. The only part left to chance was accommodation and this was because they particularly wished to be incognito and take rooms as ordinary travellers. It exposed them to some difficulties. An angry traveller refused entrance to the Commercial Room at an inn was only persuaded to go away by the plea that a wedding party was there. At another inn there were hardly any provisions: tea and two scrawny Scotch chickens without vegetables or any pudding between nine of them. But even these setbacks did not worry the Queen. She thought the expeditions perfect. Just as much as the sublime views she enjoyed riding her pony through thick bands of mist or, protected by an umbrella, waterproofs and a plaid, through beating rain. She loved being incognito but she was also touched when people recognized her and showed their loyalty as happened at an inn where the landlady, to honour her, put on a black satin dress trimmed with white ribbons and orange flowers, and the local volunteers turned out and gathered below her window to the sound of fife and drum.

Each detail of their expeditions merited a description in her journal, but two memories in particular stayed with her for ever. There was the fording of the river below a thundering waterfall in Glen Tilt where she was led through rain-swollen water by her factotum Brown on one side and by the indefatigable Duke of Athole on the other, both up to their waists in water; and, cutting right through the whinnying of the ponies and the shouts of encouragement from their leaders, and the noise of the falls, and the splashing, and the swirling water, came the thin music of the pipes, for a pair of the Duke's pipers marched first through the ford, playing as hard as they could. As clear a memory was of eating a picnic luncheon on a precipitous place on Cairn Lochan. It was a calm cloudless day when the mountains had shades of blue on them like the bloom on a plum, and after luncheon Albert wrote all their names on a piece of paper, and put it into a Selterswater bottle. Victoria described it all in her journal that night, but really it was quite unnecessary. She would never forget that picture of Albert kneeling on the turf, trying to bury the bottle with his dirk and failing because of all the stones. In the end he had to leave it half in and half out of the ground.

XVII

The Queen returned to Windsor a different person. She still missed her mother but now she had the fortitude and the common-sense not to let it upset her. Balmoral had been her anodyne and, back at home in England, she found both public and private affairs in good order. The country, said Lord Palmerston, was managing well. So, undoubtedly, was her family. Vicky, now Crown Princess of Prussia, had been given, of all things, the colonelcy of a regiment of hussars, and her plan for Bertie had been a splendid success. He had returned home full of praise for Princess Alexandra and had gone back up to Cambridge determined to marry her. As for the rest of the children, from Alice whose head was in the clouds down to baby Beatrice whose head most certainly was not, they were as happy and as well-behaved as any children could be. Baby's repertoire of astonishing remarks now included one which she hoped would excuse her from doing anything uncongenial: 'I have no time,' she would say. 'I must write letters.'

But his restless urge to work and keep going combined with his increasing debility, was proving too much for the Prince Consort. Quite unnecessarily he went regularly up to London, to attend meetings and superintend repairs being made at Marlborough House and at the Palace. He also made himself entirely responsible for the preparations for the Prince of Wales' birthday in November and for little Prince Leopold to be taken to Cannes for the winter months. All this was in addition to his normal and highly demanding routine. He became more and more debilitated and querulous, and less and less able to relax.

His friend and equerry Colonel Ponsonby had exceedingly high standards. Ordinarily he would not have dreamt of discussing private matters with anyone, but he was desperately worried. He had engaged himself to be married some ten months before, and he now went to his fiancée, a Miss Mary Bulteel, to share his troubles and ask for advice on how best he could help his master. She was adamant. He must go at once and talk to the Queen, or Colonel Phipps, as the Prince's Private Secretary, should go Phipps asked for a private audience and went.

As he told the Queen their anxieties, he saw a light die in her eyes, and he wondered how it was possible that she had failed to observe her husband's illness. In fact the change had taken place so gradually, and the deterioration in his health had corresponded so exactly with the improvement in her own, that she had not been aware of any great difference in him. But now that Phipps underlined the changes one by one, and confessed his serious concern, she realized that Albert must be very ill indeed. Her lip trembled as she promised the Colonel to do all in her power to restrain her husband, and when he left her, backing from the small audience chamber, she was staring unhappily at the ground. He found Ponsonby waiting for him. 'She did not know, by God!' he muttered. 'Ponsonby, she really did not know.'

Victoria wasted no time. She sent at once to Bagshot for Sir James Clark and saw him privately. What he said was a

283

comfort. Rest was the Prince's best medicine. He must be made to rest. That with wholesome food would give him fresh reserves of strength to face the winter.

That evening she spoke to Albert. She told him she was concerned because he did not seem himself, and she admitted that she had consulted Clark. He merely sighed and threw himself into a chair before her fire. She persevered. Was he not doing too much? Could he not cancel or at least postpone some of his less urgent engagements? No, he said shortly, he could not. Weary as he was, there could be no respite for the time being. And Clark's suggestions made him very irritable. How, he asked, could he rest when there was so much to be done and when sleep appeared to have deserted him? And how could he take nourishing food with his pathetic digestion?

She told herself that his fractiousness was natural under the circumstances. Nevertheless it surprised her. It was unlike Albert to be at the mercy of his nerves.

His irascibility grew. He was angry out of all proportion and reason when the dog Boz seized and ran off with the wig he wore when writing at his desk in the early mornings; and so brittle were his nerves that when the band played at the Prince of Wales' birthday dinner for the first time since the death of Victoria's mother, he declared it was impossible to think or converse or even eat comfortably in such a deafening row. He sent for wool floss and ostentatiously wore ear plugs for the remainder of the banquet sipping weak brandy and water, eating nothing and talking to no one.

Victoria forced herself to be patient. He was being trying but she was confident there would soon be an improvement. She was wrong. Albert felt so wretched that he himself sent for Dr Jenner and for Dr Brown of Windsor. He also asked for Sir James although Lady Clark was seriously ill at Bagshot. If his old friend could come he would be eternally grateful. Sir James went immediately because he thought it was essential to confide in his colleagues that the Prince was a natural worrier, and that if he was needlessly alarmed his recovery would be slower. Before they made the joint examination he warned them that in his experience a tactful use of euphemism was entirely justified when treating the royal family. They heard the Prince's complaints of regular headaches, stiffness in the back, griping stomach pains, sleeplessness, exhaustion, and they made a careful examination. Sir James then told him he had a seasonal illness which many people suffered from in the autumn and they prescribed rest, an invalid diet, and opiates for his stomach pains. The word 'fever' was never mentioned. Afterwards Jenner expressed some doubt as to the wisdom of giving such a wide diagnosis, but Sir James insisted it was all important for the Prince's spirits to be kept up. That, with their general prescription, would cure anything.

In the broadest sense his view was sound and the Queen recognized it as such. Encouraged by the confidence of his doctors, the Prince might have shaken off part of his depression and this would have been of inestimable value in fighting his disease, but bad news from Portugal made this impossible. King Pedro and his brother Ferdinand caught typhoid fever. Though everything possible was done for them, their condition grew worse. Both suffered acutely. After two ghastly weeks the Court and the country were plunged into grief. The brothers died in agony, both on the same day. The news was terrible enough for Victoria who had had a great affection for her cousins. To Albert, who had always been like a father to the young King, it was even worse. Already weak and nervous he could not cope with the melancholy which flooded into his heart. It made him physically sick and there was no relief in tears.

He was in this awful state when further lamentable news arrived from the continent. Stockmar wrote to say he had a duty to tell the Prince of a scandal which was circulating through Europe: that the Prince of Wales while at the Curragh Camp had had a brief affair with an actress.

Already knocked off balance by the tragedy in Portugal, Albert was quite unable to face up to this new disaster. To Colonel Phipps' embarrassment and concern he sat down heavily on the nearest chair as dejected as a beaten dog, and just like a beaten dog he cried. He sat there for several minutes trying to re-read the Baron's careful handwriting through a blur of tears. Eventually, after gulping and blowing his nose, and wiping tear drops from the paper, he managed to control himself, and sat still, numbed and bewildered. He had no strong desires himself – none, at any rate, so strong that would have made him faithless to Victoria – and he could not understand those who had. Then, as the full realization of what had happened overtook him, he was angry and indignant that the boy should have been so thoughtless and selfish as to cause pain to his parents, shock moral feelings in the country, and risk the distinct probability of losing the princess he loved. Without a word he handed the letter to Colonel Phipps to read.

His Private Secretary read through the letter twice, and said the charge should be checked. He would see to it at once and, without waiting for permission, he left the room to seek out a gossipy courtier who, if anyone at the Castle knew, was bound to know the scandal. He did. He was able to confirm the story and give particulars. Sadly Phipps returned to his master.

There was no question in Albert's mind but that Victoria ought to be told. When he was fully in control of his feelings he went to her and showed her the letter. She was less shocked than he had expected. English princes, she said, had a habit of doing this sort of thing, and the weaker their characters, the more they did it. He was a little dismayed by her understanding, and supposed she must be thinking of the gallantries of her Hanoverian uncles. But she was venomous against Bertie for causing such needless distress. She could only guess what this shaming episode might do to Albert.

After four sleepless days and nights, the Prince Consort wrote a long letter to his son at Cambridge. Victoria read it and agreed that it seemed to answer the purpose and should be sent. She also agreed that Bertie should not be told she knew of the affair, an acceptable deception because it would save embarrassment in the future. More than anything she was thankful that Albert was so calm and uncomplaining, that from somewhere he had found the energy and the will to promise to visit Bertie in Cambridge where they would talk the matter out man to man. He seemed to have found new life and his spirits had risen. He insisted on inspecting the new Military College at Sandhurst although the ceremonial was spoilt by awful weather, and on the day before he went to Cambridge he spent a morning shooting with her half-nephew Prince Charles of Leiningen.

But these signs that he was over the worst of his illness were as illusory as the flaming up of a short candle. He went up to Cambridge wracked with rheumatic pains and quite incapable of rebuking his son as he deserved. By the following Friday he could neither go out shooting nor eat any luncheon, and only for Victoria's sake did he accompany her when she inspected the Eton volunteers. How she wished he had not. That poor, pitiable figure, stumbling along in her wake was her adored husband. Panic ballooned inside her. If she looked at him once more she would break down, and it would not do for the volunteers to see their Queen in tears. And so the grotesque performance was played out: the Queen thin-lipped, marvellously controlled, talking as normally and as naturally as she could, while behind followed the Prince Consort ashen-faced, shivering perceptibly although he wore a fur-lined coat and the afternoon was freakishly warm, moving slowly because of the pain in his back and legs and with halting footsteps.

Crouched before a fire at the conclusion of that exhausting afternoon the Prince was at last persuaded to go to bed. But he could not lie still. In the small hours he was so agitated that he stirred and twisted in bed, paced up and down the room, threw himself into a chair or on to a sofa, and on to the bed again, sleepless and edgy and desperate. Despite this he insisted on going to his desk early in the morning. The papers Phipps laid before him were largely unimportant, yet he checked them as methodically as he could. And he spent much time and thought on one, the draft of a dispatch which demanded redress from the Northern States of America for violating international law and being insolent to England. He was aghast at the peremptory tone of the note. It would place the Federal government in an impossible position and might force a war on them. Though his pen

287

hand trembled so much that writing was difficult, he re-drafted the dispatch in less bellicose language. After that he laid down his pen and put his head in his hands. Colonel Phipps and the equerries helped him to a sofa. There he lay for most of the day, going in to meals for Victoria's sake although he could not swallow anything. The glass told him that his tongue was now as brown as it was leathery and he caught a fleeting glance of concern on Jenner's face when he mentioned it to the doctor.

Through that day and another sleepless night he became convinced that he was dying. Despair stole over him but not because he was very alarmed. His religion was personal and not profound, but he hoped in salvation of a kind. More frightening than death was the thought of being separated from Victoria and from his children. It was this which he found unendurable.

Victoria was often with him as his illness developed, begging him to eat a little, or try to rest, sitting beside him, looking up into his face. He looked back, trying to smile at her. She was not beautiful to the world; plain in fact, and short and fat and perhaps a little dowdy. But to him she was everything, and she had been since his dutiful marriage was blessed and raised into something precious and enduring. She was everything to him. She always would be . . .

Victoria's nightmare was the same as Albert's. The thought of their being separated was unendurable, and she was in anguish when Jenner told her the Prince had typhoid. Her only hope, that, like herself, so many had had it and recovered, she clung to stubbornly. But though additional doctors were sent from London there was no improvement and slowly, day by day, her hope corroded.

As his condition worsened Albert suffered terribly. He cried aloud with pain. In his fever he walked the corridors at night rattling doors and shouting. Sometimes he knew her, often he did not. Sometimes he was calm. At others he was delirious, imagining himself at Rosenau or in Scotland. He moved from their bed to a smaller one: then, to mollify him, the doctors wheeled him in a bed about the Castle until the ghastly procession reached the Blue Room and he decided to settle there. Victoria was against it. Her uncles George the Fourth and William the Fourth had died in this room. But the doctors insisted he be left there.

Distracted, in an agony of apprehension, the Queen went to person after person for reassurance. Old Sir James was marvellously patient with her; Miss Skerrett, Jane Churchill and her mother's Lady Augusta were like rocks of comfort. So were her children, especially Alice. It was Alice who read prayers for Albert, Alice who played hymns for him. It was Alice who at length sent for the Prince of Wales. It was Alice who so devotedly cared for her mother, treating her, rightly, as a woman losing her lover rather than as a parent or the Queen. It was Alice who came for her to lead her back to Albert's bedside when he was close to death.

Victoria had only left the Blue Room a very short time before and so she realized what the summons meant. She went with Alice, leaning on her arm. Her other children were gathered round the bed, with the Dean of Windsor, and Albert's gentlemen and servants, and the doctors, but she had eyes only for her husband.

She knelt by his side. She murmured something no one there could hear. And she tried to smile as she fondled his hand. He made no response and she knew it really was happening, the unbelievable, the dreadful thing which would end a great, great happiness. In the lamp and candlelight he looked serene. That awful straining, the horrible sweats, the restlessness were over. His lips moved once. His eyelids flickered. Quite distinctly she heard him give three long deep and satisfying breaths. And then he died.

Victoria stood up. She kissed his forehead and cried out to him; then allowed herself to be led away by Colonel Phipps.

He left her in the next room, backing from her presence as she sat on a sofa, mute and unmoving, her clenched hands on her knees, her back erect, her face working.

For two weeks, despite her agony of mind and despite the fact that she had failed again and again, she had tried to wear a brave face for Albert's sake. And for his sake she had held herself up, and carried her head high. Now that he was dead she changed. Her desolation, her long watching and her great tiredness, began to mark her features. She was no more now than a middle-aged widow, made ugly with sorrow, silent and solitary and as immobile as a stone, with the tears splashing from her cheeks.

If you have enjoyed this PAN
Book, you may like to choose
your next book from the titles
listed on the following pages.

Elizabeth Longford

VICTORIA R.I.   £1.00

'Nearly two generations have elapsed since Queen Victoria died, and yet this is the first complete and authoritative biography . . . She has done a first-class piece of work, one that will stand comparison with that model of biography, namely Sir Harold Nicolson's King George V . . . She makes her Victorian statesmen come alive – no easy task. A most admirable biography' – Sir Charles Petrie – ILLUSTRATED LONDON NEWS

'Easily the best life of Victoria that has yet appeared' – Dr. J. H. Plumb – NEW YORK TIMES

'. . . scholarly yet racily readable, witty yet wise' – SUNDAY TIMES

Tyler Whittle

THE YOUNG VICTORIA   35p

'The shabby little girl transformed into a glittering Queen'
Growing up in the taut atmosphere of the bitter feud between her ambitious mother, the Duchess of Kent, and her uncle, King William IV, the young Victoria knew early the corruption of power . . .

But she also learnt to love, and her deep affection for her governess and for Lord Melbourne, her first Prime Minister, paved the way for her lasting passion for Albert . . .

The first of three novels by Tyler Whittle about the life of Britain's longest reigning sovereign, it is a beautiful and fascinating story of love born out of tragedy . . .

Susan Howatch